D0016271

## Acclaim for **THE LEAN STARTUP**

"*The Lean Startup* isn't just about how to create a more successful entrepreneurial business; it's about what we can learn from those businesses to improve virtually everything we do. I imagine Lean Startup principles applied to government programs, to health care, and to solving the world's great problems. It's ultimately an answer to the question How can we learn more quickly what works and discard what doesn't?"

**—Tim O'Reilly, CEO, O'Reilly Media**

"Eric Ries unravels the mysteries of entrepreneurship and reveals that magic and genius are not the necessary ingredients for success but instead proposes a scientific process that can be learned and replicated. Whether you are a startup entrepreneur or corporate entrepreneur, there are important lessons here for you on your quest toward the new and unknown."

**—Tim Brown, CEO, IDEO**

"The road map for innovation for the twenty-first century. The ideas in *The Lean Startup* will help create the next industrial revolution."

**—Steve Blank, lecturer, Stanford University,
UC Berkeley Haas Business School**

"Every founding team should stop for forty-eight hours and read *The Lean Startup*. Seriously, stop and read this book now."

**—Scott Case, CEO, Startup America Partnership**

"The key lesson of this book is that startups happen in the present—that messy place between the past and the future where nothing happens according to PowerPoint. Ries's 'read and react' approach to this sport, his relentless focus on validated learning, the never-ending anxiety of hovering between 'persevere' and 'pivot,' all bear witness to his appreciation for the dynamics of entrepreneurship."

**—Geoffrey Moore, author, *Crossing the Chasm***

"If you are an entrepreneur, read this book. If you are thinking about becoming an entrepreneur, read this book. If you are just curious about entrepreneurship, read this book. Starting Lean is today's best practice for innovators. Do yourself a favor and read this book."

**—Randy Komisar, founding director of TiVo and author of the bestselling *The Monk and the Riddle***

"How do you apply the fifty-year-old ideas of Lean to the fast-paced, high-uncertainty world of startups? This book provides a brilliant, well-documented, and practical answer. It is sure to become a management classic."

**—Don Reinertsen, author, *The Principles of Product Development Flow***

"What would happen if businesses were built from the ground up to learn what their customers really wanted? *The Lean Startup* is the foundation for reimagining almost everything about how work works. Don't let the word startup in the title confuse you. This is a cookbook for entrepreneurs in organizations of all sizes."

**—Roy Bahat, president, IGN Entertainment**

"*The Lean Startup* is a foundational must-read for founders, enabling them to reduce product failures by bringing structure and science to what is usually informal and an art. It provides actionable ways to avoid product-learning mistakes, rigorously evaluate early signals from the market through validated learning, and decide whether to persevere or to pivot, all challenges that heighten the chance of entrepreneurial failure."

**—Noam Wasserman, professor, Harvard Business School**

"One of the best and most insightful new books on entrepreneurship and management I've ever read. Should be required reading not only for the entrepreneurs that I work with, but for my friends and colleagues in various industries who have inevitably grappled with many of the challenges that *The Lean Startup* addresses."

**—Eugene J. Huang, partner, True North Venture Partners**

"Every entrepreneur responsible for innovation within their organization should read this book. It entertainingly and meticulously develops a rigorous science for the innovation process through the methodology of "lean thinking." This methodology provides novel and powerful tools for companies to improve the speed and efficiency of their innovation processes through minimum viable products, validated learning, innovation accounting, and actionable metrics. These tools will help organizations large and small to sustain innovation by effectively leveraging the time, passion, and skill of their talent pools."

**—Andrea Goldsmith, professor of electrical engineering at Stanford University and cofounder of several startups**

"In business, a 'lean' enterprise is sustainable efficiency in action. Eric Ries's revolutionary Lean Startup method will help bring your new business idea to an end result that is successful *and* sustainable. You'll find innovative steps and strategies for creating and managing your own startup while learning from the real-life successes and collapses of others. This book is a must-read for entrepreneurs who are truly ready to start something great!"

**—Ken Blanchard, coauthor of *The One Minute Manager®* and *The One Minute Entrepreneur***

"Business is too important to be left to luck. Eric reveals the rigorous process that trumps luck in the invention of new products and new businesses. We've made this a centerpiece of how teams work in my company . . . it works! This book is the guided tour of the key innovative practices used inside Google, Toyota, and Facebook that work in any business."

**—Scott Cook, founder and chairman of the Executive Committee, Intuit**

# The LEAN STARTUP

# The LEAN STARTUP

## How Today's Entrepreneurs Use Continuous Innovation to Create Radically Successful Businesses

Eric Ries

Published in the United States by Crown Business, an imprint of the Crown Publishing Group, a division of Random House, Inc., New York.
www.crownpublishing.com



Crown Business books are available at special discounts for bulk purchases for sales promotions or corporate use. Special editions, including personalized covers, excerpts of existing books, or books with corporate logos, can be created in large quantities for special needs. For more information, contact Premium Sales at (212) 572–2232 or e-mail specialmarkets@randomhouse.com.

Library of Congress Cataloging-in-Publication Data
Ries, Eric, 1978–
The lean startup / Eric Ries. — 1st ed.
p. cm.
1. New business enterprises. 2. Consumers' preferences. 3. Organizational effectiveness. I. Title.
HD62.5.R545 2011
658.1'1—dc22 2011012100

ISBN 978-0-307-88789-4
eISBN 978-0-307-88791-7

Printed in the United States of America

*Book design by Lauren Dong*
*Illustrations by Fred Haynes*
*Jacket design by Marcus Gosling*

30 29 28 27 26 25

First Edition

*For Tara*

# Contents

# Foreword

Entrepreneurs are different in many ways, whether starting their own small company or inventing new products and businesses within a company like GE. But they also share certain traits. They are fast. They embrace new thinking. They are geared for disruption and innovation through uncertainty. One of the things I admire about Eric Ries's The Lean Startup is its ability to teach anyone how to do this using a scientific approach.

GE is all about constant reinvention. We iterate, innovate, and improve. Our culture embraces external thinking and invites cutting-edge practices. We do this working alongside great thinkers like Eric Ries, who help us improve the way we work.

We are adding the principles of The Lean Startup to GE's long tradition of continuous improvement, and across GE there are many projects where we are learning, iterating, and delivering outcomes in a new way. We call this new process FastWorks. Eric has been one of our advisers as we launched this tool to help us deliver better outcomes for our customers—quickly.

For GE, these concepts accelerate impact, learning, improvement, and validation. GE's founder, Thomas Edison, said he "readily absorbed ideas from every source," and we're continuing this tradition. Eric Ries is one of the people with great ideas helping us think about how a company like ours, operating at a massive scale, can be faster in everything we do, to bring more progress to our customers and to the world. I hope readers find as much inspiration and guidance in Eric's book as GE has.

—Jeff Immelt
Chairman & CEO
GE

# Introduction

Stop me if you've heard this one before. Brilliant college kids sitting in a dorm are inventing the future. Heedless of boundaries, possessed of new technology and youthful enthusiasm, they build a new company from scratch. Their early success allows them to raise money and bring an amazing new product to market. They hire their friends, assemble a superstar team, and dare the world to stop them.

Ten years and several startups ago, that was me, building my first company. I particularly remember a moment from back then: the moment I realized my company was going to fail. My cofounder and I were at our wits' end. The dot-com bubble had burst, and we had spent all our money. We tried desperately to raise more capital, and we could not. It was like a breakup scene from a Hollywood movie: it was raining, and we were arguing in the street. We couldn't even agree on where to walk next, and so we parted in anger, heading in opposite directions. As a metaphor for our company's failure, this image of the two of us, lost in the rain and drifting apart, is perfect.

It remains a painful memory. The company limped along for months afterward, but our situation was hopeless. At the time, it had seemed we were doing everything right: we had a great product, a brilliant team, amazing technology, and the right idea at the right time. And we really were on to something. We were building a way for college kids to create online profiles for the purpose of sharing . . . with employers. Oops. But despite a promising idea, we were nonetheless doomed from day one, because we did not know the process we would need to use to turn our product insights into a great company.

If you've never experienced a failure like this, it is hard to describe the feeling. It's as if the world were falling out from under you. You realize you've been duped. The stories in the magazines are lies: hard work and perseverance don't lead to success. Even worse, the many, many, many promises you've made to employees, friends, and family are not going to come true. Everyone who thought you were foolish for stepping out on your own will be proven right.

It wasn't supposed to turn out that way. In magazines and newspapers, in blockbuster movies, and on countless blogs, we hear the mantra of the successful entrepreneurs: through determination, brilliance, great timing, and—above all—a great product, you too can achieve fame and fortune.

There is a mythmaking industry hard at work to sell us that story, but I have come to believe that the story is false, the product of selection bias and after-the-fact rationalization. In fact, having worked with hundreds of entrepreneurs, I have seen firsthand how often a promising start leads to failure. The grim reality is that most startups fail. Most new products are not successful. Most new ventures do not live up to their potential.

Yet the story of perseverance, creative genius, and hard work persists. Why is it so popular? I think there is something deeply appealing about this modern-day rags-to-riches story. It makes success seem inevitable if you just have the right stuff. It means that the mundane details, the boring stuff, the small individual choices don't matter. If we build it, they will come. When we fail, as so many of us do, we have a ready-made excuse: we didn't have the right stuff. We weren't visionary enough or weren't in the right place at the right time.

After more than ten years as an entrepreneur, I came to reject that line of thinking. I have learned from both my own successes and failures and those of many others that it's the boring stuff that matters the most. Startup success is not a consequence of good genes or being in the right place at the right time. Startup success can be engineered by following the right process, which means it can be learned, which means it can be taught.

Entrepreneurship is a kind of management. No, you didn't read that wrong. We have wildly divergent associations with these two words, *entrepreneurship* and *management.* Lately, it seems that one is cool, innovative, and exciting and the other is dull, serious, and bland. It is time to look past these preconceptions.

Let me tell you a second startup story. It's 2004, and a group of founders have just started a new company. Their previous company had failed very publicly. Their credibility is at an all-time low. They have a huge vision: to change the way people communicate by using a new technology called avatars (remember, this was before James Cameron's blockbuster movie). They are following a visionary named Will Harvey, who paints a compelling picture: people connecting with their friends, hanging out online, using avatars to give them a combination of intimate connection and safe anonymity. Even better, instead of having to build all the clothing, furniture, and accessories these avatars would need to accessorize their digital lives, the customers would be enlisted to build those things and sell them to one another.

The engineering challenge before them is immense: creating virtual worlds, user-generated content, an online commerce engine, micropayments, and—last but not least—the three-dimensional avatar technology that can run on anyone's PC.

I'm in this second story, too. I'm a cofounder and chief technology officer of this company, which is called IMVU. At this point in our careers, my cofounders and I are determined to make new mistakes. We do everything wrong: instead of spending years perfecting our technology, we build a minimum viable product, an early product that is terrible, full of bugs and crash-your-computer-yes-really stability problems. Then we ship it to customers way before it's ready. And we charge money for it. After securing initial customers, we change the product constantly—much too fast by traditional standards—shipping new versions of our product dozens of times every single day.

We really did have customers in those early days—true visionary early adopters—and we often talked to them and asked for their feedback. But we emphatically did *not* do what they said. We viewed their input as only one source of information about our product and overall vision. In fact, we were much more likely to run experiments on our customers than we were to cater to their whims.

Traditional business thinking says that this approach shouldn't work, but it does, and you don't have to take my word for it. As you'll see throughout this book, the approach we pioneered at IMVU has become the basis for a new movement of entrepreneurs around the world. It builds on many previous management and product development ideas, including lean manufacturing, design thinking, customer development, and agile development. It represents a new approach to creating continuous innovation. It's called the Lean Startup.

Despite the volumes written on business strategy, the key attributes of business leaders, and ways to identify the next big thing, innovators still struggle to bring their ideas to life. This was the frustration that led us to try a radical new approach at IMVU, one characterized by an extremely fast cycle time, a focus on what customers want (without asking them), and a scientific approach to making decisions.

## ORIGINS OF THE LEAN STARTUP

I am one of those people who grew up programming computers, and so my journey to thinking about entrepreneurship and management has taken a circuitous path. I have always worked on the product development side of my industry; my partners and bosses were managers or marketers, and my peers worked in engineering and operations. Throughout my career, I kept having the experience of working incredibly hard on products that ultimately failed in the marketplace.

At first, largely because of my background, I viewed these as technical problems that required technical solutions: better architecture, a better engineering process, better discipline, focus, or product vision. These supposed fixes led to still more failure. So I read everything I could get my hands on and was blessed to have had some of the top minds in Silicon Valley as my mentors. By the time I became a cofounder of IMVU, I was hungry for new ideas about how to build a company.

I was fortunate to have cofounders who were willing to experiment with new approaches. They were fed up—as I was—by the failure of traditional thinking. Also, we were lucky to have Steve Blank as an investor and adviser. Back in 2004, Steve had just begun preaching a new idea: the business and marketing functions of a startup should be considered as important as engineering and product development and therefore deserve an equally rigorous methodology to guide them. He called that methodology Customer Development, and it offered insight and guidance to my daily work as an entrepreneur.

Meanwhile, I was building IMVU's product development team, using some of the unorthodox methods I mentioned earlier. Measured against the traditional theories of product development I had been trained on in my career, these methods did not make sense, yet I could see firsthand that they were working. I struggled to explain the practices to new employees, investors, and the founders of other companies. We lacked a common language for describing them and concrete principles for understanding them.

I began to search outside entrepreneurship for ideas that could help me make sense of my experience. I began to study other industries, especially manufacturing, from which most modern theories of management derive. I studied lean manufacturing, a process that originated in Japan with the Toyota Production System, a completely new way of thinking about the manufacturing of physical goods. I found that by applying ideas from lean manufacturing to my own entrepreneurial challenges—with a few tweaks and changes—I had the beginnings of a framework for making sense of them.

This line of thought evolved into the Lean Startup: the application of lean thinking to the process of innovation.

IMVU became a tremendous success. IMVU customers have created more than 60 million avatars. It is a profitable company with annual revenues of more than $50 million in 2011, employing more than a hundred people in our current offices in Mountain View, California. IMVU's virtual goods catalog—which seemed so risky years ago—now has more than 6 million items in it; more than 7,000 are added every day, almost all created by customers.

As a result of IMVU's success, I began to be asked for advice by other startups and venture capitalists. When I would describe my experiences at IMVU, I was often met with blank stares or extreme skepticism. The most common reply was "That could never work!" My experience so flew in the face of conventional thinking that most people, even in the innovation hub of Silicon Valley, could not wrap their minds around it.

Then I started to write, first on a blog called *Startup Lessons Learned,* and speak—at conferences and to companies, startups, and venture capitalists—to anyone who would listen. In the process of being called on to defend and explain my insights and with the collaboration of other writers, thinkers, and entrepreneurs, I had a chance to refine and develop the theory of the Lean Startup beyond its rudimentary beginnings. My hope all along was to find ways to eliminate the tremendous waste I saw all around me: startups that built products nobody wanted, new products pulled from the shelves, countless dreams unrealized.

Eventually, the Lean Startup idea blossomed into a global movement. Entrepreneurs began forming local in-person groups to discuss and apply Lean Startup ideas. There are now organized communities of practice in more than a hundred cities around the world.[1] My travels have taken me across countries and continents. Everywhere I have seen the signs of a new entrepreneurial renaissance. The Lean Startup movement is making entrepreneurship accessible to a whole new generation of founders who are hungry for new ideas about how to build successful companies.

Although my background is in high-tech software entrepreneurship, the movement has grown way beyond those roots. Thousands of entrepreneurs are putting Lean Startup principles to work in every conceivable industry. I've had the chance to work with entrepreneurs in companies of all sizes, in different industries, and even in government. This journey has taken me to places I never imagined I'd see, from the world's most elite venture capitalists, to Fortune 500 boardrooms, to the Pentagon. The most nervous I have ever been in a meeting was when

I was attempting to explain Lean Startup principles to the chief information officer of the U.S. Army, who is a three-star general (for the record, he was extremely open to new ideas, even from a civilian like me).

Pretty soon I realized that it was time to focus on the Lean Startup movement full time. My mission: to improve the success rate of new innovative products worldwide. The result is the book you are reading.

## THE LEAN STARTUP METHOD

This is a book for entrepreneurs and the people who hold them accountable. The five principles of the Lean Startup, which inform all three parts of this book, are as follows:

**1. Entrepreneurs are everywhere.** You don't have to work in a garage to be in a startup. The concept of entrepreneurship includes anyone who works within my definition of a startup: a human institution designed to create new products and services under conditions of extreme uncertainty. That means entrepreneurs are everywhere and the Lean Startup approach can work in any size company, even a very large enterprise, in any sector or industry.

**2. Entrepreneurship is management.** A startup is an institution, not just a product, and so it requires a new kind of management specifically geared to its context of extreme uncertainty. In fact, as I will argue later, I believe "entrepreneur" should be considered a job title in all modern companies that depend on innovation for their future growth.

**3. Validated learning.** Startups exist not just to make stuff, make money, or even serve customers. They exist to *learn* how to build a sustainable business. This learning can be validated scientifically by running frequent experiments that allow entrepreneurs to test each element of their vision.

**4. Build-Measure-Learn.** The fundamental activity of a startup is to turn ideas into products, measure how customers respond, and then learn whether to pivot or persevere. All successful startup processes should be geared to accelerate that feedback loop.

**5. Innovation accounting.** To improve entrepreneurial outcomes and hold innovators accountable, we need to focus on the boring stuff: how to measure progress, how to set up milestones, and how to prioritize work. This requires a new kind of accounting designed for startups—and the people who hold them accountable.

## Why Startups Fail

Why are startups failing so badly everywhere we look?

The first problem is the allure of a good plan, a solid strategy, and thorough market research. In earlier eras, these things were indicators of likely success. The overwhelming temptation is to apply them to startups too, but this doesn't work, because startups operate with too much uncertainty. Startups do not yet know who their customer is or what their product should be. As the world becomes more uncertain, it gets harder and harder to predict the future. The old management methods are not up to the task. Planning and forecasting are only accurate when based on a long, stable operating history and a relatively static environment. Startups have neither.

The second problem is that after seeing traditional management fail to solve this problem, some entrepreneurs and investors have thrown up their hands and adopted the "Just Do It" school of startups. This school believes that if management is the problem, chaos is the answer. Unfortunately, as I can attest firsthand, this doesn't work either.

It may seem counterintuitive to think that something as disruptive, innovative, and chaotic as a startup can be managed or, to be accurate, *must* be managed. Most people think of process and management as boring and dull, whereas startups are dynamic and exciting. But what is actually exciting is to see startups succeed and change the world. The passion, energy, and vision that people bring to these new ventures are resources too precious to waste. We can—and must—do better. This book is about how.

## HOW THIS BOOK IS ORGANIZED

This book is divided into three parts: "Vision," "Steer," and "Accelerate."

"Vision" makes the case for a new discipline of entrepreneurial management. I identify who is an entrepreneur, define a startup, and articulate a new way for startups to gauge if they are making progress, called validated learning. To achieve that learning, we'll see that startups—in a garage or inside an enterprise—can use scientific experimentation to discover how to build a sustainable business.

"Steer" dives into the Lean Startup method in detail, showing one major turn through the core Build-Measure-Learn feedback loop. Beginning with leap-of-faith assumptions that cry out for rigorous testing, you'll learn how to build a minimum viable product to test those assumptions, a new accounting system for evaluating whether you're making progress, and a method for deciding whether to pivot (changing course with one foot anchored to the ground) or persevere.

In "Accelerate," we'll explore techniques that enable Lean Startups to speed through the Build-Measure-Learn feedback loop as quickly as possible, even as they scale. We'll explore lean manufacturing concepts that are applicable to startups, too, such as the power of small batches. We'll also discuss organizational design, how products grow, and how to apply Lean Startup principles beyond the proverbial garage, even inside the world's largest companies.

## MANAGEMENT'S SECOND CENTURY

As a society, we have a proven set of techniques for managing big companies and we know the best practices for building physical products. But when it comes to startups and innovation, we are still shooting in the dark. We are relying on vision, chasing the "great men" who can make magic happen, or trying to analyze our new products to death. These are new problems, born of the success of management in the twentieth century.

This book attempts to put entrepreneurship and innovation on a rigorous footing. We are at the dawn of management's second century. It is our challenge to do something great with the opportunity we have been given. The Lean Startup movement seeks to ensure that those of us who long to build the next big thing will have the tools we need to change the world.

# Part One

# VISION

# 1
# START

## ENTREPRENEURIAL MANAGEMENT

Building a startup is an exercise in institution building; thus, it necessarily involves management. This often comes as a surprise to aspiring entrepreneurs, because their associations with these two words are so diametrically opposed. Entrepreneurs are rightly wary of implementing traditional management practices early on in a startup, afraid that they will invite bureaucracy or stifle creativity.

Entrepreneurs have been trying to fit the square peg of their unique problems into the round hole of general management for decades. As a result, many entrepreneurs take a "just do it" attitude, avoiding all forms of management, process, and discipline. Unfortunately, this approach leads to chaos more often than it does to success. I should know: my first startup failures were all of this kind.

The tremendous success of general management over the last century has provided unprecedented material abundance, but those management principles are ill suited to handle the chaos and uncertainty that startups must face.

o o o

I believe that entrepreneurship requires a managerial discipline to harness the entrepreneurial opportunity we have been given.

There are more entrepreneurs operating today than at any previous time in history. This has been made possible by dramatic changes in the global economy. To cite but one example, one often hears commentators lament the loss of manufacturing jobs in the United States over the previous two decades, but one rarely hears about a corresponding loss of manufacturing capability. That's because total manufacturing output in the United States is *increasing* (by 15 percent in the last decade) even as jobs continue to be lost (see the charts below). In effect, the huge productivity increases made possible by modern management and technology have created more productive capacity than firms know what to do with.[1]

We are living through an unprecedented worldwide entrepreneurial renaissance, but this opportunity is laced with peril.

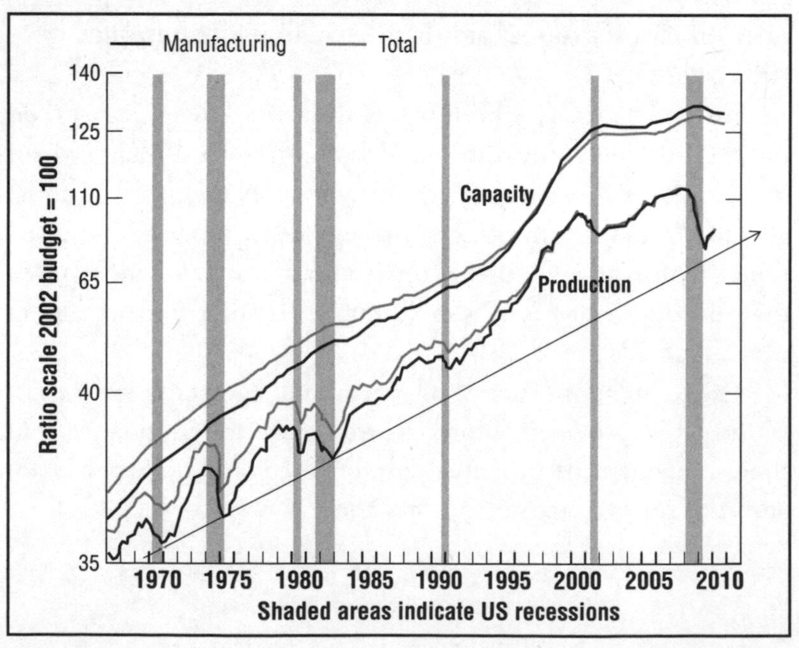

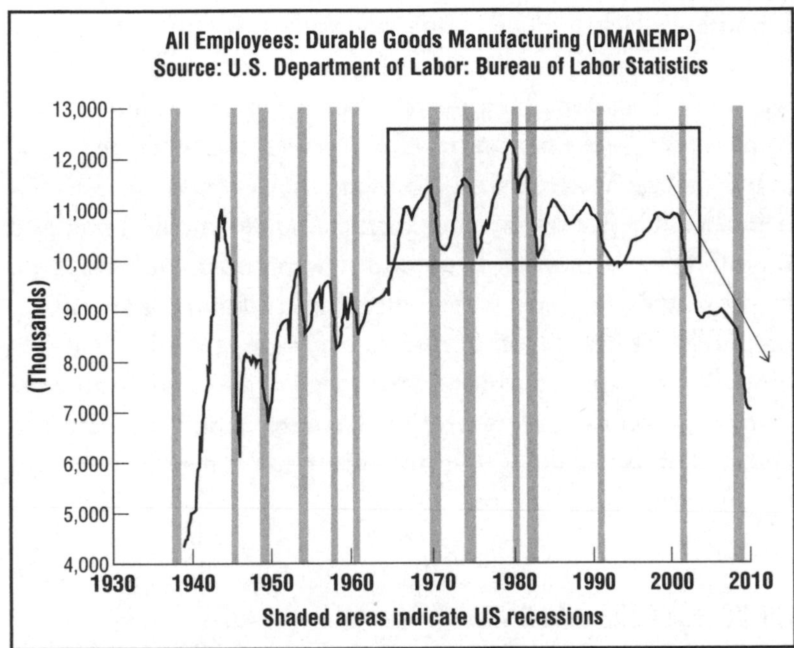
All Employees: Durable Goods Manufacturing (DMANEMP)
Source: U.S. Department of Labor: Bureau of Labor Statistics
13,000
12,000
11,000
10,000
9,000
8,000
7,000
6,000
5,000
4,000
(Thousands)
1930
1940
1950
1960
1970
1980
1990
2000
2010
Shaded areas indicate US recessions

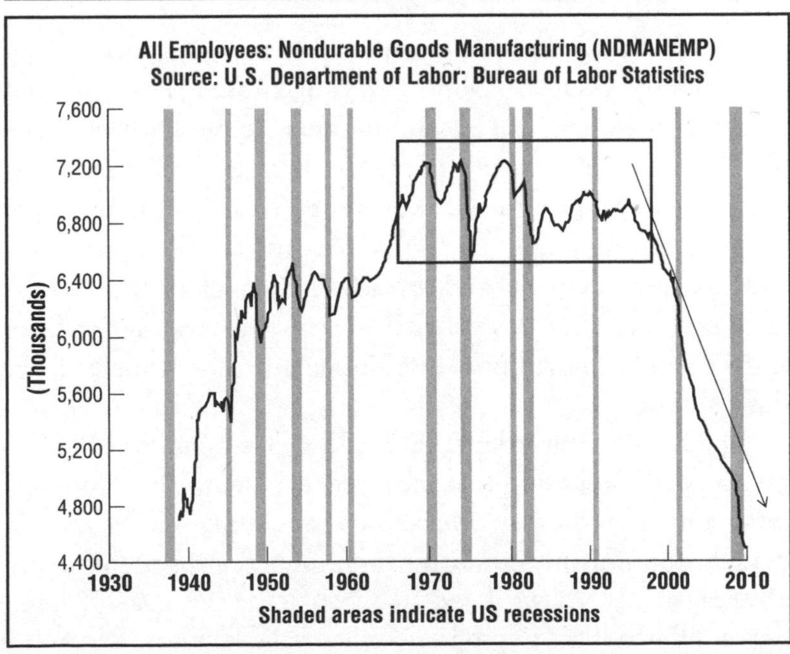
All Employees: Nondurable Goods Manufacturing (NDMANEMP)
Source: U.S. Department of Labor: Bureau of Labor Statistics
7,600
7,200
6,800
6,400
6,000
5,600
5,200
4,800
4,400
(Thousands)
1930
1940
1950
1960
1970
1980
1990
2000
2010
Shaded areas indicate US recessions

Because we lack a coherent management paradigm for new innovative ventures, we're throwing our excess capacity around with wild abandon. Despite this lack of rigor, we are finding some ways to make money, but for every success there are far too many failures: products pulled from shelves mere weeks after being launched, high-profile startups lauded in the press and forgotten a few months later, and new products that wind up being used by nobody. What makes these failures particularly painful is not just the economic damage done to individual employees, companies, and investors; they are also a colossal waste of our civilization's most precious resource: the time, passion, and skill of its people. The Lean Startup movement is dedicated to preventing these failures.

## THE ROOTS OF THE LEAN STARTUP

The Lean Startup takes its name from the lean manufacturing revolution that Taiichi Ohno and Shigeo Shingo are credited with developing at Toyota. Lean thinking is radically altering the way supply chains and production systems are run. Among its tenets are drawing on the knowledge and creativity of individual workers, the shrinking of batch sizes, just-in-time production and inventory control, and an acceleration of cycle times. It taught the world the difference between value-creating activities and waste and showed how to build quality into products from the inside out.

The Lean Startup adapts these ideas to the context of entrepreneurship, proposing that entrepreneurs judge their progress differently from the way other kinds of ventures do. Progress in manufacturing is measured by the production of high-quality physical goods. As we'll see in Chapter 3, the Lean Startup uses a different unit of progress, called validated learning. With scientific learning as our yardstick, we can discover and eliminate the sources of waste that are plaguing entrepreneurship.

A comprehensive theory of entrepreneurship should address all the functions of an early-stage venture: vision and concept, product development, marketing and sales, scaling up, partnerships and distribution, and structure and organizational design. It has to provide a method for measuring progress in the context of extreme uncertainty. It can give entrepreneurs clear guidance on how to make the many trade-off decisions they face: whether and when to invest in process; formulating, planning, and creating infrastructure; when to go it alone and when to partner; when to respond to feedback and when to stick with vision; and how and when to invest in scaling the business. Most of all, it must allow entrepreneurs to make testable predictions.

For example, consider the recommendation that you build cross-functional teams and hold them accountable to what we call *learning milestones* instead of organizing your company into strict functional departments (marketing, sales, information technology, human resources, etc.) that hold people accountable for performing well in their specialized areas (see Chapter 7). Perhaps you agree with this recommendation, or perhaps you are skeptical. Either way, if you decide to implement it, I predict that you pretty quickly will get feedback from your teams that the new process is reducing their productivity. They will ask to go back to the old way of working, in which they had the opportunity to "stay efficient" by working in larger batches and passing work between departments.

It's safe to predict this result, and not just because I have seen it many times in the companies I work with. It is a straightforward prediction of the Lean Startup theory itself. When people are used to evaluating their productivity locally, they feel that a good day is one in which they did their job well all day. When I worked as a programmer, that meant eight straight hours of programming without interruption. That was a good day. In contrast, if I was interrupted with questions, process, or—heaven forbid—meetings, I felt bad. What did I really accomplish that day? Code and product features were tangible to me; I could see them, understand them, and show them off. Learning, by contrast, is frustratingly intangible.

The Lean Startup asks people to start measuring their productivity differently. Because startups often accidentally build something nobody wants, it doesn't matter much if they do it on time and on budget. The goal of a startup is to figure out the right thing to build—the thing customers want and will pay for—as quickly as possible. In other words, the Lean Startup is a new way of looking at the development of innovative new products that emphasizes fast iteration and customer insight, a huge vision, and great ambition, all at the same time.

○ ○ ○

Henry Ford is one of the most successful and celebrated entrepreneurs of all time. Since the idea of management has been bound up with the history of the automobile since its first days, I believe it is fitting to use the automobile as a metaphor for a startup.

An internal combustion automobile is powered by two important and very different feedback loops. The first feedback loop is deep inside the engine. Before Henry Ford was a famous CEO, he was an engineer. He spent his days and nights tinkering in his garage with the precise mechanics of getting the engine cylinders to move. Each tiny explosion within the cylinder provides the motive force to turn the wheels but also drives the ignition of the next explosion. Unless the timing of this feedback loop is managed precisely, the engine will sputter and break down.

Startups have a similar engine that I call the *engine of growth*. The markets and customers for startups are diverse: a toy company, a consulting firm, and a manufacturing plant may not seem like they have much in common, but, as we'll see, they operate with the same engine of growth.

Every new version of a product, every new feature, and every new marketing program is an attempt to improve this engine of growth. Like Henry Ford's tinkering in his garage, not all of these changes turn out to be improvements. New product development happens in fits and starts. Much of the time in a startup's life is spent tuning the engine by making improvements in product, marketing, or operations.

The second important feedback loop in an automobile is between the driver and the steering wheel. This feedback is so immediate and automatic that we often don't think about it, but it is steering that differentiates driving from most other forms of transportation. If you have a daily commute, you probably know the route so well that your hands seem to steer you there on their own accord. We can practically drive the route in our sleep. Yet if I asked you to close your eyes and write down exactly how to get to your office—not the street directions but every action you need to take, every push of hand on wheel and foot on pedals—you'd find it impossible. The choreography of driving is incredibly complex when one slows down to think about it.

By contrast, a rocket ship requires just this kind of in-advance calibration. It must be launched with the most precise instructions on what to do: every thrust, every firing of a booster, and every change in direction. The tiniest error at the point of launch could yield catastrophic results thousands of miles later.

Unfortunately, too many startup business plans look more like they are planning to launch a rocket ship than drive a car. They prescribe the steps to take and the results to expect in excruciating detail, and as in planning to launch a rocket, they are set up in such a way that even tiny errors in assumptions can lead to catastrophic outcomes.

One company I worked with had the misfortune of forecasting significant customer adoption—in the millions—for one of its new products. Powered by a splashy launch, the company successfully executed its plan. Unfortunately, customers did not flock to the product in great numbers. Even worse, the company had invested in massive infrastructure, hiring, and support to handle the influx of customers it expected. When the customers failed to materialize, the company had committed itself so completely that they could not adapt in time. They had "achieved failure"—successfully, faithfully, and rigorously executing a plan that turned out to have been utterly flawed.

The Lean Startup method, in contrast, is designed to teach you how to drive a startup. Instead of making complex plans that are based on a lot of assumptions, you can make constant adjustments with a steering wheel called the *Build-Measure-Learn* feedback loop. Through this process of steering, we can learn when and if it's time to make a sharp turn called a *pivot* or whether we should *persevere* along our current path. Once we have an engine that's revved up, the Lean Startup offers methods to scale and grow the business with maximum acceleration.

Throughout the process of driving, you always have a clear idea of where you're going. If you're commuting to work, you don't give up because there's a detour in the road or you made a wrong turn. You remain thoroughly focused on getting to your destination.

Startups also have a true north, a destination in mind: creating a thriving and world-changing business. I call that a startup's *vision*. To achieve that vision, startups employ a *strategy*, which includes a business model, a product road map, a point of view about partners and competitors, and ideas about who the customer will be. The *product* is the end result of this strategy (see the chart on page 23).

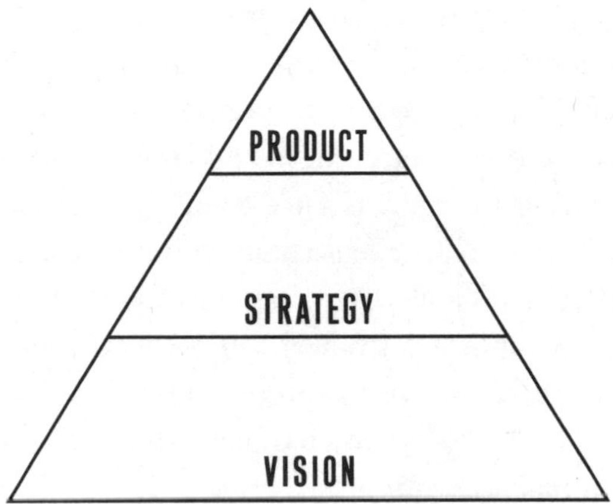


Products change constantly through the process of optimization, what I call *tuning the engine*. Less frequently, the strategy may have to change (called a pivot). However, the overarching vision rarely changes. Entrepreneurs are committed to seeing the startup through to that destination. Every setback is an opportunity for learning how to get where they want to go (see the chart below).

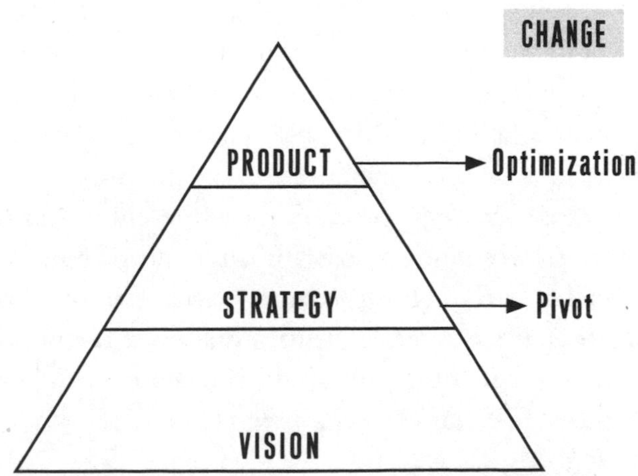

In real life, a startup is a portfolio of activities. A lot is happening simultaneously: the engine is running, acquiring new customers and serving existing ones; we are tuning, trying to improve our product, marketing, and operations; and we are steering, deciding if and when to pivot. The challenge of entrepreneurship is to balance all these activities. Even the smallest startup faces the challenge of supporting existing customers while trying to innovate. Even the most established company faces the imperative to invest in innovation lest it become obsolete. As companies grow, what changes is the mix of these activities in the company's portfolio of work.

○ ○ ○

Entrepreneurship is management. And yet, imagine a modern manager who is tasked with building a new product in the context of an established company. Imagine that she goes back to her company's chief financial officer (CFO) a year later and says, "We have failed to meet the growth targets we predicted. In fact, we have almost no new customers and no new revenue. However, we have learned an incredible amount and are on the cusp of a breakthrough new line of business. All we need is another year." Most of the time, this would be the last report this intrapreneur would give her employer. The reason is that in general management, a failure to deliver results is due to either a failure to plan adequately or a failure to execute properly. Both are significant lapses, yet new product development in our modern economy routinely requires exactly this kind of failure on the way to greatness. In the Lean Startup movement, we have come to realize that these internal innovators are actually entrepreneurs, too, and that entrepreneurial management can help them succeed; this is the subject of the next chapter.

# 2
# DEFINE

## WHO, EXACTLY, IS AN ENTREPRENEUR?

As I travel the world talking about the Lean Startup, I'm consistently surprised that I meet people in the audience who seem out of place. In addition to the more traditional startup entrepreneurs I meet, these people are general managers, mostly working in very large companies, who are tasked with creating new ventures or product innovations. They are adept at organizational politics: they know how to form autonomous divisions with separate profit and loss statements (P&Ls) and can shield controversial teams from corporate meddling. The biggest surprise is that they are visionaries. Like the startup founders I have worked with for years, they can see the future of their industries and are prepared to take bold risks to seek out new and innovative solutions to the problems their companies face.

Mark, for example, is a manager for an extremely large company who came to one of my lectures. He is the leader of a division that recently had been chartered to bring his company into the twenty-first century by building a new suite of products designed to take advantage of the Internet. When he came to talk to me afterward, I started to give him the standard advice about how to create innovation teams inside big companies, and he stopped me in midstream: "Yeah, I've read *The Innovator's Dilemma.*[1] I've got that all taken care of." He was a long-term employee of the company and a successful manager to boot, so managing internal politics was the least of his problems. I should have known; his success was a testament to his ability to navigate the company's corporate policies, personnel, and processes to get things done.

Next, I tried to give him some advice about the future, about cool new highly leveraged product development technologies. He interrupted me again: "Right. I know all about the Internet, and I have a vision for how our company needs to adapt to it or die."

Mark has all the entrepreneurial *prerequisites* nailed—proper team structure, good personnel, a strong vision for the future, and an appetite for risk taking—and so it finally occurred to me to ask why he was coming to me for advice. He said, "It's as if we have all of the raw materials: kindling, wood, paper, flint, even some sparks. But where's the fire?" The theories of management that Mark had studied treat innovation like a "black box" by focusing on the structures companies need to put in place to form internal startup teams. But Mark found himself working *inside the black box*—and in need of guidance.

What Mark was missing was a process for converting the raw materials of innovation into real-world breakthrough successes. Once a team is set up, what should it do? What process should it use? How should it be held accountable to performance milestones? These are questions the Lean Startup methodology is designed to answer.

My point? Mark is an entrepreneur just like a Silicon Valley high-tech founder with a garage startup. He needs the principles of the Lean Startup just as much as the folks I thought of as classic entrepreneurs do.

Entrepreneurs who operate inside an established organization sometimes are called "intrapreneurs" because of the special circumstances that attend building a startup within a larger company. As I have applied Lean Startup ideas in an ever-widening variety of companies and industries, I have come to believe that intrapreneurs have much more in common with the rest of the community of entrepreneurs than most people believe. Thus, when I use the term *entrepreneur,* I am referring to the whole startup ecosystem regardless of company size, sector, or stage of development.

This book is for entrepreneurs of all stripes: from young visionaries with little backing but great ideas to seasoned visionaries within larger companies such as Mark—and the people who hold them accountable.

## IF I'M AN ENTREPRENEUR, WHAT'S A STARTUP?

The Lean Startup is a set of practices for helping entrepreneurs increase their odds of building a successful startup. To set the record straight, it's important to define what a startup is:

> A startup is a human institution designed to create a new product or service under conditions of extreme uncertainty.

I've come to realize that the most important part of this definition is what it omits. It says nothing about size of the company, the industry, or the sector of the economy. Anyone who is creating a new product or business under conditions of extreme uncertainty is an entrepreneur whether he or she knows it or not and whether working in a government agency, a venture-backed company, a nonprofit, or a decidedly for-profit company with financial investors.

Let's take a look at each of the pieces. The word *institution* connotes bureaucracy, process, even lethargy. How can that be part of a startup? Yet successful startups are full of activities associated with building an institution: hiring creative employees, coordinating their activities, and creating a company culture that delivers results.

We often lose sight of the fact that a startup is not just about a product, a technological breakthrough, or even a brilliant idea. A startup is greater than the sum of its parts; it is an acutely human enterprise.

The fact that a startup's product or service is a new innovation is also an essential part of the definition and a tricky part too. I prefer to use the broadest definition of *product,* one that encompasses any source of value for the people who become customers. Anything those customers experience from their interaction with a company should be considered part of that company's product. This is true of a grocery store, an e-commerce website, a consulting service, and a nonprofit social service agency. In every case, the organization is dedicated to uncovering a new source of value for customers and cares about the impact of its product on those customers.

It's also important that the word *innovation* be understood broadly. Startups use many kinds of innovation: novel scientific discoveries, repurposing an existing technology for a new use, devising a new business model that unlocks value that was hidden, or simply bringing a product or service to a new location or a previously underserved set of customers. In all these cases, innovation is at the heart of the company's success.

There is one more important part of this definition: the context in which the innovation happens. Most businesses—large and small alike—are excluded from this context. Startups are designed to confront situations of extreme uncertainty. To open up a new business that is an exact clone of an existing business all the way down to the business model, pricing, target customer, and product may be an attractive economic investment, but it is not a startup because its success depends only on execution—so much so that this success can be modeled with high accuracy. (This is why so many small businesses can be financed with simple bank loans; the level of risk and uncertainty is understood well enough that a loan officer can assess its prospects.)

Most tools from general management are not designed to flourish in the harsh soil of extreme uncertainty in which startups thrive. The future is unpredictable, customers face a growing array of alternatives, and the pace of change is ever increasing. Yet most startups—in garages and enterprises alike—still are managed by using standard forecasts, product milestones, and detailed business plans.

## THE SNAPTAX STORY

In 2009, a startup decided to try something really audacious. They wanted to liberate taxpayers from expensive tax stores by automating the process of collecting information typically found on W-2 forms (the end-of-year statement that most employees receive from their employer that summarizes their taxable wages for the year). The startup quickly ran into difficulties. Even though many consumers had access to a printer/scanner in their home or office, few knew how to use those devices. After numerous conversations with potential customers, the team lit upon the idea of having customers take photographs of the forms directly from their cell phone. In the process of testing this concept, customers asked something unexpected: would it be possible to finish *the whole tax return* right on the phone itself?

That was not an easy task. Traditional tax preparation requires consumers to wade through hundreds of questions, many forms, and a lot of paperwork. This startup tried something novel by deciding to ship an early version of its product that could do much less than a complete tax package. The initial version worked only for consumers with a very simple return to file, and it worked only in California.

Instead of having consumers fill out a complex form, they allowed the customers to use the phone's camera to take a picture of their W-2 forms. From that single picture, the company developed the technology to compile and file most of the 1040 EZ tax return. Compared with the drudgery of traditional tax filing, the new product—called SnapTax—provides a magical experience. From its modest beginning, SnapTax grew into a significant startup success story. Its nationwide launch in 2011 showed that customers loved it, to the tune of more than 350,000 downloads in the first three weeks.

This is the kind of amazing innovation you'd expect from a new startup.

However, the name of this company may surprise you. SnapTax was developed by Intuit, America's largest producer of finance, tax, and accounting tools for individuals and small businesses. With more than 7,700 employees and annual revenues in the billions, Intuit is not a typical startup.[2]

The team that built SnapTax doesn't look much like the archetypal image of entrepreneurs either. They don't work in a garage or eat ramen noodles. Their company doesn't lack for resources. They are paid a full salary and benefits. They come into a regular office every day. Yet they are entrepreneurs.

Stories like this one are not nearly as common inside large corporations as they should be. After all, SnapTax competes directly with one of Intuit's flagship products: the fully featured TurboTax desktop software. Usually, companies like Intuit fall into the trap described in Clayton Christensten's *The Innovator's Dilemma:* they are very good at creating incremental improvements to existing products and serving existing customers, which Christensen called *sustaining innovation,* but struggle to create breakthrough new products—*disruptive innovation*—that can create new sustainable sources of growth.

One remarkable part of the SnapTax story is what the team leaders said when I asked them to account for their unlikely success. Did they hire superstar entrepreneurs from outside the company? No, they assembled a team from within Intuit. Did they face constant meddling from senior management, which is the bane of innovation teams in many companies? No, their executive sponsors created an "island of freedom" where they could experiment as necessary. Did they have a huge team, a large budget, and lots of marketing dollars? Nope, they started with a team of five.

What allowed the SnapTax team to innovate was not their genes, destiny, or astrological signs but a process deliberately facilitated by Intuit's senior management. Innovation is a bottoms-up, decentralized, and unpredictable thing, but that doesn't mean it cannot be managed. It can, but to do so requires a new management discipline, one that needs to be mastered not just by practicing entrepreneurs seeking to build the next big thing but also by the people who support them, nurture them, and hold them accountable. In other words, cultivating entrepreneurship is the responsibility of senior management.Today, a cutting-edge company such as Intuit can point to success stories like SnapTax because it has recognized the need for a new management paradigm. This is a realization that was years in the making.[3]

## A SEVEN-THOUSAND-PERSON LEAN STARTUP

In 1983, Intuit's founder, the legendary entrepreneur Scott Cook, had the radical notion (with cofounder Tom Proulx) that personal accounting should happen by computer. Their success was far from inevitable; they faced numerous competitors, an uncertain future, and an initially tiny market. A decade later, the company went public and subsequently fended off well-publicized attacks from larger incumbents, including the software behemoth Microsoft. Partly with the help of famed venture capitalist John Doerr, Intuit became a fully diversified enterprise, a member of the Fortune 1000 that now provides dozens of market-leading products across its major divisions.

This is the kind of entrepreneurial success we're used to hearing about: a ragtag team of underdogs who eventually achieve fame, acclaim, and significant riches.

Flash-forward to 2002. Cook was frustrated. He had just tabulated ten years of data on all of Intuit's new product introductions and had concluded that the company was getting a measly return on its massive investments. Simply put, too many of its new products were failing. By traditional standards, Intuit is an extremely well-managed company, but as Scott dug into the root causes of those failures, he came to a difficult conclusion: the prevailing management paradigm he and his company had been practicing was inadequate to the problem of continuous innovation in the modern economy.

By fall 2009, Cook had been working to change Intuit's management culture for several years. He came across my early work on the Lean Startup and asked me to give a talk at Intuit. In Silicon Valley this is not the kind of invitation you turn down. I admit I was curious. I was still at the beginning of my Lean Startup journey and didn't have much appreciation for the challenges faced by a Fortune 1000 company like his.

My conversations with Cook and Intuit chief executive officer (CEO) Brad Smith were my initiation into the thinking of modern general managers, who struggle with entrepreneurship every bit as much as do venture capitalists and founders in a garage. To combat these challenges, Scott and Brad are going back to Intuit's roots. They are working to build entrepreneurship and risk taking into all their divisions.

For example, consider one of Intuit's flagship products. Because TurboTax does most of its sales around tax season in the United States, it used to have an extremely conservative culture. Over the course of the year, the marketing and product teams would conceive one major initiative that would be rolled out just in time for tax season. Now they test over five hundred different changes in a two-and-a-half-month tax season. They're running up to seventy different tests per week. The team can make a change live on its website on Thursday, run it over the weekend, read the results on Monday, and come to conclusions starting Tuesday; then they rebuild new tests on Thursday and launch the next set on Thursday night.

As Scott put it, "Boy, the amount of learning they get is just immense now. And what it does is develop entrepreneurs, because when you have only one test, you don't have entrepreneurs, you have politicians, because you have to sell. Out of a hundred good ideas, you've got to sell your idea. So you build up a society of politicians and salespeople. When you have five hundred tests you're running, then everybody's ideas can run. And then you create entrepreneurs who run and learn and can retest and relearn as opposed to a society of politicians. So we're trying to drive that throughout our organization, using examples which have nothing to do with high tech, like the website example. Every business today has a website. You don't have to be high tech to use fast-cycle testing."

This kind of change is hard. After all, the company has a significant number of existing customers who continue to demand exceptional service and investors who expect steady, growing returns.

Scott says,

> It goes against the grain of what people have been taught in business and what leaders have been taught. The problem isn't with the teams or the entrepreneurs. They love the chance to quickly get their baby out into the market. They love the chance to have the customer vote instead of the suits voting. The real issue is with the leaders and the middle managers. There are many business leaders who have been successful because of analysis. They think they're analysts, and their job is to do great planning and analyzing and have a plan.

The amount of time a company can count on holding on to market leadership to exploit its earlier innovations is shrinking, and this creates an imperative for even the most entrenched companies to invest in innovation. In fact, I believe a company's only sustainable path to long-term economic growth is to build an "innovation factory" that uses Lean Startup techniques to create disruptive innovations on a continuous basis. In other words, established companies need to figure out how to accomplish what Scott Cook did in 1983, but on an industrial scale and with an established cohort of managers steeped in traditional management culture.

Ever the maverick, Cook asked me to put these ideas to the test, and so I gave a talk that was simulcast to all seven thousand–plus Intuit employees during which I explained the theory of the Lean Startup, repeating my definition: an organization designed to create new products and services under conditions of extreme uncertainty.

What happened next is etched in my memory. CEO Brad Smith had been sitting next to me as I spoke. When I was done, he got up and said before all of Intuit's employees, "Folks, listen up. You heard Eric's definition of a startup. It has three parts, and we here at Intuit match *all three parts* of that definition."

Scott and Brad are leaders who realize that something new is needed in management thinking. Intuit is proof that this kind of thinking can work in established companies. Brad explained to me how they hold themselves accountable for their new innovation efforts by measuring two things: the number of customers using products that didn't exist three years ago and the percentage of revenue coming from offerings that did not exist three years ago.

Under the old model, it took an average of 5.5 years for a successful new product to start generating $50 million in revenue. Brad explained to me, "We've generated $50 million in offerings that did not exist twelve months ago in the last year. Now it's not one particular offering. It's a combination of a whole bunch of innovation happening, but that's the kind of stuff that's creating some energy for us, that we think we can truly short-circuit the ramp by killing things that don't make sense fast and doubling down on the ones that do." For a company as large as Intuit, these are modest results and early days. They have decades of legacy systems and legacy thinking to overcome. However, their leadership in adopting entrepreneurial management is starting to pay off.

Leadership requires creating conditions that enable employees to do the kinds of experimentation that entrepreneurship requires. For example, changes in TurboTax enabled the Intuit team to develop five hundred experiments per tax season. Before that, marketers with great ideas couldn't have done those tests even if they'd wanted to, because they didn't have a system in place through which to change the website rapidly. Intuit invested in systems that increased the speed at which tests could be built, deployed, and analyzed.

As Cook says, "Developing these experimentation systems is

the responsibility of senior management; they have to be put in by the leadership. It's moving leaders from playing Caesar with their thumbs up and down on every idea to—instead—putting in the culture and the systems so that teams can move and innovate at the speed of the experimentation system."

# 3

# LEARN

As an entrepreneur, nothing plagued me more than the question of whether my company was making progress toward creating a successful business. As an engineer and later as a manager, I was accustomed to measuring progress by making sure our work proceeded according to plan, was high quality, and cost about what we had projected.

After many years as an entrepreneur, I started to worry about measuring progress in this way. What if we found ourselves building something that nobody wanted? In that case what did it matter if we did it on time and on budget? When I went home at the end of a day's work, the only things I knew for sure were that I had kept people busy and spent money that day. I hoped that my team's efforts took us closer to our goal. If we wound up taking a wrong turn, I'd have to take comfort in the fact that at least we'd learned something important.

Unfortunately, "learning" is the oldest excuse in the book for a failure of execution. It's what managers fall back on when they fail to achieve the results we promised. Entrepreneurs, under pressure to succeed, are wildly creative when it comes to demonstrating what we have learned. We can all tell a good story when our job, career, or reputation depends on it.

However, learning is cold comfort to employees who are following an entrepreneur into the unknown. It is cold comfort to the investors who allocate precious money, time, and energy to entrepreneurial teams. It is cold comfort to the organizations—large and small—that depend on entrepreneurial innovation to survive. You can't take learning to the bank; you can't spend it or invest it. You cannot give it to customers and cannot return it to limited partners. Is it any wonder that learning has a bad name in entrepreneurial and managerial circles?

Yet if the fundamental goal of entrepreneurship is to engage in organization building under conditions of extreme uncertainty, its most vital function is learning. We must learn the truth about which elements of our strategy are working to realize our vision and which are just crazy. We must learn what customers really want, not what they say they want or what we think they should want. We must discover whether we are on a path that will lead to growing a sustainable business.

In the Lean Startup model, we are rehabilitating learning with a concept I call *validated learning.* Validated learning is not after-the-fact rationalization or a good story designed to hide failure. It is a rigorous method for demonstrating progress when one is embedded in the soil of extreme uncertainty in which startups grow. Validated learning is the process of demonstrating empirically that a team has discovered valuable truths about a startup's present and future business prospects. It is more concrete, more accurate, and faster than market forecasting or classical business planning. It is the principal antidote to the lethal problem of achieving failure: successfully executing a plan that leads nowhere.

## VALIDATED LEARNING AT IMVU

Let me illustrate this with an example from my career. Many audiences have heard me recount the story of IMVU's founding and the many mistakes we made in developing our first product. I'll now elaborate on one of those mistakes to illustrate validated learning clearly.

Those of us involved in the founding of IMVU aspired to be serious strategic thinkers. Each of us had participated in previous ventures that had failed, and we were loath to repeat that experience. Our main concerns in the early days dealt with the following questions: What should we build and for whom? What market could we enter and dominate? How could we build durable value that would not be subject to erosion by competition?[1]

## Brilliant Strategy

We decided to enter the instant messaging (IM) market. In 2004, that market had hundreds of millions of consumers actively participating worldwide. However, the majority of the customers who were using IM products were not paying for the privilege. Instead, large media and portal companies such as AOL, Microsoft, and Yahoo! operated their IM networks as a loss leader for other services while making modest amounts of money through advertising.

IM is an example of a market that involves strong *network effects.* Like most communication networks, IM is thought to follow Metcalfe's law: the value of a network as a whole is proportional to the square of the number of participants. In other words, the more people in the network, the more valuable the network. This makes intuitive sense: the value to each participant is driven primarily by how many other people he or she can communicate with. Imagine a world in which you own the only telephone; it would have no value. Only when other people also have a telephone does it become valuable.

In 2004, the IM market was locked up by a handful of

incumbents. The top three networks controlled more than 80 percent of the overall usage and were in the process of consolidating their gains in market share at the expense of a number of smaller players.[2] The common wisdom was that it was more or less impossible to bring a new IM network to market without spending an extraordinary amount of money on marketing.

The reason for that wisdom is simple. Because of the power of network effects, IM products have high switching costs. To switch from one network to another, customers would have to convince their friends and colleagues to switch with them. This extra work for customers creates a barrier to entry in the IM market: with all consumers locked in to an incumbent's product, there are no customers left with whom to establish a beachhead.

At IMVU we settled on a strategy of building a product that would combine the large mass appeal of traditional IM with the high revenue per customer of three-dimensional (3D) video games and virtual worlds. Because of the near impossibility of bringing a new IM network to market, we decided to build an IM add-on product that would interoperate with the existing networks. Thus, customers would be able to adopt the IMVU virtual goods and avatar communication technology without having to switch IM providers, learn a new user interface, and—most important—bring their friends with them.

In fact, we thought this last point was essential. For the add-on product to be useful, customers would *have* to use it with their existing friends. Every communication would come embedded with an invitation to join IMVU. Our product would be inherently viral, spreading throughout the existing IM networks like an epidemic. To achieve that viral growth, it was important that our add-on product support as many of the existing IM networks as possible and work on all kinds of computers.

## Six Months to Launch

With this strategy in place, my cofounders and I began a period of intense work. As the chief technology officer, it was my responsibility, among other things, to write the software that would support IM interoperability across networks. My cofounders and I worked for months, putting in crazy hours struggling to get our first product released. We gave ourselves a hard deadline of six months—180 days—to launch the product and attract our first paying customers. It was a grueling schedule, but we were determined to launch on time.

The add-on product was so large and complex and had so many moving parts that we had to cut a lot of corners to get it done on time. I won't mince words: the first version was terrible. We spent endless hours arguing about which bugs to fix and which we could live with, which features to cut and which to try to cram in. It was a wonderful and terrifying time: we were full of hope about the possibilities for success and full of fear about the consequences of shipping a bad product.

Personally, I was worried that the low quality of the product would tarnish my reputation as an engineer. People would think I didn't know how to build a quality product. All of us feared tarnishing the IMVU brand; after all, we were charging people money for a product that didn't work very well. We all envisioned the damning newspaper headlines: "Inept Entrepreneurs Build Dreadful Product."

As launch day approached, our fears escalated. In our situation, many entrepreneurial teams give in to fear and postpone the launch date. Although I understand this impulse, I am glad we persevered, since delay prevents many startups from getting the feedback they need. Our previous failures made us more afraid of another, even worse, outcome than shipping a bad product: building something that nobody wants. And so, teeth clenched and apologies at the ready, we released our product to the public.

## Launch

And then—nothing happened! It turned out that our fears were unfounded, because nobody even tried our product. At first I was relieved because at least nobody was finding out how bad the product was, but soon that gave way to serious frustration. After all the hours we had spent arguing about which features to include and which bugs to fix, our value proposition was so far off that customers weren't getting far enough into the experience to find out how bad our design choices were. Customers wouldn't even download our product.

Over the ensuing weeks and months, we labored to make the product better. We brought in a steady flow of customers through our online registration and download process. We treated each day's customers as a brand-new report card to let us know how we were doing. We eventually learned how to change the product's positioning so that customers at least would download it. We were making improvements to the underlying product continuously, shipping bug fixes and new changes daily. However, despite our best efforts, we were able to persuade only a pathetically small number of people to buy the product.

In retrospect, one good decision we made was to set clear revenue targets for those early days. In the first month we intended to make $300 in total revenue, and we did—barely. Many friends and family members were asked (okay, begged). Each month our small revenue targets increased, first to $350 and then to $400. As they rose, our struggles increased. We soon ran out of friends and family; our frustration escalated. We were making the product better every day, yet our customers' behavior remained unchanged: they still wouldn't use it.

Our failure to move the numbers prodded us to accelerate our efforts to bring customers into our office for in-person interviews and usability tests. The quantitative targets created the motivation to engage in qualitative inquiry and guided us in the questions we asked; this is a pattern we'll see throughout this book.

I wish I could say that I was the one to realize our mistake and suggest the solution, but in truth, I was the last to admit the problem. In short, our entire strategic analysis of the market was utterly wrong. We figured this out empirically, through experimentation, rather than through focus groups or market research. Customers could not tell us what they wanted; most, after all, had never heard of 3D avatars. Instead, they revealed the truth through their action or inaction as we struggled to make the product better.

## Talking to Customers

Out of desperation, we decided to talk to some potential customers. We brought them into our office, and said, "Try this new product; it's IMVU." If the person was a teenager, a heavy user of IM, or a tech early adopter, he or she would engage with us. In constrast, if it was a mainstream person, the response was, "Right. So exactly what would you like me to do?" We'd get nowhere with the mainstream group; they thought IMVU was too weird.

Imagine a seventeen-year-old girl sitting down with us to look at this product. She chooses her avatar and says, "Oh, this is really fun." She's customizing the avatar, deciding how she's going to look. Then we say, "All right, it's time to download the instant messaging add-on," and she responds, "What's that?"

"Well, it's this thing that interoperates with the instant messaging client." She's looking at us and thinking, "I've never heard of that, my friends have never heard of that, why do you want me to do that?" It required a lot of explanation; an instant messaging add-on was not a product category that existed in her mind.

But since she was in the room with us, we were able to talk her into doing it. She downloads the product, and then we say, "Okay, invite one of your friends to chat." And she says, "No way!" We say, "Why not?" And she says, "Well, I don't know if this thing is cool yet. You want me to risk inviting one of my friends? What are they going to think of me? If it sucks, they're going to think I suck, right?" And we say, "No, no, it's going to be so much fun once you get the person in there; it's a *social* product." She looks at us, her face filled with doubt; you can see that this is a deal breaker. Of course, the first time I had that experience, I said, "It's all right, it's just this one person, send her away and get me a new one." Then the second customer comes in and says the same thing. Then the third customer comes in, and it's the same thing. You start to see patterns, and no matter how stubborn you are, there's obviously something wrong.

Customers kept saying, "I want to use it by myself. I want to try it out first to see if it's really cool before I invite a friend." Our team was from the video game industry, so we understood what that meant: single-player mode. So we built a single-player version. We'd bring new customers into our office. They'd customize the avatar and download the product like before. Then they would go into single-player mode, and we'd say, "Play with your avatar and dress it up; check out the cool moves it can make." Followed by, "Okay, you did that by yourself; now it's time to invite one of your friends." You can see what's coming. They'd say, "No way! This isn't cool." And we'd say, "Well, we *told* you it wasn't going to be cool! What is the point of a single-player experience for a social product?" See, we thought we should get a gold star just for listening to our customers. Except our customers still didn't like the product. They would look at us and say, "Listen, old man, you don't understand. What is the deal with this crazy business of inviting friends before I know if it's cool?" It was a total deal breaker.

Out of further desperation, we introduced a feature called ChatNow that allows you to push a button and be randomly matched with somebody else anywhere in the world. The only thing you have in common is that you both pushed the button at the same time. All of a sudden, in our customer service tests, people were saying, "Oh, this is fun!"

So we'd bring them in, they'd use ChatNow, and maybe they would meet somebody they thought was cool. They'd say, "Hey, that guy was neat; I want to add him to my buddy list. Where's my buddy list?" And we'd say, "Oh, no, you don't want a new buddy list; you want to use your regular AOL buddy list." Remember, this was how we planned to harness the interoperability that would lead to network effects and viral growth. Picture the customer looking at us, asking, "What do you want me to do exactly?" And we'd say, "Well, just give the stranger your AIM screen name so you can put him on your buddy list." You could see their eyes go wide, and they'd say, "Are you kidding me? A stranger on my AIM buddy list?" To which we'd respond, "Yes; otherwise you'd have to download a whole new IM client with a new buddy list." And they'd say, "Do you have any idea how many IM clients I already run?"

"No. One or two, maybe?" That's how many clients each of us in the office used. To which the teenager would say, "Duh! I run eight." We had no idea how many instant messaging clients there were in the world.

We had the incorrect preconception that it's a challenge to learn new software and it's tricky to move your friends over to a new buddy list. Our customers revealed that this was nonsense.

We wanted to draw diagrams on the whiteboard that showed why our strategy was brilliant, but our customers didn't understand concepts like network effects and switching costs. If we tried to explain why they should behave the way we predicted, they'd just shake their heads at us, bewildered.

We had a mental model for how people used software that was years out of date, and so eventually, painfully, after dozens of meetings like that, it started to dawn on us that the IM add-on concept was fundamentally flawed.[3]

Our customers did not want an IM add-on; they wanted a stand-alone IM network. They did not consider having to learn how to use a new IM program a barrier; on the contrary, our early adopters used many different IM programs simultaneously. Our customers were not intimidated by the idea of having to take their friends with them to a new IM network; it turned out that they enjoyed that challenge. Even more surprising, our assumption that customers would want to use avatar-based IM primarily with their existing friends was also wrong. They wanted to make new friends, an activity that 3D avatars are particularly well suited to facilitating. Bit by bit, customers tore apart our seemingly brilliant initial strategy.

## Throwing My Work Away

Perhaps you can sympathize with our situation and forgive my obstinacy. After all, it was my work over the prior months that needed to be thrown away. I had slaved over the software that was required to make our IM program interoperate with other networks, which was at the heart of our original strategy. When it came time to pivot and abandon that original strategy, almost all of my work—thousands of lines of code—was thrown out. I felt betrayed. I was a devotee of the latest in software development methods (known collectively as agile development), which promised to help drive waste out of product development. However, despite that, I had committed the biggest waste of all: building a product that our customers refused to use. That was *really* depressing.

I wondered: in light of the fact that my work turned out to be a waste of time and energy, would the company have been just as well off if I had spent the last six months on a beach sipping umbrella drinks? Had I really been needed? Would it have been better if I had not done any work at all?

There is, as I mentioned at the beginning of this chapter, always one last refuge for people aching to justify their own failure. I consoled myself that if we hadn't built this first product—mistakes and all—we never would have learned these important insights about customers. We never would have learned that our strategy was flawed. There is truth in this excuse: what we learned during those critical early months set IMVU on a path that would lead to our eventual breakout success.

For a time, this "learning" consolation made me feel better, but my relief was short-lived. Here's the question that bothered me most of all: if the goal of those months was to learn these important insights about customers, why did it take so long? How much of our effort contributed to the essential lessons we needed to learn? Could we have learned those lessons earlier if I hadn't been so focused on making the product "better" by adding features and fixing bugs?

## VALUE VS. WASTE

In other words, which of our efforts are value-creating and which are wasteful? This question is at the heart of the lean manufacturing revolution; it is the first question any lean manufacturing adherent is trained to ask. Learning to see waste and then systematically eliminate it has allowed lean companies such as Toyota to dominate entire industries. In the world of software, the agile development methodologies I had practiced until that time had their origins in lean thinking. They were designed to eliminate waste too.

Yet those methods had led me down a road in which the majority of my team's efforts were wasted. Why?

The answer came to me slowly over the subsequent years. Lean thinking defines value as providing benefit to the customer; anything else is waste. In a manufacturing business, customers don't care how the product is assembled, only that it works correctly. But in a startup, who the customer is and what the customer might find valuable are unknown, part of the very uncertainty that is an essential part of the definition of a startup. I realized that as a startup, we needed a new definition of value. The real progress we had made at IMVU was what we had learned over those first months about what creates value for customers.

Anything we had done during those months that did not contribute to our learning was a form of waste. Would it have been possible to learn the same things with less effort? Clearly, the answer is yes.

For one thing, think of all the debate and prioritization of effort that went into features that customers would never discover. If we had shipped sooner, we could have avoided that waste. Also consider all the waste caused by our incorrect strategic assumptions. I had built interoperability for more than a dozen different IM clients and networks. Was this really necessary to test our assumptions? Could we have gotten the same feedback from our customers with half as many networks? With only three? With only one? Since the customers of all IM networks found our product equally unattractive, the level of learning would have been the same, but our effort would have been dramatically less.

Here's the thought that kept me up nights: did we have to

support any networks at all? Is it possible that we could have discovered how flawed our assumptions were without building anything? For example, what if we simply had offered customers the opportunity to download the product from us solely on the basis of its proposed features before building anything? Remember, almost no customers were willing to use our original product, so we wouldn't have had to do much apologizing when we failed to deliver. (Note that this is different from asking customers what they want. Most of the time customers don't know what they want in advance.) We could have conducted an experiment, offering customers the chance to try something and then measuring their behavior.

Such thought experiments were extremely disturbing to me because they undermined my job description. As the head of product development, I thought my job was to ensure the timely delivery of high-quality products and features. But if many of those features were a waste of time, what should I be doing instead? How could we avoid this waste?

I've come to believe that learning is the essential unit of progress for startups. The effort that is not absolutely necessary for learning what customers want can be eliminated. I call this *validated learning* because it is always demonstrated by positive improvements in the startup's core metrics. As we've seen, it's easy to kid yourself about what you think customers want. It's also easy to learn things that are completely irrelevant. Thus, validated learning is backed up by empirical data collected from real customers.

## WHERE DO YOU FIND VALIDATION?

As I can attest, anybody who fails in a startup can claim that he or she has learned a lot from the experience. They can tell a compelling story. In fact, in the story of IMVU so far, you might have noticed something missing. Despite my claims that we learned a lot in those early months, lessons that led to our eventual success, I haven't offered any evidence to back that up. In hindsight, it's easy to make such claims and sound credible (and you'll see some evidence later in the book), but imagine us in IMVU's early months trying to convince investors, employees, family members, and most of all ourselves that we had not squandered our time and resources. What evidence did we have?

Certainly our stories of failure were entertaining, and we had fascinating theories about what we had done wrong and what we needed to do to create a more successful product. However, the proof did not come until we put those theories into practice and built subsequent versions of the product that showed superior results with actual customers.

The next few months are where the true story of IMVU begins, not with our brilliant assumptions and strategies and whiteboard gamesmanship but with the hard work of discovering what customers really wanted and adjusting our product and strategy to meet those desires. We adopted the view that our job was to find a synthesis between our vision and what customers would accept; it wasn't to capitulate to what customers thought they wanted or to tell customers what they ought to want.

As we came to understand our customers better, we were able to improve our products. As we did that, the fundamental metrics of our business changed. In the early days, despite our efforts to improve the product, our metrics were stubbornly flat. We treated each day's customers as a new report card. We'd pay attention to the percentage of new customers who exhibited product behaviors such as downloading and buying our product. Each day, roughly the same number of customers would buy the product, and that number was pretty close to zero despite the many improvements.

However, once we pivoted away from the original strategy, things started to change. Aligned with a superior strategy, our product development efforts became magically more productive—not because we were working harder but because we were working smarter, aligned with our customers' real needs. Positive changes in metrics became the quantitative validation that our learning was real. This was critically important because we could show our stakeholders—employees, investors, and ourselves—that we were making genuine progress, not deluding ourselves. It is also the right way to think about productivity in a startup: not in terms of how much stuff we are building but in terms of how much validated learning we're getting for our efforts.[4]

For example, in one early experiment, we changed our entire website, home page, and product registration flow to replace "avatar chat" with "3D instant messaging." New customers were split automatically between these two versions of the site; half saw one, and half saw the other. We were able to measure the difference in behavior between the two groups. Not only were the people in the experimental group more likely to sign up for the product, they were more likely to become long-term paying customers.

We had plenty of failed experiments too. During one period in which we believed that customers weren't using the product because they didn't understand its many benefits, we went so far as to pay customer service agents to act as virtual tour guides for new customers. Unfortunately, customers who got that VIP treatment were no more likely to become active or paying customers.

Even after ditching the IM add-on strategy, it still took months to understand *why* it hadn't worked. After our pivot and many failed experiments, we finally figured out this insight: customers wanted to use IMVU to make *new* friends online. Our customers intuitively grasped something that we were slow to realize. All the existing social products online were centered on customers' real-life identity. IMVU's avatar technology, however, was uniquely well suited to help people get to know each other online without compromising safety or opening themselves up to identity theft. Once we formed this hypothesis, our experiments became much more likely to produce positive results. Whenever we would change the product to make it easier for people to find and keep new friends, we discovered that customers were more likely to engage. This is true startup productivity: systematically figuring out the right things to build.

These were just a few experiments among hundreds that we ran week in and week out as we started to learn which customers would use the product and why. Each bit of knowledge we gathered suggested new experiments to run, which moved our metrics closer and closer to our goal.

## THE AUDACITY OF ZERO

Despite IMVU's early success, our gross numbers were still pretty small. Unfortunately, because of the traditional way businesses are evaluated, this is a dangerous situation. The irony is that it is often easier to raise money or acquire other resources when you have zero revenue, zero customers, and zero traction than when you have a small amount. Zero invites imagination, but small numbers invite questions about whether large numbers will ever materialize. Everyone knows (or thinks he or she knows) stories of products that achieved breakthrough success overnight. As long as nothing has been released and no data have been collected, it is still possible to imagine overnight success in the future. Small numbers pour cold water on that hope.

This phenomenon creates a brutal incentive: postpone getting any data until you are certain of success. Of course, as we'll see, such delays have the unfortunate effect of increasing the amount of wasted work, decreasing essential feedback, and dramatically increasing the risk that a startup will build something nobody wants.

However, releasing a product and hoping for the best is not a good plan either, because this incentive is real. When we launched IMVU, we were ignorant of this problem. Our earliest investors and advisers thought it was quaint that we had a $300-per-month revenue plan at first. But after several months with our revenue hovering around $500 per month, some began to lose faith, as did some of our advisers, employees, and even spouses. In fact, at one point, some investors were seriously recommending that we pull the product out of the market and return to stealth mode. Fortunately, as we pivoted and experimented, incorporating what we learned into our product development and marketing efforts, our numbers started to improve.

But not by much! On the one hand, we were lucky to see a growth pattern that started to look like the famous hockey stick graph. On the other hand, the graph went up only to a few thousand dollars per month. These early graphs, although promising, were not by themselves sufficient to combat the loss of faith caused by our early failure, and we lacked the language of validated learning to provide an alternative concept to rally around. We were quite fortunate that some of our early investors understood its importance and were willing to look beyond our small gross numbers to see the real progress we were making. (You'll see the exact same graphs they did in Chapter 7.)

Thus, we can mitigate the waste that happens because of the audacity of zero with validated learning. What we needed to demonstrate was that our product development efforts were leading us toward massive success without giving in to the temptation to fall back on vanity metrics and "success theater"—the work we do to make ourselves look successful. We could have tried marketing gimmicks, bought a Super Bowl ad, or tried flamboyant public relations (PR) as a way of juicing our gross numbers. That would have given investors the illusion of traction, but only for a short time. Eventually, the fundamentals of the business would win out and the PR bump would pass. Because we would have squandered precious resources on theatrics instead of progress, we would have been in real trouble.

Sixty million avatars later, IMVU is still going strong. Its legacy is not just a great product, an amazing team, and promising financial results but a whole new way of measuring the progress of startups.

## LESSONS BEYOND IMVU

I have had many opportunities to teach the IMVU story as a business case ever since Stanford's Graduate School of Business wrote an official study about IMVU's early years.[5] The case is now part of the entrepreneurship curriculum at several business schools, including Harvard Business School, where I serve as an entrepreneur in residence. I've also told these stories at countless workshops, lectures, and conferences.

Every time I teach the IMVU story, students have an overwhelming temptation to focus on the tactics it illustrates: launching a low-quality early prototype, charging customers from day one, and using low-volume revenue targets as a way to drive accountability. These are useful techniques, but they are not the moral of the story. There are too many exceptions. Not every kind of customer will accept a low-quality prototype, for example. If the students are more skeptical, they may argue that the techniques do not apply to their industry or situation, but work only because IMVU is a software company, a consumer Internet business, or a non-mission-critical application.

None of these takeaways is especially useful. The Lean Startup is not a collection of individual tactics. It is a principled approach to new product development. The only way to make sense of its recommendations is to understand the underlying principles that make them work. As we'll see in later chapters, the Lean Startup model has been applied to a wide variety of businesses and industries: manufacturing, clean tech, restaurants, and even laundry. The tactics from the IMVU story may or may not make sense in your particular business.

Instead, the way forward is to learn to see every startup in any industry as a grand experiment. The question is not "Can this product be built?" In the modern economy, almost any product that can be imagined can be built. The more pertinent questions are "Should this product be built?" and "Can we build a sustainable business around this set of products and services?" To answer those questions, we need a method for systematically breaking down a business plan into its component parts and testing each part empirically.

In other words, we need the scientific method. In the Lean Startup model, every product, every feature, every marketing campaign—everything a startup does—is understood to be an experiment designed to achieve validated learning. This experimental approach works across industries and sectors, as we'll see in Chapter 4.

# 4
# EXPERIMENT

I come across many startups that are struggling to answer the following questions: Which customer opinions should we listen to, if any? How should we prioritize across the many features we could build? Which features are essential to the product's success and which are ancillary? What can be changed safely, and what might anger customers? What might please today's customers at the expense of tomorrow's? What should we work on next?

These are some of the questions teams struggle to answer if they have followed the "let's just ship a product and see what happens" plan. I call this the "just do it" school of entrepreneurship after Nike's famous slogan.[1] Unfortunately, if the plan is to see what happens, a team is guaranteed to succeed—at seeing what happens—but won't necessarily gain validated learning. This is one of the most important lessons of the scientific method: if you cannot fail, you cannot learn.

## FROM ALCHEMY TO SCIENCE

The Lean Startup methodology reconceives a startup's efforts as experiments that test its strategy to see which parts are brilliant and which are crazy. A true experiment follows the scientific method. It begins with a clear hypothesis that makes predictions about what is supposed to happen. It then tests those predictions empirically. Just as scientific experimentation is informed by theory, startup experimentation is guided by the startup's vision. The goal of every startup experiment is to discover how to build a sustainable business around that vision.

## Think Big, Start Small

Zappos is the world's largest online shoe store, with annual gross sales in excess of $1 billion. It is known as one of the most successful, customer-friendly e-commerce businesses in the world, but it did not start that way.

Founder Nick Swinmurn was frustrated because there was no central online site with a great selection of shoes. He envisioned a new and superior retail experience. Swinmurn could have waited a long time, insisting on testing his complete vision complete with warehouses, distribution partners, and the promise of significant sales. Many early e-commerce pioneers did just that, including infamous dot-com failures such as Webvan and Pets.com.

Instead, he started by running an experiment. His hypothesis was that customers were ready and willing to buy shoes online. To test it, he began by asking local shoe stores if he could take pictures of their inventory. In exchange for permission to take the pictures, he would post the pictures online and come back to buy the shoes at full price if a customer bought them online.

Zappos began with a tiny, simple product. It was designed to answer one question above all: is there already sufficient demand for a superior online shopping experience for shoes? However, a well-designed startup experiment like the one Zappos began with does more than test a single aspect of a business plan. In the course of testing this first assumption, many other assumptions were tested as well. To sell the shoes, Zappos had to interact with customers: taking payment, handling returns, and dealing with customer support. This is decidedly different from market research. If Zappos had relied on existing market research or conducted a survey, it could have asked what customers thought they wanted. By building a product instead, albeit a simple one, the company learned much more:

1. It had more accurate data about customer demand because it was observing real customer behavior, not asking hypothetical questions.
2. It put itself in a position to interact with real customers and learn about their needs. For example, the business plan might call for discounted pricing, but how are customer perceptions of the product affected by the discounting strategy?
3. It allowed itself to be surprised when customers behaved in unexpected ways, revealing information Zappos might not have known to ask about. For example, what if customers returned the shoes?

Zappos' initial experiment provided a clear, quantifiable outcome: either a sufficient number of customers would buy the shoes or they would not. It also put the company in a position to observe, interact with, and learn from real customers and partners. This qualitative learning is a necessary companion to quantitative testing. Although the early efforts were decidedly small-scale, that did not prevent the huge Zappos vision from being realized. In fact, in 2009 Zappos was acquired by the e-commerce giant Amazon.com for a reported $1.2 billion.[2]

## For Long-Term Change, Experiment Immediately

Caroline Barlerin is a director in the global social innovation division at Hewlett-Packard (HP), a multinational company with more than three hundred thousand employees and more than $100 billion in annual sales. Caroline, who leads global community involvement, is a social entrepreneur working to get more of HP's employees to take advantage of the company's policy on volunteering.

Corporate guidelines encourage every employee to spend up to four hours a month of company time volunteering in his or her community; that volunteer work could take the form of any philanthropic effort: painting fences, building houses, or even using pro bono or work-based skills outside the company. Encouraging the latter type of volunteering was Caroline's priority. Because of its talent and values, HP's combined workforce has the potential to have a monumental positive impact. A designer could help a nonprofit with a new website design. A team of engineers could wire a school for Internet access.

Caroline's project is just beginning, and most employees do not know that this volunteering policy exists, and only a tiny fraction take advantage of it. Most of the volunteering has been of the low-impact variety, involving manual labor, even when the volunteers were highly trained experts. Barlerin's vision is to take the hundreds of thousands of employees in the company and transform them into a force for social good.

This is the kind of corporate initiative undertaken every day at companies around the world. It doesn't look like a startup by the conventional definition or what we see in the movies. On the surface it seems to be suited to traditional management and planning. However, I hope the discussion in Chapter 2 has prompted you to be a little suspicious. Here's how we might analyze this project using the Lean Startup framework.

Caroline's project faces extreme uncertainty: there had never been a volunteer campaign of this magnitude at HP before. How confident should she be that she knows the real reasons people aren't volunteering? Most important, how much does she really know about how to change the behavior of hundreds of thousand people in more than 170 countries? Barlerin's goal is to inspire her colleagues to make the world a better place. Looked at that way, her plan seems full of untested assumptions—and a lot of vision.

In accordance with traditional management practices, Barlerin is spending time planning, getting buy-in from various departments and other managers, and preparing a road map of initiatives for the first eighteen months of her project. She also has a strong accountability framework with metrics for the impact her project should have on the company over the next four years. Like many entrepreneurs, she has a business plan that lays out her intentions nicely. Yet despite all that work, she is—so far—creating one-off wins and no closer to knowing if her vision will be able to scale.

One assumption, for example, might be that the company's long-standing values included a commitment to improving the community but that recent economic trouble had resulted in an increased companywide strategic focus on short-term profitability. Perhaps longtime employees would feel a desire to reaffirm their values of giving back to the community by volunteering. A second assumption could be that they would find it more satisfying and therefore more sustainable to use their actual workplace skills in a volunteer capacity, which would have a greater impact on behalf of the organizations to which they donated their time. Also lurking within Caroline's plans are many practical assumptions about employees' willingness to take the time to volunteer, their level of commitment and desire, and the way to best reach them with her message.

The Lean Startup model offers a way to test these hypotheses rigorously, immediately, and thoroughly. Strategic planning takes months to complete; these experiments could begin immediately. By starting small, Caroline could prevent a tremendous amount of waste down the road without compromising her overall vision. Here's what it might look like if Caroline were to treat her project as an experiment.

## Break It Down

The first step would be to break down the grand vision into its component parts. The two most important assumptions entrepreneurs make are what I call the value hypothesis and the growth hypothesis.

The *value hypothesis* tests whether a product or service really delivers value to customers once they are using it. What's a good indicator that employees find donating their time valuable? We could survey them to get their opinion, but that would not be very accurate because most people have a hard time assessing their feelings objectively.

Experiments provide a more accurate gauge. What could we see in real time that would serve as a proxy for the value participants were gaining from volunteering? We could find opportunities for a small number of employees to volunteer and then look at the retention rate of those employees. How many of them sign up to volunteer again? When an employee voluntarily invests their time and attention in this program, that is a strong indicator that they find it valuable.

For the *growth hypothesis,* which tests how new customers will discover a product or service, we can do a similar analysis. Once the program is up and running, how will it spread among the employees, from initial early adopters to mass adoption throughout the company? A likely way this program could expand is through viral growth. If that is true, the most important thing to measure is behavior: would the early participants actively spread the word to other employees?

In this case, a simple experiment would involve taking a very small number—a dozen, perhaps—of existing long-term employees and providing an exceptional volunteer opportunity for them. Because Caroline's hypothesis was that employees would be motivated by their desire to live up to HP's historical commitment to community service, the experiment would target employees who felt the greatest sense of disconnect between their daily routine and the company's expressed values. The point is not to find the average customer but to find *early adopters:* the customers who feel the need for the product most acutely. Those customers tend to be more forgiving of mistakes and are especially eager to give feedback.

Next, using a technique I call the *concierge minimum viable product* (described in detail in Chapter 6), Caroline could make sure the first few participants had an experience that was as good as she could make it, completely aligned with her vision. Unlike in a focus group, her goal would be to measure what the customers actually did. For example, how many of the first volunteers actually complete their volunteer assignments? How many volunteer a second time? How many are willing to recruit a colleague to participate in a subsequent volunteer activity?

Additional experiments can expand on this early feedback and learning. For example, if the growth model requires that a certain percentage of participants share their experiences with colleagues and encourage their participation, the degree to which that takes place can be tested even with a very small sample of people. If ten people complete the first experiment, how many do we expect to volunteer again? If they are asked to recruit a colleague, how many do we expect will do so? Remember that these are supposed to be the kinds of early adopters with the most to gain from the program.

Put another way, what if all ten early adopters decline to volunteer again? That would be a highly significant—and very negative—result. If the numbers from such early experiments don't look promising, there is clearly a problem with the strategy. That doesn't mean it's time to give up; on the contrary, it means it's time to get some immediate qualitative feedback about how to improve the program. Here's where this kind of experimentation has an advantage over traditional market research. We don't have to commission a survey or find new people to interview. We already have a cohort of people to talk to as well as knowledge about their actual behavior: the participants in the initial experiment.

This entire experiment could be conducted in a matter of weeks, less than one-tenth the time of the traditional strategic planning process. Also, it can happen in parallel with strategic planning while the plan is still being formulated. Even when experiments produce a negative result, those failures prove instructive and can influence the strategy. For example, what if no volunteers can be found who are experiencing the conflict of values within the organization that was such an important assumption in the business plan? If so, congratulations: it's time to pivot (a concept that is explored in more detail in Chapter 8).[3]

## AN EXPERIMENT IS A PRODUCT

In the Lean Startup model, an experiment is more than just a theoretical inquiry; it is also a first product. If this or any other experiment is successful, it allows the manager to get started with his or her campaign: enlisting early adopters, adding employees to each further experiment or iteration, and eventually starting to build a product. By the time that product is ready to be distributed widely, it will already have established customers. It will have solved real problems and offer detailed specifications for what needs to be built. Unlike a traditional strategic planning or market research process, this specification will be rooted in feedback on what is working today rather than in anticipation of what might work tomorrow.

To see this in action, consider an example from Kodak. Kodak's history is bound up with cameras and film, but today it also operates a substantial online business called Kodak Gallery. Mark Cook is Kodak Gallery's vice president of products, and he is working to change Kodak Gallery's culture of development to embrace experimentation.

Mark explained, "Traditionally, the product manager says, 'I just want this.' In response, the engineer says, 'I'm going to build it.' Instead, I try to push my team to first answer four questions:

1. Do consumers recognize that they have the problem you are trying to solve?
2. If there was a solution, would they buy it?
3. Would they buy it from us?
4. Can we build a solution for that problem?"

The common tendency of product development is to skip straight to the fourth question and build a solution before confirming that customers have the problem. For example, Kodak Gallery offered wedding cards with gilded text and graphics on its site. Those designs were popular with customers who were getting married, and so the team redesigned the cards to be used at other special occasions, such as for holidays. The market research and design process indicated that customers would like the new cards, and that finding justified the significant effort that went into creating them.

Days before the launch, the team realized the cards were too difficult to understand from their depiction on the website; people couldn't see how beautiful they were. They were also hard to produce. Cook realized that they had done the work backward. He explained, "Until we could figure out how to sell and make the product, it wasn't worth spending any engineering time on."

Learning from that experience, Cook took a different approach when he led his team through the development of a new set of features for a product that makes it easier to share photos taken at an event. They believed that an online "event album" would provide a way for people who attended a wedding, a conference, or another gathering to share photos with other attendees. Unlike other online photo sharing services, Kodak Gallery's event album would have strong privacy controls, assuring that the photos would be shared only with people who attended the same event.

In a break with the past, Cook led the group through a process of identifying risks and assumptions before building anything and then testing those assumptions experimentally.

There were two main hypotheses underlying the proposed event album:

1. The team assumed that customers would want to create the albums in the first place.
2. It assumed that event participants would upload photos to event albums created by friends or colleagues.

The Kodak Gallery team built a simple prototype of the event album. It lacked many features—so many, in fact, that the team was reluctant to show it to customers. However, even at that early stage, allowing customers to use the prototype helped the team refute their hypotheses. First, creating an album was not as easy as the team had predicted; *none* of the early customers were able to create one. Further, customers complained that the early product version lacked essential features.

Those negative results demoralized the team. The usability problems frustrated them, as did customer complains about missing features, many of which matched the original road map. Cook explained that even though the product was missing features, the project was not a failure. The initial product—flaws and all—confirmed that users did have the desire to create event albums, which was extremely valuable information. Where customers complained about missing features, this suggested that the team was on the right track. The team now had early evidence that those features were in fact important. What about features that were on the road map but that customers didn't complain about? Maybe those features weren't as important as they initially seemed.

Through a beta launch the team continued to learn and iterate. While the early users were enthusiastic and the numbers were promising, the team made a major discovery. Through the use of online surveying tool KISSinsights, the team learned that many customers wanted to be able to arrange the order of pictures before they would invite others to contribute. Knowing they weren't ready to launch, Cook held off his division's general manager by explaining how iterating and experimenting before beginning the marketing campaign would yield far better results. In a world where marketing launch dates were often set months in advance, waiting until the team had really solved the problem was a break from the past.

This process represented a dramatic change for Kodak Gallery; employees were used to being measured on their progress at completing tasks. As Cook says, "Success is not delivering a feature; success is learning how to solve the customer's problem."[4]

## THE VILLAGE LAUNDRY SERVICE

In India, due to the cost of a washing machine, less than seven percent of the population have one in their homes. Most people either hand wash their clothing at home or pay a Dhobi to do it for them. Dhobis take the clothes to the nearest river, wash them in the river water, bang them against rocks to get them clean, and hang them to dry, which takes two to seven days. The result? Clothes are returned in about ten days and are probably not that clean.

Akshay Mehra had been working at Procter & Gamble Singapore for eight years when he sensed an opportunity. As the brand manager of the Tide and Pantene brands for India and ASEAN countries, he thought he could make laundry services available to people who previously could not afford them. Returning to India, Akshay joined the Village Laundry Services (VLS), created by Innosight Ventures. VLS began a series of experiments to test its business assumptions.

For their first experiment, VLS mounted a consumer-grade laundry machine on the back of a pickup truck parked on a street corner in Bangalore. The experiment cost less than $8,000 and had the simple goal of proving that people would hand over their laundry and pay to have it cleaned. The entrepreneurs did not clean the laundry on the truck, which was more for marketing and show, but took it off-site to be cleaned and brought it back to their customers by the end of the day.

The VLS team continued the experiment for a week, parking the truck on different street corners, digging deeper to discover all they could about their potential customers. They wanted to know how they could encourage people to come to the truck. Did cleaning speed matter? Was cleanliness a concern? What were people asking for when they left their laundry with them?

They discovered that customers were happy to give them their laundry to clean. However, those customers were suspicious of the washing machine mounted on the back of the truck, concerned that VLS would take their laundry and run. To address that concern, VLS created a slightly more substantial mobile cart that looked more like a kiosk.

VLS also experimented with parking the carts in front of a local minimarket chain. Further iterations helped VLS figure out which services people were most interested in and what price they were willing to pay. They discovered that customers often wanted their clothes ironed and were willing to pay double the price to get their laundry back in four hours rather than twenty-four hours.

As a result of those early experiments, VLS created an end product that was a three-foot by four-foot mobile kiosk that included an energy-efficient, consumer-grade washing machine, a dryer, and an extra-long extension cord. The kiosk used Western detergents and was supplied daily with fresh clean water delivered by VLS.

Since then, the Village Laundry Service has grown substantially, with fourteen locations operational in Bangalore, Mysore, and Mumbai. As CEO Akshay Mehra shared with me, "We have serviced 116,000 kgs. in 2010 (vs. 30,600 kg. in 2009). And almost 60 percent of the business is coming from repeat customers. We have serviced more than 10,000 customers in the past year alone across all the outlets."[5]

## A LEAN STARTUP IN GOVERNMENT?

On July 21, 2010, President Obama signed the Dodd–Frank Wall Street Reform and Consumer Protection Act into law. One of its landmark provisions created a new federal agency, the

Consumer Federal Protection Bureau (CFPB). This agency is tasked with protecting American citizens from predatory lending by financial services companies such as credit card companies, student lenders, and payday loan offices. The plan calls for it to accomplish this by setting up a call center where trained case workers will field calls directly from the public.

Left to its own devices, a new government agency would probably hire a large staff with a large budget to develop a plan that is expensive and time-consuming. However, the CFPB is considering doing things differently. Despite its $500 million budget and high-profile origins, the CPFB is really a startup.

President Obama tasked his chief technology officer, Aneesh Chopra, with collecting ideas for how to set up the new startup agency, and that is how I came to be involved. On one of Chopra's visits to Silicon Valley, he invited a number of entrepreneurs to make suggestions for ways to cultivate a startup mentality in the new agency. In particular, his focus was on leveraging technology and innovation to make the agency more efficient, cost-effective, and thorough.

My suggestion was drawn straight from the principles of this chapter: treat the CFPB as an experiment, identify the elements of the plan that are assumptions rather than facts, and figure out ways to test them. Using these insights, we could build a minimum viable product and have the agency up and running—on a micro scale—long before the official plan was set in motion.

The number one assumption underlying the current plan is that once Americans know they can call the CFPB for help with financial fraud and abuse, there will be a significant volume of citizens who do that. This sounds reasonable, as it is based on market research about the amount of fraud that affects Americans each year. However, despite all that research, it is still an assumption. If the actual call volume differs markedly from that in the plan, it will require significant revision. What if Americans who are subjected to financial abuse don't view themselves as victims and therefore don't seek help? What if they have very different notions of what problems are important? What if they call the agency seeking help for problems that are outside its purview?

Once the agency is up and running with a $500 million budget and a correspondingly large staff, altering the plan will be expensive and time-consuming, but why wait to get feedback? To start experimenting immediately, the agency could start with the creation of a simple hotline number, using one of the new breed of low-cost and fast setup platforms such as Twilio. With a few hours' work, they could add simple voice prompts, offering callers a menu of financial problems to choose from. In the first version, the prompts could be drawn straight from the existing research. Instead of a caseworker on the line, each prompt could offer the caller useful information about how to solve her or his problem.

Instead of marketing this hotline to the whole country, the agency could run the experiment in a much more limited way: start with a small geographic area, perhaps as small as a few city blocks, and instead of paying for expensive television or radio advertising to let people know about the service, use highly targeted advertising. Flyers on billboards, newspaper advertisements to those blocks, or specially targeted online ads would be a good start. Since the target area is so small, they could afford to pay a premium to create a high level of awareness in the target zone. The total cost would remain quite small.

As a comprehensive solution to the problem of financial abuse, this minimum viable product is not very good compared with what a $500 million agency could accomplish. But it is also not very expensive. This product could be built in a matter of days or weeks, and the whole experiment probably would cost only a few thousand dollars.

What we would learn from this experiment would be invaluable. On the basis of the selections of those first callers, the agency could immediately start to get a sense of what kinds of problems Americans believe they have, not just what they "should" have. The agency could begin to test marketing messages: What motivates people to call? It could start to extrapolate real-world trends: What percentage of people in the target area actually call? The extrapolation would not be perfect, but it would establish a baseline behavior that would be far more accurate than market research.

Most important, this product would serve as a seed that could germinate into a much more elaborate service. With this beginning, the agency could engage in a continuous process of improvement, slowly but surely adding more and better solutions. Eventually, it would staff the hotline with caseworkers, perhaps at first addressing only one category of problems, to give the caseworkers the best chance of success. By the time the official plan was ready for implementation, this early service could serve as a real-world template.

The CFPB is just getting started, but already they are showing signs of following an experimental approach. For example, instead of doing a geographically limited rollout, they are segmenting their first products by use case. They have established a preliminary order of financial products to provide consumer services for, with credit cards coming first. As their first experiment unfolds, they will have the opportunity to closely monitor all of the other complaints and consumer feedback they receive. This data will influence the depth, breadth, and sequence of future offerings.

As David Forrest, the CFPB's chief technology officer, told me, "Our goal is to give American citizens an easy way to tell us about the problems they see out there in the consumer financial marketplace. We have an opportunity to closely monitor what the public is telling us and react to new information. Markets change all the time and our job is to change with them."[6]

○ ○ ○

The entrepreneurs and managers profiled in this book are smart, capable, and extremely results-oriented. In many cases, they are in the midst of building an organization in a way consistent with the best practices of current management thinking. They face the same challenges in both the public and private sectors, regardless of industry. As we've seen, even the seasoned managers and executives at the world's best-run companies struggle to consistently develop and launch innovative new products.

Their challenge is to overcome the prevailing management thinking that puts its faith in well-researched plans. Remember, planning is a tool that only works in the presence of a long and stable operating history. And yet, do any of us feel that the world around us is getting more and more stable every day? Changing such a mind-set is hard but critical to startup success. My hope is that this book will help managers and entrepreneurs make this change.

# Part Two

# STEER

# How Vision Leads to Steering

At its heart, a startup is a catalyst that transforms ideas into products. As customers interact with those products, they generate feedback and data. The feedback is both qualitative (such as what they like and don't like) and quantitative (such as how many people use it and find it valuable). As we saw in Part One, the products a startup builds are really experiments; the learning about how to build a sustainable business is the outcome of those experiments. For startups, that information is much more important than dollars, awards, or mentions in the press, because it can influence and reshape the next set of ideas.

We can visualize this three-step process with this simple diagram:

**BUILD-MEASURE-LEARN FEEDBACK LOOP**

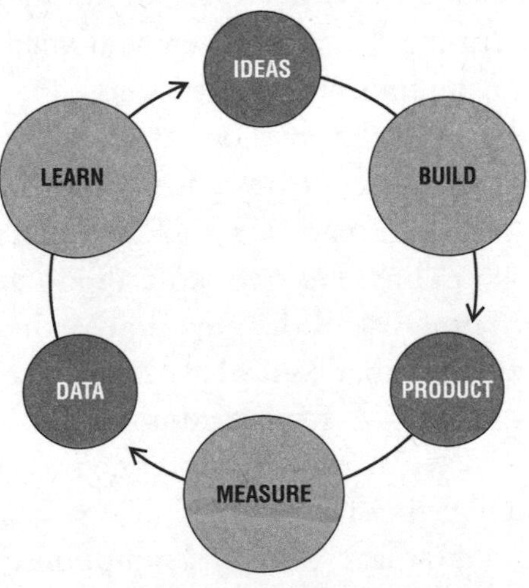


**Minimize *TOTAL* time through the loop**

This Build-Measure-Learn feedback loop is at the core of the Lean Startup model. In Part Two, we will examine it in great detail.

Many people have professional training that emphasizes one element of this feedback loop. For engineers, it's learning to build things as efficiently as possible. Some managers are experts at strategizing and learning at the whiteboard. Plenty of entrepreneurs focus their energies on the individual nouns: having the best product idea or the best-designed initial product or obsessing over data and metrics. The truth is that none of these activities by itself is of paramount importance. Instead, we need to focus our energies on minimizing the *total* time through this feedback loop. This is the essence of steering a startup and is the subject of Part Two. We will walk through a complete turn of the Build-Measure-Learn feedback loop, discussing each of the components in detail.

The purpose of Part One was to explore the importance of learning as the measure of progress for a startup. As I hope is evident by now, by focusing our energies on validated learning, we can avoid much of the waste that plagues startups today. As in lean manufacturing, learning where and when to invest energy results in saving time and money.

To apply the scientific method to a startup, we need to identify which hypotheses to test. I call the riskiest elements of a startup's plan, the parts on which everything depends, *leap-of-faith* assumptions. The two most important assumptions are the value hypothesis and the growth hypothesis. These give rise to tuning variables that control a startup's engine of growth. Each iteration of a startup is an attempt to rev this engine to see if it will turn. Once it is running, the process repeats, shifting into higher and higher gears.

Once clear on these leap-of-faith assumptions, the first step is to enter the Build phase as quickly as possible with a minimum viable product (MVP). The MVP is that version of the product that enables a full turn of the Build-Measure-Learn loop with a minimum amount of effort and the least amount of development time. The minimum viable product lacks many features that may prove essential later on. However, in some ways, creating a MVP requires extra work: we must be able to measure its impact. For example, it is inadequate to build a prototype that is evaluated solely for internal quality by engineers and designers. We also need to get it in front of potential customers to gauge their reactions. We may even need to try selling them the prototype, as we'll soon see.

When we enter the Measure phase, the biggest challenge will be determining whether the product development efforts are leading to real progress. Remember, if we're building something that nobody wants, it doesn't much matter if we're doing it on time and on budget. The method I recommend is called *innovation accounting,* a quantitative approach that allows us to see whether our engine-tuning efforts are bearing fruit. It also allows us to create *learning milestones,* which are an alternative to traditional business and product milestones. Learning milestones are useful for entrepreneurs as a way of assessing their progress accurately and objectively; they are also invaluable to managers and investors who must hold entrepreneurs accountable. However, not all metrics are created equal, and in Chapter 7 I'll clarify the danger of *vanity metrics* in contrast to the nuts-and-bolts usefulness of *actionable metrics,* which help to analyze customer behavior in ways that support innovation accounting.

Finally, and most important, there's the *pivot.* Upon completing the Build-Measure-Learn loop, we confront the most difficult question any entrepreneur faces: whether to pivot the original strategy or persevere. If we've discovered that one of our hypotheses is false, it is time to make a major change to a new strategic hypothesis.

The Lean Startup method builds capital-efficient companies because it allows startups to recognize that it's time to pivot sooner, creating less waste of time and money. Although we write the feedback loop as Build-Measure-Learn because the activities happen in that order, our planning really works in the reverse order: we figure out what we need to learn, use innovation accounting to figure out what we need to measure to know if we are gaining validated learning, and then figure out what product we need to build to run that experiment and get that measurement. All of the techniques in Part Two are designed to minimize the total time through the Build-Measure-Learn feedback loop.

# 5

# LEAP

In 2004, three college sophomores arrived in Silicon Valley with their fledgling college social network. It was live on a handful of college campuses. It was not the market-leading social network or even the first college social network; other companies had launched sooner and with more features. With 150,000 registered users, it made very little revenue, yet that summer they raised their first $500,000 in venture capital. Less than a year later, they raised an additional $12.7 million.

Of course, by now you've guessed that these three college sophomores were Mark Zuckerberg, Dustin Moskovitz, and Chris Hughes of Facebook. Their story is now world famous. Many things about it are remarkable, but I'd like to focus on only one: how Facebook was able to raise so much money when its actual usage was so small.[1]

By all accounts, what impressed investors the most were two facts about Facebook's early growth. The first fact was the raw amount of time Facebook's active users spent on the site. More than half of the users came back to the site every single day.[2] This is an example of how a company can validate its value hypothesis—that customers find the product valuable. The second impressive thing about Facebook's early traction was the rate at which it had taken over its first few college campuses. The rate of growth was staggering: Facebook launched on February 4, 2004, and by the end of that month almost three-quarters of Harvard's undergraduates were using it, without a dollar of marketing or advertising having been spent. In other words, Facebook also had validated its growth hypothesis. These two hypotheses represent two of the most important *leap-of-faith* questions any new startup faces.[3]

At the time, I heard many people criticize Facebook's early investors, claiming that Facebook had "no business model" and only modest revenues relative to the valuation offered by its investors. They saw in Facebook a return to the excesses of the dot-com era, when companies with little revenue raised massive amounts of cash to pursue a strategy of "attracting eyeballs" and "getting big fast." Many dot-com-era startups planned to make money later by selling the eyeballs they had bought to other advertisers. In truth, those dot-com failures were little more than middlemen, effectively paying money to acquire customers' attention and then planning to resell it to others. Facebook was different, because it employed a different engine of growth. It paid nothing for customer acquisition, and its high engagement meant that it was accumulating massive amounts of customer attention every day. There was never any question that attention would be valuable to advertisers; the only question was how much they would pay.

Many entrepreneurs are attempting to build the next Facebook, yet when they try to apply the lessons of Facebook and other famous startup success stories, they quickly get confused. Is the lesson of Facebook that startups should not charge customers money in the early days? Or is it that startups should never spend money on marketing? These questions cannot be answered in the abstract; there are an almost infinite number of counterexamples for any technique. Instead, as we saw in Part One, startups need to conduct experiments that help determine what techniques will work in their unique circumstances. For startups, the role of strategy is to help figure out the right questions to ask.

## STRATEGY IS BASED ON ASSUMPTIONS

Every business plan begins with a set of assumptions. It lays out a strategy that takes those assumptions as a given and proceeds to show how to achieve the company's vision. Because the assumptions haven't been proved to be true (they are assumptions, after all) and in fact are often erroneous, the goal of a startup's early efforts should be to test them as quickly as possible.

What traditional business strategy excels at is helping managers identify clearly what assumptions are being made in a particular business. The first challenge for an entrepreneur is to build an organization that can test these assumptions systematically. The second challenge, as in all entrepreneurial situations, is to perform that rigorous testing without losing sight of the company's overall vision.

Many assumptions in a typical business plan are unexceptional. These are well-established facts drawn from past industry experience or straightforward deductions. In Facebook's case, it was clear that advertisers would pay for customers' attention. Hidden among these mundane details are a handful of assumptions that require more courage to state—in the present tense—with a straight face: we assume that customers have a significant desire to use a product like ours, or we assume that supermarkets will carry our product. Acting as if these assumptions are true is a classic entrepreneur superpower. They are called *leaps of faith* precisely because the success of the entire venture rests on them. If they are true, tremendous opportunity awaits. If they are false, the startup risks total failure.

Most leaps of faith take the form of an argument by analogy. For example, one business plan I remember argued as follows: "Just as the development of progressive image loading allowed the widespread use of the World Wide Web over dial-up, so too our progressive rendering technology will allow our product to run on low-end personal computers." You probably have no idea what progressive image loading or rendering is, and it doesn't much matter. But you know the argument (perhaps you've even used it):

> Previous technology X was used to win market Y because of attribute Z. We have a new technology X2 that will enable us to win market Y2 because we too have attribute Z.

The problem with analogies like this is that they obscure the true leap of faith. That is their goal: to make the business seem less risky. They are used to persuade investors, employees, or partners to sign on. Most entrepreneurs would cringe to see their leap of faith written this way:

> Large numbers of people already wanted access to the World Wide Web. They knew what it was, they could afford it, but they could not get access to it because the time it took to load images was too long. When progressive image loading was introduced, it allowed people to get onto the World Wide Web and tell their friends about it. Thus, company X won market Y.
>
> Similarly, there is already a large number of potential customers who want access to our product right now. They know they want it, they can afford it, but they cannot access it because the rendering is too slow. When we debut our product with progressive rendering technology,

> they will flock to our software and tell their friends, and we will win market Y2.

There are several things to notice in this revised statement. First, it's important to identify the facts clearly. Is it really true that progressive image loading caused the adoption of the World Wide Web, or was this just one factor among many? More important, is it really true that there are large numbers of potential customers out there who want our solution right now? The earlier analogy was designed to convince stakeholders that a reasonable first step is to build the new startup's technology and see if customers will use it. The restated approach should make clear that what is needed is to do some empirical testing first: let's make sure that there really are hungry customers out there eager to embrace our new technology.

## Analogs and Antilogs

There is nothing intrinsically wrong with basing strategy on comparisons to other companies and industries. In fact, that approach can help you discover assumptions that are not really leaps of faith. For example, the venture capitalist Randy Komisar, whose book *Getting to Plan B* discussed the concept of leaps of faith in great detail, uses a framework of "analogs" and "antilogs" to plot strategy.

He explains the analog-antilog concept by using the iPod as an example. "If you were looking for analogs, you would have to look at the Walkman," he says. "It solved a critical question that Steve Jobs never had to ask himself: Will people listen to music in a public place using earphones? We think of that as a nonsense question today, but it is fundamental. When Sony asked the question, they did not have the answer. Steve Jobs had [the answer] in the analog [version]" Sony's Walkman was the analog. Jobs then had to face the fact that although people were willing to download music, they were not willing to pay for it. "Napster was an antilog. That antilog had to lead him to address his business in a particular way," Komisar says. "Out of these analogs and antilogs come a series of unique, unanswered questions. Those are leaps of faith that I, as an entrepreneur, am taking if I go through with this business venture. They are going to make or break my business. In the iPod business, one of those leaps of faith was that people would pay for music." Of course that leap of faith turned out to be correct.[4]

## Beyond "The Right Place at the Right Time"

There are any number of famous entrepreneurs who made millions because they seemed to be in the right place at the right time. However, for every successful entrepreneur who was in the right place in the right time, there are many more who were there, too, in that right place at the right time but still managed to fail. Henry Ford was joined by nearly five hundred other entrepreneurs in the early twentieth century. Imagine being an automobile entrepreneur, trained in state-of-the-art engineering, on the ground floor of one of the biggest market opportunities in history. Yet the vast majority managed to make no money at all.[5] We saw the same phenomenon with Facebook, which faced early competition from other college-based social networks whose head start proved irrelevant.

What differentiates the success stories from the failures is that the successful entrepreneurs had the foresight, the ability, and the tools to discover which parts of their plans were working brilliantly and which were misguided, and adapt their strategies accordingly.

## Value and Growth

As we saw in the Facebook story, two leaps of faith stand above all others: the value creation hypothesis and the growth hypothesis. The first step in understanding a new product or service is to figure out if it is fundamentally value-creating or value-destroying. I use the language of economics in referring to value rather than profit, because entrepreneurs include people who start not-for-profit social ventures, those in public sector startups, and internal change agents who do not judge their success by profit alone. Even more confusing, there are many organizations that are wildly profitable in the short term but ultimately value-destroying, such as the organizers of Ponzi schemes, and fraudulent or misguided companies (e.g., Enron and Lehman Brothers).

A similar thing is true for growth. As with value, it's essential that entrepreneurs understand the reasons behind a startup's growth. There are many value-destroying kinds of growth that should be avoided. An example would be a business that grows through continuous fund-raising from investors and lots of paid advertising but does not develop a value-creating product.

Such businesses are engaged in what I call success theater, using the appearance of growth to make it seem that they are successful. One of the goals of innovation accounting, which is discussed in depth in Chapter 7, is to help differentiate these false startups from true innovators. Traditional accounting judges new ventures by the same standards it uses for established companies, but these indications are not reliable predictors of a startup's future prospects. Consider companies such as Amazon.com that racked up huge losses on their way to breakthrough success.

Like its traditional counterpart, innovation accounting requires that a startup have and maintain a quantitative financial model that can be used to evaluate progress rigorously. However, in a startup's earliest days, there is not enough data to make an informed guess about what this model might look like. A startup's earliest strategic plans are likely to be hunch- or intuition-guided, and that is a good thing. To translate those instincts into data, entrepreneurs must, in Steve Blank's famous phrase, "get out of the building" and start learning.

## GENCHI GEMBUTSU

The importance of basing strategic decisions on firsthand understanding of customers is one of the core principles that underlies the Toyota Production System. At Toyota, this goes by the Japanese term *genchi gembutsu,* which is one of the most important phrases in the lean manufacturing vocabulary. In English, it is usually translated as a directive to "go and see for yourself" so that business decisions can be based on deep firsthand knowledge. Jeffrey Liker, who has extensively documented the "Toyota Way," explains it this way:

> In my Toyota interviews, when I asked what distinguishes the Toyota Way from other management approaches, the most common first response was *genchi gembutsu*—whether I was in manufacturing, product development, sales, distribution, or public affairs. You cannot be sure you really understand any part of any business problem unless you go and see for yourself firsthand. It is unacceptable to take anything for granted or to rely on the reports of others.[6]

To demonstrate, take a look at the development of Toyota's Sienna minivan for the 2004 model year. At Toyota, the manager responsible for the design and development of a new model is called the chief engineer, a cross-functional leader who oversees the entire process from concept to production. The 2004 Sienna was assigned to Yuji Yokoya, who had very little experience in North America, which was the Sienna's primary market. To figure out how to improve the minivan, he proposed an audacious entrepreneurial undertaking: a road trip spanning all fifty U.S. states, all thirteen provinces and territories of Canada, and all parts of Mexico. In all, he logged more than 53,000 miles of driving. In small towns and large cities, Yokoya would rent a current-model Sienna, driving it in addition to talking to and observing real customers. From those firsthand observations, Yokoya was able to start testing his critical assumptions about what North American consumers wanted in a minivan.

It is common to think of selling to consumers as easier than selling to enterprises, because customers lack the complexity of multiple departments and different people playing different roles in the purchasing process. Yokoya discovered this was untrue for his customers: "The parents and grandparents may own the minivan. But it's the kids who rule it. It's the kids who occupy the rear two-thirds of the vehicle. And it's the kids who are the most critical—and the most appreciative of their environment. If I learned anything in my travels, it was the new Sienna would need kid appeal."[7] Identifying these assumptions helped guide the car's development. For example, Yokoya spent an unusual amount of the Sienna's development budget on internal comfort features, which are critical to a long-distance family road trip (such trips are much more common in America than in Japan).

The results were impressive, boosting the Sienna's market share dramatically. The 2004 model's sales were 60 percent higher than those in 2003. Of course, a product like the Sienna is a classic *sustaining innovation*, the kind that the world's best-managed established companies, such as Toyota, excel at. Entrepreneurs face a different set of challenges because they operate with much higher uncertainty. While a company working on a sustaining innovation knows enough about who and where their customers are to use *genchi gembutsu* to discover what customers want, startups' early contact with potential customers merely reveals what assumptions require the most urgent testing.

## GET OUT OF THE BUILDING

Numbers tell a compelling story, but I always remind entrepreneurs that metrics are people, too. No matter how many intermediaries lie between a company and its customers, at the end of the day, customers are breathing, thinking, buying individuals. Their behavior is measurable and changeable. Even when one is selling to large institutions, as in a business-to-business model, it helps to remember that those businesses are made up of individuals. All successful sales models depend on breaking down the monolithic view of organizations into the disparate people that make them up.

As Steve Blank has been teaching entrepreneurs for years, the facts that we need to gather about customers, markets, suppliers, and channels exist only "outside the building." Startups need extensive contact with potential customers to understand them, so get out of your chair and get to know them.

The first step in this process is to confirm that your leap-of-faith questions are based in reality, that the customer has a significant problem worth solving.[8] When Scott Cook conceived Intuit in 1982, he had a vision—at that time quite radical—that someday consumers would use personal computers to pay bills and keep track of expenses. When Cook left his consulting job to take the entrepreneurial plunge, he didn't start with stacks of market research or in-depth analysis at the whiteboard. Instead, he picked up two phone books: one for Palo Alto, California, where he was living at the time, and the other for Winnetka, Illinois.

Calling people at random, he inquired if he could ask them a few questions about the way they managed their finances. Those early conversations were designed to answer this leap-of-faith question: do people find it frustrating to pay bills by hand? It turned out that they did, and this early validation gave Cook the confirmation he needed to get started on a solution.[9]

Those early conversations did not delve into the product features of a proposed solution; that attempt would have been foolish. The average consumers at that time were not conversant enough with personal computers to have an opinion about whether they'd want to use them in a new way. Those early conversations were with mainstream customers, not early adopters. Still, the conversations yielded a fundamental insight: if Intuit could find a way to solve this problem, there could be a large mainstream audience on which it could build a significant business.

## Design and the Customer Archetype

The goal of such early contact with customers is not to gain definitive answers. Instead, it is to clarify at a basic, coarse level that we understand our potential customer and what problems they have. With that understanding, we can craft a *customer archetype,* a brief document that seeks to humanize the proposed target customer. This archetype is an essential guide for product development and ensures that the daily prioritization decisions that every product team must make are aligned with the customer to whom the company aims to appeal.

There are many techniques for building an accurate customer archetype that have been developed over long years of practice in the design community. Traditional approaches such as interaction design or design thinking are enormously helpful. To me, it has always seemed ironic that many of these approaches are highly experimental and iterative, using techniques such as rapid prototyping and in-person customer observations to guide designers' work. Yet because of the way design agencies traditionally have been compensated, all this work culminates in a monolithic deliverable to the client. All of a sudden, the rapid learning and experimentation stops; the assumption is that the designers have learned all there is to know. For startups, this is an unworkable model. No amount of design can anticipate the many complexities of bringing a product to life in the real world.

In fact, a new breed of designers is developing brand-new techniques under the banner of Lean User Experience (Lean UX). They recognize that the customer archetype is a hypothesis, not a fact. The customer profile should be considered provisional until the strategy has shown via validated learning that we can serve this type of customer in a sustainable way.[10]

## ANALYSIS PARALYSIS

There are two ever-present dangers when entrepreneurs conduct market research and talk to customers. Followers of the just-do-it school of entrepreneurship are impatient to get started and don't want to spend time analyzing their strategy. They'd rather start building immediately, often after just a few cursory customer conversations. Unfortunately, because customers don't really know what they want, it's easy for these entrepreneurs to delude themselves that they are on the right path.

Other entrepreneurs can fall victim to analysis paralysis,

endlessly refining their plans. In this case, talking to customers, reading research reports, and whiteboard strategizing are all equally unhelpful. The problem with most entrepreneurs' plans is generally not that they don't follow sound strategic principles but that the facts upon which they are based are wrong. Unfortunately, most of these errors cannot be detected at the whiteboard because they depend on the subtle interactions between products and customers.

If too much analysis is dangerous but none can lead to failure, how do entrepreneurs know when to stop analyzing and start building? The answer is a concept called the minimum viable product, the subject of Chapter 6.

# 6
# TEST

Groupon is one of the fastest-growing companies of all time. Its name comes from "group coupons," an ingenious idea that has spawned an entire industry of social commerce imitators. However, it didn't start out successful. When customers took Groupon up on its first deal, a whopping twenty people bought two-for-one pizza in a restaurant on the first floor of the company's Chicago offices—hardly a world-changing event.

In fact, Groupon wasn't originally meant to be about commerce at all. The founder, Andrew Mason, intended his company to become a "collective activism platform" called The Point. Its goal was to bring people together to solve problems they couldn't solve on their own, such as fund-raising for a cause or boycotting a certain retailer. The Point's early results were disappointing, however, and at the end of 2008 the founders decided to try something new. Although they still had grand ambitions, they were determined to keep the new product simple. They built a minimum viable product. Does this sound like a billion-dollar company to you? Mason tells the story:

> We took a WordPress Blog and we skinned it to say Groupon and then every day we would do a new post. It was totally ghetto. We would sell T-shirts on the first

> version of Groupon. We'd say in the write-up, "This T-shirt will come in the color red, size large. If you want a different color or size, e-mail that to us." We didn't have a form to add that stuff. It was just so cobbled together.
>
> It was enough to prove the concept and show that it was something that people really liked. The actual coupon generation that we were doing was all FileMaker. We would run a script that would e-mail the coupon PDF to people. It got to the point where we'd sell 500 sushi coupons in a day, and we'd send 500 PDFs to people with Apple Mail at the same time. Really until July of the first year it was just a scrambling to grab the tiger by the tail. It was trying to catch up and reasonably piece together a product.[1]

Handmade PDFs, a pizza coupon, and a simple blog were enough to launch Groupon into record-breaking success; it is on pace to become the fastest company in history to achieve $1 billion in sales. It is revolutionizing the way local businesses find new customers, offering special deals to consumers in more than 375 cities worldwide.[2]

○ ○ ○

A minimum viable product (MVP) helps entrepreneurs start the process of learning as quickly as possible.[3] It is not necessarily the smallest product imaginable, though; it is simply the fastest way to get through the Build-Measure-Learn feedback loop with the minimum amount of effort.

Contrary to traditional product development, which usually involves a long, thoughtful incubation period and strives for product perfection, the goal of the MVP is to begin the process of learning, not end it. Unlike a prototype or concept test, an

MVP is designed not just to answer product design or technical questions. Its goal is to test fundamental business hypotheses.

## WHY FIRST PRODUCTS AREN'T MEANT TO BE PERFECT

At IMVU, when we were raising money from venture investors, we were embarrassed. First of all, our product was still buggy and low-quality. Second, although we were proud of our business results, they weren't exactly earth-shattering. The good news was that we were on a hockey-stick-shaped growth curve. The bad news was that the hockey stick went up to only about $8,000 per month of revenue. These numbers were so low that we'd often have investors ask us, "What are the units on these charts? Are those numbers in thousands?" We'd have to reply, "No, sir, those are in ones."

However, those early results were extremely significant in predicting IMVU's future path. As you'll see in Chapter 7, we were able to validate two of our leap-of-faith assumptions: IMVU was providing value for customers, and we had a working engine of growth. The gross numbers were small because we were selling the product to visionary early customers called *early adopters.* Before new products can be sold successfully to the mass market, they have to be sold to early adopters. These people are a special breed of customer. They accept—in fact prefer—an 80 percent solution; you don't need a perfect solution to capture their interest.[4]

Early technology adopters lined up around the block for Apple's original iPhone even though it lacked basic features such as copy and paste, 3G Internet speed, and support for corporate e-mail. Google's original search engine could answer queries about specialized topics such as Stanford University and the Linux operating system, but it would be years before it could "organize the world's information." However, this did not stop early adopters from singing its praises.

Early adopters use their imagination to fill in what a product is missing. They prefer that state of affairs, because what they care about above all is being the first to use or adopt a new product or technology. In consumer products, it's often the thrill of being the first one on the block to show off a new basketball shoe, music player, or cool phone. In enterprise products, it's often about gaining a competitive advantage by taking a risk with something new that competitors don't have yet. Early adopters are suspicious of something that is too polished: if it's ready for everyone to adopt, how much advantage can one get by being early? As a result, additional features or polish beyond what early adopters demand is a form of wasted resources and time.

This is a hard truth for many entrepreneurs to accept. After all, the vision entrepreneurs keep in their heads is of a high-quality mainstream product that will change the world, not one used by a small niche of people who are willing to give it a shot before it's ready. That world-changing product is polished, slick, and ready for prime time. It wins awards at trade shows and, most of all, is something you can proudly show Mom and Dad. An early, buggy, incomplete product feels like an unacceptable compromise. How many of us were raised with the expectation that we would put our best work forward? As one manager put it to me recently, "I know for me, the MVP feels a little dangerous—in a good way—since I have always been such a perfectionist."

Minimum viable products range in complexity from extremely simple smoke tests (little more than an advertisement) to actual early prototypes complete with problems and missing features. Deciding exactly how complex an MVP needs to be cannot be done formulaically. It requires judgment. Luckily, this judgment is not difficult to develop: most entrepreneurs and product development people dramatically overestimate how many features are needed in an MVP. When in doubt, simplify.

For example, consider a service sold with a one-month free trial. Before a customer can use the service, he or she has to sign up for the trial. One obvious assumption, then, of the business model is that customers will sign up for a free trial once they have a certain amount of information about the service. A critical question to consider is whether customers will in fact sign up for the free trial given a certain number of promised features (the value hypothesis).

Somewhere in the business model, probably buried in a single cell in a spreadsheet, it specifies the "percentage of customers who see the free trial offer who then sign up." Maybe in our projections we say that this number should be 10 percent. If you think about it, this is a leap-of-faith question. It really should be represented in giant letters in a bold red font: WE ASSUME 10 PERCENT OF CUSTOMERS WILL SIGN UP.

Most entrepreneurs approach a question like this by building the product and then checking to see how customers react to it. I consider this to be exactly backward because it can lead to a lot of waste. First, if it turns out that we're building something nobody wants, the whole exercise will be an avoidable expense of time and money. If customers won't sign up for the free trial, they'll never get to experience the amazing features that await them. Even if they do sign up, there are many other opportunities for waste. For example, how many features do we really need to include to appeal to early adopters? Every extra feature is a form of waste, and if we delay the test for these extra features, it comes with a tremendous potential cost in terms of learning and cycle time.

The lesson of the MVP is that any additional work beyond

what was required to start learning is waste, no matter how important it might have seemed at the time.

To demonstrate, I'll share several MVP techniques from actual Lean Startups. In each case, you'll witness entrepreneurs avoiding the temptation to overbuild and overpromise.

## THE VIDEO MINIMUM VIABLE PRODUCT

Drew Houston is the CEO of Dropbox, a Silicon Valley company that makes an extremely easy-to-use file-sharing tool. Install its application, and a Dropbox folder appears on your computer desktop. Anything you drag into that folder is uploaded automatically to the Dropbox service and then instantly replicated across all your computers and devices.

The founding team was made up of engineers, as the product demanded significant technical expertise to build. It required, for example, integration with a variety of computer platforms and operating systems: Windows, Macintosh, iPhone, Android, and so on. Each of these implementations happens at a deep level of the system and requires specialized know-how to make the user experience exceptional. In fact, one of Dropbox's biggest competitive advantages is that the product works in such a seamless way that the competition struggles to emulate it.

These are not the kind of people one would think of as marketing geniuses. In fact, none of them had ever worked in a marketing job. They had prominent venture capital backers and could have been expected to apply the standard engineering thinking to building the business: build it and they will come. But Dropbox did something different.

In parallel with their product development efforts, the founders wanted feedback from customers about what really mattered to them. In particular, Dropbox needed to test its leap-of-faith question: if we can provide a superior customer experience, will people give our product a try? They believed—rightly, as it turned out—that file synchronization was a problem that most people didn't know they had. Once you experience the solution, you can't imagine how you ever lived without it.

This is not the kind of entrepreneurial question you can ask or expect an answer to in a focus group. Customers often don't know what they want, and they often had a hard time understanding Dropbox when the concept was explained. Houston learned this the hard way when he tried to raise venture capital. In meeting after meeting, investors would explain that this "market space" was crowded with existing products, none of them had made very much money, and the problem wasn't a very important one. Drew would ask: "Have you personally tried those other products?" When they would say yes, he'd ask: "Did they work seamlessly for you?" The answer was almost always no. Yet in meeting after meeting, the venture capitalists could not imagine a world in line with Drew's vision. Drew, in contrast, believed that if the software "just worked like magic," customers would flock to it.

The challenge was that it was impossible to demonstrate the working software in a prototype form. The product required that they overcome significant technical hurdles; it also had an online service component that required high reliability and availability. To avoid the risk of waking up after years of development with a product nobody wanted, Drew did something unexpectedly easy: he made a video.

The video is banal, a simple three-minute demonstration of the technology as it is meant to work, but it was targeted at a community of technology early adopters. Drew narrates the video personally, and as he's narrating, the viewer is watching his screen. As he describes the kinds of files he'd like to synchronize, the viewer can watch his mouse manipulate his computer. Of course, if you're paying attention, you start to notice that the files he's moving around are full of in-jokes and humorous references that were appreciated by this community of early adopters. Drew recounted, "It drove hundreds of thousands of people to the website. Our beta waiting list went from 5,000 people to 75,000 people literally overnight. It totally blew us away." Today, Dropbox is one of Silicon Valley's hottest companies, rumored to be worth more than $1 billion.[5]

In this case, the video was the minimum viable product. The MVP validated Drew's leap-of-faith assumption that customers wanted the product he was developing not because they said so in a focus group or because of a hopeful analogy to another business, but because they actually signed up.

## THE CONCIERGE MINIMUM VIABLE PRODUCT

Consider another kind of MVP technique: the *concierge MVP.* To understand how this technique works, meet Manuel Rosso, the CEO of an Austin, Texas–based startup called Food on the Table. Food on the Table creates weekly meal plans and grocery lists that are based on food you and your family enjoy, then hooks into your local grocery stores to find the best deals on the ingredients.

After you sign up for the site, you walk through a little setup in which you identify your main grocery store and check off the foods your family likes. Later, you can pick another nearby store if you want to compare prices. Next, you're presented with a list of items that are based on your preferences and asked: "What are you in the mood for this week?" Make your choices, select the number of meals you're ready to plan, and choose what you care about most in terms of time, money, health, or variety. At this point, the site searches through recipes that match your needs, prices out the cost of the meal for you, and lets you print out your shopping list.[6]

Clearly, this is an elaborate service. Behind the scenes, a team of professional chefs devise recipes that take advantage of items that are on sale at local grocery stores around the country. Those recipes are matched via computer algorithm to each family's unique needs and preferences. Try to visualize the work involved: databases of almost every grocery store in the country must be maintained, including what's on sale at each one this week. Those groceries have to be matched to appropriate recipes and then appropriately customized, tagged, and sorted. If a recipe calls for broccoli rabe, is that the same ingredient as the broccoli on sale at the local market?

After reading that description, you might be surprised to learn that Food on the Table (FotT) began life with a single customer. Instead of supporting thousands of grocery stores around the country as it does today, FotT supported just one. How did the company choose which store to support? The founders didn't—until they had their first customer. Similarly, they began life with no recipes whatsoever—until their first customer was ready to begin her meal planning. In fact, the company served its first customer without building any software, without signing any business development partnerships, and without hiring any chefs.

Manuel, along with VP of product Steve Sanderson, went to local supermarkets and moms' groups in his hometown of Austin. Part of their mission was the typical observation of customers that is a part of design thinking and other ideation techniques. However, Manuel and his team were also on the hunt for something else: their first customer.

As they met potential customers in those settings, they would interview them the way any good market researcher would, but at the end of each interview they would attempt to make a sale. They'd describe the benefits of FotT, name a weekly subscription fee, and invite the customer to sign up. Most times they were rejected. After all, most people are not early adopters and will not sign up for a new service sight unseen. But eventually someone did.

That one early adopter got the concierge treatment. Instead of interacting with the FotT product via impersonal software, she got a personal visit each week from the CEO of the company. He and the VP of product would review what was on sale at her preferred grocery store and carefully select recipes on the basis of her preferences, going so far as to learn her favorite recipes for items she regularly cooked for her family. Each week they would hand her—in person—a prepared packet containing a shopping list and relevant recipes, solicit her feedback, and make changes as necessary. Most important, each week they would collect a check for $9.95.

Talk about inefficient! Measured according to traditional criteria, this is a terrible system, entirely nonscalable and a complete waste of time. The CEO and VP of product, instead of building their business, are engaged in the drudgery of solving just one customer's problem. Instead of marketing themselves to millions, they sold themselves to one. Worst of all, their efforts didn't appear to be leading to anything tangible. They had no product, no meaningful revenue, no databases of recipes, not even a lasting organization.

However, viewed through the lens of the Lean Startup, they were making monumental progress. Each week they were learning more and more about what was required to make their product a success. After a few weeks they were ready for another customer. Each customer they brought on made it easier to get the next one, because FotT could focus on the same grocery store, getting to know its products and the kinds of people who shopped there well. Each new customer got the concierge treatment: personal in-home visits, the works. But after a few more customers, the overhead of serving them one-on-one started to increase.

Only at the point where the founders were too busy to bring on additional customers did Manuel and his team start to invest in automation in the form of product development. Each iteration of their minimum viable product allowed them to save a little more time and serve a few more customers: delivering the recipes and shopping list via e-mail instead of via an in-home visit, starting to parse lists of what was on sale automatically via software instead of by hand, even eventually taking credit card payments online instead of a handwritten check.

Before long, they had built a substantial service offering, first in the Austin area and eventually nationwide. But along the way, their product development team was always focused on scaling something that was working rather than trying to invent something that might work in the future. As a result, their development efforts involved far less waste than is typical for a venture of this kind.

It is important to contrast this with the case of a small business, in which it is routine to see the CEO, founder, president, and owner serving customers directly, one at a time. In a concierge MVP, this personalized service is not the product but a learning activity designed to test the leap-of-faith assumptions in the company's growth model. In fact, a common outcome of a concierge MVP is to invalidate the company's proposed growth model, making it clear that a different approach is needed. This can happen even if the initial MVP is profitable for the company. Without a formal growth model, many companies get caught in the trap of being satisfied with a small profitable business when a pivot (change in course or strategy) might lead to more significant growth. The only way to know is to have tested the growth model systematically with real customers.

## PAY NO ATTENTION TO THE EIGHT PEOPLE BEHIND THE CURTAIN

Meet Max Ventilla and Damon Horowitz, technologists with a vision to build a new type of search software designed to answer the kinds of questions that befuddle state-of-the-art companies such as Google. Google befuddled? Think about it. Google and its peers excel at answering factual questions: What is the tallest mountain in the world? Who was the twenty-third president of the United States? But for more subjective questions, Google struggles. Ask, "What's a good place to go out for a drink after the ball game in my city?" and the technology fails. What's interesting about this class of queries is that they are relatively easy for a *person* to answer. Imagine being at a cocktail party surrounded by friends. How likely would you be to get a high-quality answer to your subjective question? You almost certainly would get one. Unlike factual queries, because these subjective questions have no single right answer, today's technology struggles to answer them. Such questions depend on the person answering them, his or her personal experience, taste, and assessment of what you're looking for.

To solve this problem, Max and Damon created a product called Aardvark. With their deep technical knowledge and industry experience, it would have been reasonable to expect them to dive in and start programming. Instead, they took six months to figure out what they should be building. But they didn't spend that year at the whiteboard strategizing or engage in a lengthy market research project.

Instead, they built a series of functioning products, each designed to test a way of solving this problem for their customers. Each product was then offered to beta testers, whose behavior was used to validate or refute each specific hypothesis (see examples in sidebar).

The following list of projects are examples from Aardvark's ideation period.[7]

**Rekkit.** A service to collect your ratings from across the web and give better recommendations to you.

**Ninjapa.** A way that you could open accounts in various applications through a single website and manage your data across multiple sites.

**The Webb.** A central number that you could call and talk to a person who could do anything for you that you could do online.

**Web Macros.** A way to record sequences of steps on websites so that you could repeat common actions, even across sites, and share "recipes" for how you accomplished online tasks.

**Internet Button Company.** A way to package steps taken on a website and smart form-fill functionality. People could encode buttons and share buttons à la social bookmarking.

Max and Damon had a vision that computers could be used to create a virtual personal assistant to which their customers could ask questions. Because the assistant was designed for subjective questions, the answers required human judgment. Thus, the early Aardvark experiments tried many variations on this theme, building a series of prototypes for ways customers could interact with the virtual assistant and get their questions answered. All the early prototypes failed to engage the customers.

As Max describes it, "We self-funded the company and released very cheap prototypes to test. What became Aardvark was the sixth prototype. Each prototype was a two- to four-week effort. We used humans to replicate the back end as much as possible. We invited one hundred to two hundred friends to try the prototypes and measured how many of them came back. The results were unambiguously negative until Aardvark."

Because of the short time line, none of the prototypes involved advanced technology. Instead, they were MVPs designed to test a more important question: what would be required to get customers to engage with the product and tell their friends about it?

"Once we chose Aardvark," Ventilla says, "we continued to run with humans replicating pieces of the backend for nine months. We hired eight people to manage queries, classify conversations, etc. We actually raised our seed and series A rounds before the system was automated—the assumption was that the lines between humans and artificial intelligence would cross, and we at least proved that we were building stuff people would respond to.

"As we refined the product, we would bring in six to twelve people weekly to react to mockups, prototypes, or simulations that we were working on. It was a mix of existing users and people who never saw the product before. We had our engineers join for many of these sessions, both so that they could make modifications in real time, but also so we could all experience the pain of a user not knowing what to do."[8]

The Aardvark product they settled on worked via instant messaging (IM). Customers could send Aardvark a question via IM, and Aardvark would get them an answer that was drawn from the customer's social network: the system would seek out the customer's friends and friends of friends and pose the question to them. Once it got a suitable answer, it would report back to the initial customer.

Of course, a product like that requires a very important algorithm: given a question about a certain topic, who is the best person in the customer's social network to answer that question? For example, a question about restaurants in San Francisco shouldn't be routed to someone in Seattle. More challenging still, a question about computer programming probably shouldn't be routed to an art student.

Throughout their testing process, Max and Damon encountered many difficult technological problems like these. Each time, they emphatically refused to solve them at that early stage. Instead, they used *Wizard of Oz testing* to fake it. In a Wizard of Oz test, customers believe they are interacting with the actual product, but behind the scenes human beings are doing the work. Like the concierge MVP, this approach is incredibly inefficient. Imagine a service that allowed customers to ask questions of human researchers—for free—and expect a real-time response. Such a service (at scale) would lose money, but it is easy to build on a micro scale. At that scale, it allowed Max and Damon to answer these all-important questions: If we can solve the tough technical problems behind this artificial intelligence product, will people use it? Will their use lead to the creation of a product that has real value?

It was this system that allowed Max and Damon to pivot over and over again, rejecting concepts that seemed promising but that would not have been viable. When they were ready to start scaling, they had a ready-made road map of what to build. The result: Aardvark was acquired for a reported $50 million—by Google.[9]

## THE ROLE OF QUALITY AND DESIGN IN AN MVP

One of the most vexing aspects of the minimum viable product is the challenge it poses to traditional notions of quality. The best professionals and craftspersons alike aspire to build quality products; it is a point of pride.

Modern production processes rely on high quality as a way to boost efficiency. They operate using W. Edwards Deming's famous dictum that the customer is the most important part of the production process. This means that we must focus our energies exclusively on producing outcomes that the customer perceives as valuable. Allowing sloppy work into our process inevitably leads to excessive variation. Variation in process yields products of varying quality in the eyes of the customer that at best require rework and at worst lead to a lost customer. Most modern business and engineering philosophies focus on producing high-quality experiences for customers as a primary principle; it is the foundation of Six Sigma, lean manufacturing, design thinking, extreme programming, and the software craftsmanship movement.

These discussions of quality presuppose that the company already knows what attributes of the product the customer will perceive as worthwhile. In a startup, this is a risky assumption to make. Often we are not even sure who the customer is. Thus, for startups, I believe in the following quality principle:

> If we do not know who the customer is, we do not know what quality is.

Even a "low-quality" MVP can act in service of building a great high-quality product. Yes, MVPs sometimes are perceived as low-quality by customers. If so, we should use this as an opportunity to learn what attributes customers care about. This is infinitely better than mere speculation or whiteboard strategizing, because it provides a solid empirical foundation on which to build future products.

Sometimes, however, customers react quite differently. Many famous products were released in a "low-quality" state, and customers loved them. Imagine if Craig Newmark, in the early days of Craigslist, had refused to publish his humble e-mail newsletter because it lacked sufficient high design. What if the founders of Groupon had felt "two pizzas for the price of one" was beneath them?

I have had many similar experiences. In the early days of IMVU, our avatars were locked in one place, unable to move around the screen. The reason? We were building an MVP and had not yet tackled the difficult task of creating the technology that would allow avatars to walk around the virtual environments they inhabit. In the video game industry, the standard is that 3D avatars should move fluidly as they walk, avoid obstacles in their path, and take an intelligent route toward their destination. Famous best-selling games such as Electronic Arts' *The Sims* work on this principle. We didn't want to ship a low-quality version of this feature, so we opted instead to ship with stationary avatars.

Feedback from the customers was very consistent: they wanted the ability to move their avatars around the environment. We took this as bad news because it meant we would have to spend considerable amounts of time and money on a high-quality solution similar to *The Sims*. But before we committed ourselves to that path, we decided to try another MVP. We used a simple hack, which felt almost like cheating. We changed the product so that customers could click where they wanted their avatar to go, and the avatar would teleport there instantly. No walking, no obstacle avoidance. The avatar disappeared and then reappeared an instant later in the new place. We couldn't even afford fancy teleportation graphics or sound effects. We felt lame shipping this feature, but it was all we could afford.

You can imagine our surprise when we started to get positive customer feedback. We never asked about the movement feature directly (we were too embarrassed). But when asked to name the top things about IMVU they liked best, customers consistently listed avatar "teleportation" among the top three (unbelievably, they often specifically described it as "more advanced than *The Sims*"). This inexpensive compromise outperformed many features of the product we were most proud of, features that had taken much more time and money to produce.

Customers don't care how much time something takes to build. They care only if it serves their needs. Our customers preferred the quick teleportation feature because it allowed them to get where they wanted to go as fast as possible. In retrospect, this makes sense. Wouldn't we all like to get wherever we're going in an instant? No lines, no hours on a plane or sitting on the tarmac, no connections, no cabs or subways. Beam me up, Scotty. Our expensive "real-world" approach was beaten handily by a cool fantasy-world feature that cost much less but that our customers preferred.

So which version of the product is low-quality, again?

MVPs require the courage to put one's assumptions to the test. If customers react the way we expect, we can take that as confirmation that our assumptions are correct. If we release a poorly designed product and customers (even early adopters) cannot figure out how to use it, that will confirm our need to invest in superior design. But we must always ask: what if they don't care about design in the same way we do?

Thus, the Lean Startup method is not opposed to building high-quality products, but only in service of the goal of winning over customers. We must be willing to set aside our traditional professional standards to start the process of validated learning as soon as possible. But once again, this does not mean operating in a sloppy or undisciplined way. (This is an important caveat. There is a category of quality problems that have the net effect of slowing down the Build-Measure-Learn feedback loop. Defects make it more difficult to evolve the product. They actually interfere with our ability to learn and so are dangerous to tolerate in any production process. We will consider methods for figuring out when to make investments in preventing these kinds of problems in Part Three.)

As you consider building your own minimum viable product, let this simple rule suffice: remove any feature, process, or effort that does not contribute directly to the learning you seek.

## SPEED BUMPS IN BUILDING AN MVP

Building an MVP is not without risks, both real and imagined. Both can derail a startup effort unless they are understood ahead of time. The most common speed bumps are legal issues, fears about competitors, branding risks, and the impact on morale.

For startups that rely on patent protection, there are special challenges with releasing an early product. In some jurisdictions, the window for filing a patent begins when the product is released to the general public, and depending on the way the MVP is structured, releasing it may start this clock. Even if your startup is not in one of those jurisdictions, you may want international patent protection and may wind up having to abide by these more stringent requirements. (In my opinion, issues like this are one of the many ways in which current patent law inhibits innovation and should be remedied as a matter of public policy.)

In many industries, patents are used primarily for defensive purposes, as a deterrent to hold competitors at bay. In such cases, the patent risks of an MVP are minor compared with the learning benefits. However, in industries in which a new scientific breakthrough is at the heart of a company's competitive advantage, these risks need to be balanced more carefully. In all cases, entrepreneurs should seek legal counsel to ensure that they understand the risks fully.

Legal risks may be daunting, but you may be surprised to learn that the most common objection I have heard over the years to building an MVP is fear of competitors—especially large established companies—stealing a startup's ideas. If only it were so easy to have a good idea stolen! Part of the special challenge of being a startup is the near impossibility of having your idea, company, or product be noticed by anyone, let alone a competitor. In fact, I have often given entrepreneurs fearful of this issue the following assignment: take one of your ideas (one of your lesser insights, perhaps), find the name of the relevant product manager at an established company who has responsibility for that area, and try to get that company to steal your idea. Call them up, write them a memo, send them a press release—go ahead, try it. The truth is that most managers in most companies are already overwhelmed with good ideas. Their challenge lies in prioritization and execution, and it is those challenges that give a startup hope of surviving.[10]

If a competitor can outexecute a startup once the idea is known, the startup is doomed anyway. The reason to build a new team to pursue an idea is that you believe you can accelerate through the Build-Measure-Learn feedback loop faster than anyone else can. If that's true, it makes no difference what the competition knows. If it's not true, a startup has much bigger problems, and secrecy won't fix them. Sooner or later, a successful startup will face competition from fast followers. A head start is rarely large enough to matter, and time spent in stealth mode—away from customers—is unlikely to provide a head start. The only way to win is to learn faster than anyone else.

Many startups plan to invest in building a great brand, and an MVP can seem like a dangerous branding risk. Similarly, entrepreneurs in existing organizations often are constrained by the fear of damaging the parent company's established brand. In either of these cases, there is an easy solution: launch the MVP under a different brand name. In addition, a long-term reputation is only at risk when companies engage in vocal launch activities such as PR and building hype. When a product fails to live up to those pronouncements, real long-term damage can happen to a corporate brand. But startups have the advantage of being obscure, having a pathetically small number of customers, and not having much exposure. Rather than lamenting them, use these advantages to experiment under the radar and then do a public marketing launch once the product has proved itself with real customers.[11]

Finally, it helps to prepare for the fact that MVPs often result in bad news. Unlike traditional concept tests or prototypes, they are designed to speak to the full range of business questions, not just design or technical ones, and they often provide a needed dose of reality. In fact, piercing the reality distortion field is quite uncomfortable. Visionaries are especially afraid of a false negative: that customers will reject a flawed MVP that is too small or too limited. It is precisely this attitude that one sees when companies launch fully formed products without prior testing. They simply couldn't bear to test them in anything less than their full splendor. Yet there is wisdom in the visionary's fear. Teams steeped in traditional product development methods are trained to make go/kill decisions on a regular basis. That is the essence of the waterfall or stage-gate development model. If an MVP fails, teams are liable to give up hope and abandon the project altogether. But this is a solvable problem.

## FROM THE MVP TO INNOVATION ACCOUNTING

The solution to this dilemma is a commitment to iteration. You have to commit to a locked-in agreement—ahead of time—that no matter what comes of testing the MVP, you will not give up hope. Successful entrepreneurs do not give up at the first sign of trouble, nor do they persevere the plane right into the ground. Instead, they possess a unique combination of perseverance and flexibility. The MVP is just the first step on a journey of learning. Down that road—after many iterations—you may learn that some element of your product or strategy is flawed and decide it is time to make a change, which I call a pivot, to a different method for achieving your vision.

Startups are especially at risk when outside stakeholders and investors (especially corporate CFOs for internal projects) have a crisis of confidence. When the project was authorized or the investment made, the entrepreneur promised that the new product would be world-changing. Customers were supposed to flock to it in record numbers. Why are so few actually doing so?

In traditional management, a manager who promises to deliver something and fails to do so is in trouble. There are only two possible explanations: a failure of execution or a failure to plan appropriately. Both are equally inexcusable. Entrepreneurial managers face a difficult problem: because the plans and projections we make are full of uncertainty, how can we claim success when we inevitably fail to deliver what we promised? Put another way, how does the CFO or VC know that we're failing because we learned something critical and not because we were goofing off or misguided?

The solution to this problem resides at the heart of the Lean Startup model. We all need a disciplined, systematic approach to figuring out if we're making progress and discovering if we're actually achieving validated learning. I call this system innovation accounting, an alternative to traditional accounting designed specifically for startups. It is the subject of Chapter 7.

# 7

# MEASURE

At the beginning, a startup is little more than a model on a piece of paper. The financials in the business plan include projections of how many customers the company expects to attract, how much it will spend, and how much revenue and profit that will lead to. It's an ideal that's usually far from where the startup is in its early days.

A startup's job is to (1) rigorously measure where it is right now, confronting the hard truths that assessment reveals, and then (2) devise experiments to learn how to move the real numbers closer to the ideal reflected in the business plan.

Most products—even the ones that fail—do not have zero traction. Most products have some customers, some growth, and some positive results. One of the most dangerous outcomes for a startup is to bumble along in the land of the living dead. Employees and entrepreneurs tend to be optimistic by nature. We want to keep believing in our ideas even when the writing is on the wall. This is why the myth of perseverance is so dangerous. We all know stories of epic entrepreneurs who managed to pull out a victory when things seemed incredibly bleak. Unfortunately, we don't hear stories about the countless nameless others who persevered too long, leading their companies to failure.

## WHY SOMETHING AS SEEMINGLY DULL AS ACCOUNTING WILL CHANGE YOUR LIFE

People are accustomed to thinking of accounting as dry and boring, a necessary evil used primarily to prepare financial reports and survive audits, but that is because accounting is something that has become taken for granted. Historically, under the leadership of people such as Alfred Sloan at General Motors, accounting became an essential part of the method of exerting centralized control over far-flung divisions. Accounting allowed GM to set clear milestones for each of its divisions and then hold each manager accountable for his or her division's success in reaching those goals. All modern corporations use some variation of that approach. Accounting is the key to their success.

Unfortunately, standard accounting is not helpful in evaluating entrepreneurs. Startups are too unpredictable for forecasts and milestones to be accurate.

I recently met with a phenomenal startup team. They are well financed, have significant customer traction, and are growing rapidly. Their product is a leader in an emerging category of enterprise software that uses consumer marketing techniques to sell into large companies. For example, they rely on employee-to-employee viral adoption rather than a traditional sales process, which might target the chief information officer or the head of information technology (IT). As a result, they have the opportunity to use cutting-edge experimental techniques as they constantly revise their product. During the meeting, I asked the team a simple question that I make a habit of asking startups whenever we meet: are you making your product better? They always say yes. Then I ask: how do you know? I invariably get this answer: well, we are in engineering and we made a number of changes last month, and our customers seem to like them, and our overall numbers are higher this month. We must be on the right track.

This is the kind of storytelling that takes place at most startup board meetings. Most milestones are built the same way: hit a certain product milestone, maybe talk to a few customers, and see if the numbers go up. Unfortunately, this is not a good indicator of whether a startup is making progress. How do we know that the changes we've made are related to the results we're seeing? More important, how do we know that we are drawing the right lessons from those changes?

To answer these kinds of questions, startups have a strong need for a new kind of accounting geared specifically to disruptive innovation. That's what innovation accounting is.

## An Accountability Framework That Works Across Industries

Innovation accounting enables startups to prove objectively that they are learning how to grow a sustainable business. Innovation accounting begins by turning the leap-of-faith assumptions discussed in Chapter 5 into a quantitative financial model. Every business plan has some kind of model associated with it, even if it's written on the back of a napkin. That model provides assumptions about what the business will look like at a successful point in the future.

For example, the business plan for an established manufacturing company would show it growing in proportion to its sales volume. As the profits from the sales of goods are reinvested in marketing and promotions, the company gains new customers. The rate of growth depends primarily on three things: the profitability of each customer, the cost of acquiring new customers, and the repeat purchase rate of existing customers. The higher these values are, the faster the company will grow and the more profitable it will be. These are the drivers of the company's growth model.

By contrast, a marketplace company that matches buyers and sellers such as eBay will have a different growth model. Its success depends primarily on the network effects that make it the premier destination for both buyers and sellers to transact business. Sellers want the marketplace with the highest number of potential customers. Buyers want the marketplace with the most competition among sellers, which leads to the greatest availability of products and the lowest prices. (In economics, this sometimes is called supply-side increasing returns and demand-side increasing returns.) For this kind of startup, the important thing to measure is that the network effects are working, as evidenced by the high retention rate of new buyers and sellers. If people stick with the product with very little attrition, the marketplace will grow no matter how the company acquires new customers. The growth curve will look like a compounding interest table, with the rate of growth depending on the "interest rate" of new customers coming to the product.

Though these two businesses have very different drivers of growth, we can still use a common framework to hold their leaders accountable. This framework supports accountability even when the model changes.

## HOW INNOVATION ACCOUNTING WORKS—THREE LEARNING MILESTONES

Innovation accounting works in three steps: first, use a minimum viable product to establish real data on where the company is right now. Without a clear-eyed picture of your current status—no matter how far from the goal you may be—you cannot begin to track your progress.

Second, startups must attempt to tune the engine from the baseline toward the ideal. This may take many attempts. After the startup has made all the micro changes and product optimizations it can to move its baseline toward the ideal, the company reaches a decision point. That is the third step: pivot or persevere.

If the company is making good progress toward the ideal, that means it's learning appropriately and using that learning effectively, in which case it makes sense to continue. If not, the management team eventually must conclude that its current product strategy is flawed and needs a serious change. When a company pivots, it starts the process all over again, reestablishing a new baseline and then tuning the engine from there. The sign of a successful pivot is that these engine-tuning activities are more productive after the pivot than before.

## Establish the Baseline

For example, a startup might create a complete prototype of its product and offer to sell it to real customers through its main marketing channel. This single MVP would test most of the startup's assumptions and establish baseline metrics for each assumption simultaneously. Alternatively, a startup might prefer to build separate MVPs that are aimed at getting feedback on one assumption at a time. Before building the prototype, the company might perform a smoke test with its marketing materials. This is an old direct marketing technique in which customers are given the opportunity to preorder a product that has not yet been built. A smoke test measures only one thing: whether customers are interested in trying a product. By itself, this is insufficient to validate an entire growth model. Nonetheless, it can be very useful to get feedback on this assumption before committing more money and other resources to the product.

These MVPs provide the first example of a *learning milestone.* An MVP allows a startup to fill in real baseline data in its growth model—conversion rates, sign-up and trial rates, customer lifetime value, and so on—and this is valuable as the foundation for learning about customers and their reactions to a product even if that foundation begins with extremely bad news.

When one is choosing among the many assumptions in a business plan, it makes sense to test the riskiest assumptions first. If you can't find a way to mitigate these risks toward the ideal that is required for a sustainable business, there is no point in testing the others. For example, a media business that is selling advertising has two basic assumptions that take the form of questions: Can it capture the attention of a defined customer segment on an ongoing basis? and can it sell that attention to advertisers? In a business in which the advertising rates for a particular customer segment are well known, the far riskier assumption is the ability to capture attention. Therefore, the first experiments should involve content production rather than advertising sales. Perhaps the company will produce a pilot episode or issue to see how customers engage.

## Tuning the Engine

Once the baseline has been established, the startup can work toward the second learning milestone: tuning the engine. Every product development, marketing, or other initiative that a startup undertakes should be targeted at improving one of the drivers of its growth model. For example, a company might spend time improving the design of its product to make it easier for new customers to use. This presupposes that the *activation rate* of new customers is a driver of growth and that its baseline is lower than the company would like. To demonstrate validated learning, the design changes must improve the activation rate of new customers. If they do not, the new design should be judged a failure. This is an important rule: a good design is one that changes customer behavior for the better.

Compare two startups. The first company sets out with a clear baseline metric, a hypothesis about what will improve that metric, and a set of experiments designed to test that hypothesis. The second team sits around debating what would improve the product, implements several of those changes at once, and celebrates if there is any positive increase in any of the numbers. Which startup is more likely to be doing effective work and achieving lasting results?

### Pivot or Persevere

Over time, a team that is learning its way toward a sustainable business will see the numbers in its model rise from the horrible baseline established by the MVP and converge to something like the ideal one established in the business plan. A startup that fails to do so will see that ideal recede ever farther into the distance. When this is done right, even the most powerful reality distortion field won't be able to cover up this simple fact: if we're not moving the drivers of our business model, we're not making progress. That becomes a sure sign that it's time to pivot.

## INNOVATION ACCOUNTING AT IMVU

Here's what innovation accounting looked like for us in the early days of IMVU. Our minimum viable product had many defects and, when we first released it, extremely low sales. We naturally assumed that the lack of sales was related to the low quality of the product, so week after week we worked on improving the quality of the product, trusting that our efforts were worthwhile. At the end of each month, we would have a board meeting at which we would present the results. The night before the board meeting, we'd run our standard analytics, measuring conversion rates, customer counts, and revenue to show what a good job we had done. For several meetings in a row, this caused a last-minute panic because the quality improvements were not yielding any change in customer behavior. This led to some frustrating board meetings at which we could show great product "progress" but not much in the way of business results. After a while, rather than leave it to the last minute, we began to track our metrics more frequently, tightening the feedback loop with product development. This was even more depressing. Week in, week out, our product changes were having no effect.

## Improving a Product on Five Dollars a Day

We tracked the "funnel metrics" behaviors that were critical to our engine of growth: customer registration, the download of our application, trial, repeat usage, and purchase. To have enough data to learn, we needed just enough customers using our product to get real numbers for each behavior. We allocated a budget of five dollars per day: enough to buy clicks on the then-new Google AdWords system. In those days, the minimum you could bid for a click was 5 cents, but there was no overall minimum to your spending. Thus, we could afford to open an account and get started even though we had very little money.[1]

Five dollars bought us a hundred clicks—every day. From a marketing point of view this was not very significant, but for learning it was priceless. Every single day we were able to measure our product's performance with a brand new set of customers. Also, each time we revised the product, we got a brand new report card on how we were doing the very next day.

For example, one day we would debut a new marketing

message aimed at first-time customers. The next day we might change the way new customers were initiated into the product. Other days, we would add new features, fix bugs, roll out a new visual design, or try a new layout for our website. Every time, we told ourselves we were making the product better, but that subjective confidence was put to the acid test of real numbers.

Day in and day out we were performing random trials. Each day was a new experiment. Each day's customers were independent of those of the day before. Most important, even though our gross numbers were growing, it became clear that our funnel metrics were not changing.

Here is a graph from one of IMVU's early board meetings:

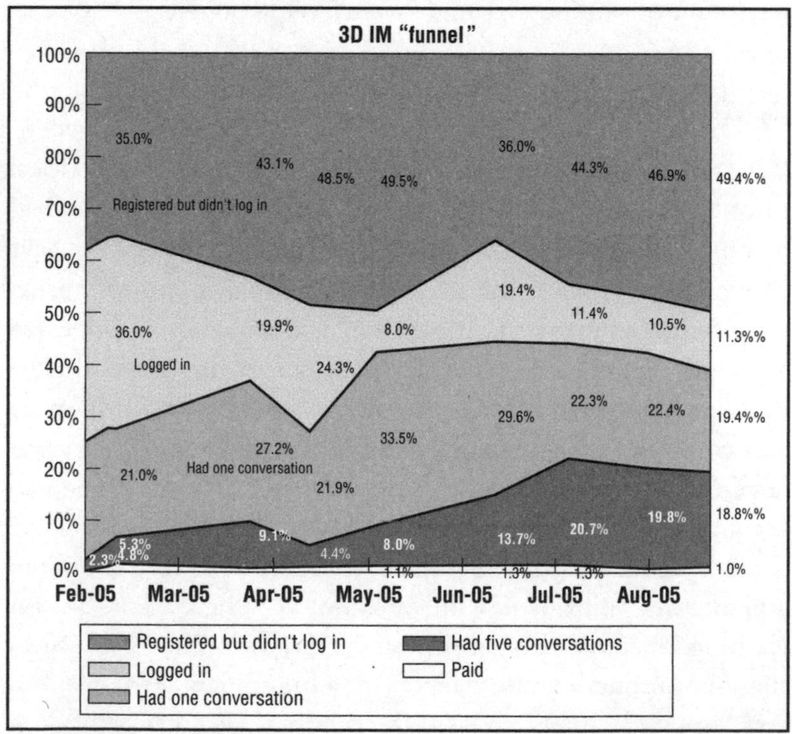


This graph represents approximately seven months of work. Over that period, we were making constant improvements to the IMVU product, releasing new features on a daily basis. We were conducting a lot of in-person customer interviews, and our product development team was working extremely hard.

## Cohort Analysis

To read the graph, you need to understand something called *cohort analysis*. This is one of the most important tools of startup analytics. Although it sounds complex, it is based on a simple premise. Instead of looking at cumulative totals or gross numbers such as total revenue and total number of customers, one looks at the performance of each group of customers that comes into contact with the product independently. Each group is called a cohort. The graph shows the conversion rates to IMVU of new customers who joined in each indicated month. Each conversion rate shows the percentage of customer who registered in that month who subsequently went on to take the indicated action. Thus, among all the customers who joined IMVU in February 2005, about 60 percent of them logged in to our product at least one time.

Managers with an enterprise sales background will recognize this funnel analysis as the traditional sales funnel that is used to manage prospects on their way to becoming customers. Lean Startups use it in product development, too. This technique is useful in many types of business, because every company depends for its survival on sequences of customer behavior called flows. Customer flows govern the interaction of customers with a company's products. They allow us to understand a business quantitatively and have much more predictive power than do traditional gross metrics.

If you look closely, you'll see that the graph shows some clear trends. Some product improvements are helping—a little. The percentage of new customers who go on to use the product at least five times has grown from less than 5 percent to almost 20 percent. Yet despite this fourfold increase, the percentage of new customers who pay money for IMVU is stuck at around 1 percent. Think about that for a moment. After months and months of work, thousands of individual improvements, focus groups, design sessions, and usability tests, the percentage of new customers who subsequently pay money is exactly the same as it was at the onset even though many more customers are getting a chance to try the product.

Thanks to the power of cohort analysis, we could not blame this failure on the legacy of previous customers who were resistant to change, external market conditions, or any other excuse. Each cohort represented an independent report card, and try as we might, we were getting straight C's. This helped us realize we had a problem.

I was in charge of the product development team, small though it was in those days, and shared with my cofounders the sense that the problem had to be with my team's efforts. I worked harder, tried to focus on higher- and higher-quality features, and lost a lot of sleep. Our frustration grew. When I could think of nothing else to do, I was finally ready to turn to the last resort: talking to customers. Armed with our failure to make progress tuning our engine of growth, I was ready to ask the right questions.

Before this failure, in the company's earliest days, it was easy to talk to potential customers and come away convinced we were on the right track. In fact, when we would invite customers into the office for in-person interviews and usability tests, it was easy to dismiss negative feedback. If they didn't want to use the product, I assumed they were not in our target market. "Fire that customer," I'd say to the person responsible for recruiting for our tests. "Find me someone in our target demographic." If the next customer was more positive, I would take it as confirmation that I was right in my targeting. If not, I'd fire another customer and try again.

By contrast, once I had data in hand, my interactions with customers changed. Suddenly I had urgent questions that needed answering: Why aren't customers responding to our product "improvements"? Why isn't our hard work paying off? For example, we kept making it easier and easier for customers to use IMVU with their existing friends. Unfortunately, customers didn't want to engage in that behavior. Making it easier to use was totally beside the point. Once we knew what to look for, genuine understanding came much faster. As was described in Chapter 3, this eventually led to a critically important pivot: away from an IM add-on used with existing friends and toward a stand-alone network one can use to make new friends. Suddenly, our worries about productivity vanished. Once our efforts were aligned with what customers really wanted, our experiments were much more likely to change their behavior for the better.

This pattern would repeat time and again, from the days when we were making less than a thousand dollars in revenue per month all the way up to the time we were making millions. In fact, this is the sign of a successful pivot: the new experiments you run are overall more productive than the experiments you were running before.

This is the pattern: poor quantitative results force us to declare failure and create the motivation, context, and space for more qualitative research. These investigations produce new ideas—new hypotheses—to be tested, leading to a possible pivot. Each pivot unlocks new opportunities for further experimentation, and the cycle repeats. Each time we repeat this simple rhythm: establish the baseline, tune the engine, and make a decision to pivot or persevere.

## OPTIMIZATION VERSUS LEARNING

Engineers, designers, and marketers are all skilled at optimization. For example, direct marketers are experienced at split testing value propositions by sending a different offer to two similar groups of customers so that they can measure differences in the response rates of the two groups. Engineers, of course, are skilled at improving a product's performance, just as designers are talented at making products easier to use. All these activities in a well-run traditional organization offer incremental benefit for incremental effort. As long as we are executing the plan well, hard work yields results.

However, these tools for product improvement do not work the same way for startups. If you are building the wrong thing, optimizing the product or its marketing will not yield significant results. A startup has to measure progress against a high bar: evidence that a sustainable business can be built around its products or services. That's a standard that can be assessed only if a startup has made clear, tangible predictions ahead of time.

In the absence of those predictions, product and strategy decisions are far more difficult and time-consuming. I often see this in my consulting practice. I've been called in many times to help a startup that feels that its engineering team "isn't working hard enough." When I meet with those teams, there are always improvements to be made and I recommend them, but invariably the real problem is not a lack of development talent, energy, or effort. Cycle after cycle, the team is working hard, but the business is not seeing results. Managers trained in a traditional model draw the logical conclusion: our team is not working hard, not working effectively, or not working efficiently.

Thus the downward cycle begins: the product development team valiantly tries to build a product according to the specifications it is receiving from the creative or business leadership. When good results are not forthcoming, business leaders assume that any discrepancy between what was planned and what was built is the cause and try to specify the next iteration in greater detail. As the specifications get more detailed, the planning process slows down, batch size increases, and feedback is delayed. If a board of directors or CFO is involved as a stakeholder, it doesn't take long for personnel changes to follow.

A few years ago, a team that sells products to large media companies invited me to help them as a consultant because they were concerned that their engineers were not working hard enough. However, the fault was not in the engineers; it was in the process the whole company was using to make decisions. They had customers but did not know them very well. They were deluged with feature requests from customers, the internal sales team, and the business leadership. Every new insight became an emergency that had to be addressed immediately. As a result, long-term projects were hampered by constant interruptions. Even worse, the team had no clear sense of whether any of the changes they were making mattered to customers. Despite the constant tuning and tweaking, the business results were consistently mediocre.

Learning milestones prevent this negative spiral by emphasizing a more likely possibility: the company is executing—with discipline!—a plan that does not make sense. The innovation accounting framework makes it clear when the company is stuck and needs to change direction.

In the example above, early in the company's life, the product development team was incredibly productive because the company's founders had identified a large unmet need in the target market. The initial product, while flawed, was popular with early adopters. Adding the major features that customers asked for seemed to work wonders, as the early adopters spread the word about the innovation far and wide. But unasked and unanswered were other lurking questions: Did the company have a working engine of growth? Was this early success related to the daily work of the product development team? In most cases, the answer was no; success was driven by decisions the team had made in the past. None of its current initiatives were having any impact. But this was obscured because the company's gross metrics were all "up and to the right."

As we'll see in a moment, this is a common danger. Companies of any size that have a working engine of growth can come to rely on the wrong kind of metrics to guide their actions. This is what tempts managers to resort to the usual bag of success theater tricks: last-minute ad buys, channel stuffing, and whiz-bang demos, in a desperate attempt to make the gross numbers look better. Energy invested in success theater is energy that could have been used to help build a sustainable business. I call the traditional numbers used to judge startups "vanity metrics," and innovation accounting requires us to avoid the temptation to use them.

## VANITY METRICS: A WORD OF CAUTION

To see the danger of vanity metrics clearly, let's return once more to the early days of IMVU. Take a look at the following graph, which is from the same era in IMVU's history as that shown earlier in this chapter. It covers the same time period as the cohort-style graph on page 122; in fact, it is from the same board presentation.

This graph shows the traditional gross metrics for IMVU so far: total registered users and total paying customers (the gross revenue graph looks almost the same). From this viewpoint, things look much more exciting. That's why I call these vanity

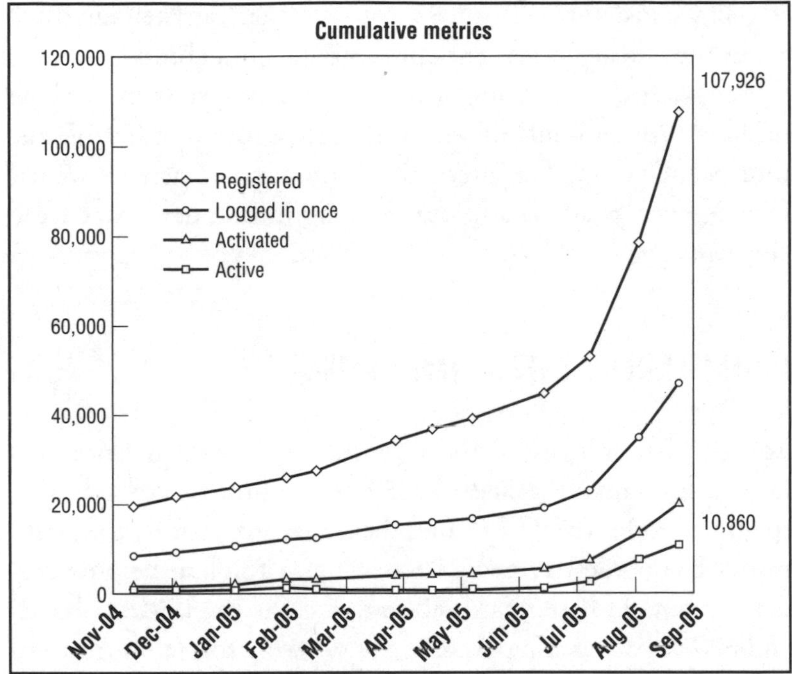


metrics: they give the rosiest possible picture. You'll see a traditional hockey stick graph (the ideal in a rapid-growth company). As long as you focus on the top-line numbers (signing up more customers, an increase in overall revenue), you'll be forgiven for thinking this product development team is making great progress. The company's growth engine is working. Each month it is able to acquire customers and has a positive return on investment. The excess revenue from those customers is reinvested the next month in acquiring more. That's where the growth is coming from.

But think back to the same data presented in a cohort style. IMVU is adding new customers, but it is not improving the yield on each new group. The engine is turning, but the efforts to tune the engine are not bearing much fruit. From the traditional graph alone, you cannot tell whether IMVU is on pace to build a sustainable business; you certainly can't tell anything about the efficacy of the entrepreneurial team behind it.

Innovation accounting will not work if a startup is being misled by these kinds of vanity metrics: gross number of customers and so on. The alternative is the kind of metrics we use to judge our business and our learning milestones, what I call *actionable metrics.*

## ACTIONABLE METRICS VERSUS VANITY METRICS

To get a better sense of the importance of good metrics, let's look at a company called Grockit. Its founder, Farbood Nivi, spent a decade working as a teacher at two large for-profit education companies, Princeton Review and Kaplan, helping students prepare for standardized tests such as the GMAT, LSAT, and SAT. His engaging classroom style won accolades from his students and promotions from his superiors; he was honored with Princeton Review's National Teacher of the Year award. But Farb was frustrated with the traditional teaching methods used by those companies. Teaching six to nine hours per day to thousands of students, he had many opportunities to experiment with new approaches.[2]

Over time, Farb concluded that the traditional lecture model of education, with its one-to-many instructional approach, was inadequate for his students. He set out to develop a superior approach, using a combination of teacher-led lectures, individual homework, and group study. In particular, Farb was fascinated by how effective the student-to-student peer-driven learning method was for his students. When students could help each other, they benefited in two ways. First, they could get customized instruction from a peer who was much less intimidating than a teacher. Second, they could reinforce their learning by teaching it to others. Over time, Farb's classes became increasingly social—and successful.

As this unfolded, Farb felt more and more that his physical presence in the classroom was less important. He made an important connection: "I have this social learning model in my classroom. There's all this social stuff going on on the web." His idea was to bring social peer-to-peer learning to people who could not afford an expensive class from Kaplan or Princeton Review or an even more expensive private tutor. From this insight Grockit was born.

Farb explains, "Whether you're studying for the SAT or you're studying for algebra, you study in one of three ways. You spend some time with experts, you spend some time on your own, and you spend some time with your peers. Grockit offers these three same formats of studying. What we do is we apply technology and algorithms to optimize those three forms."

Farb is the classic entrepreneurial visionary. He recounts his original insight this way: "Let's forget educational design up until now, let's forget what's possible and just redesign learning with today's students and today's technology in mind. There were plenty of multi-billion-dollar organizations in the education space, and I don't think they were innovating in the way that we needed them to and I didn't think we needed them anymore. To me, it's really all about the students and I didn't feel like the students were being served as well as they could."

Today Grockit offers many different educational products, but in the beginning Farb followed a lean approach. Grockit built a minimum viable product, which was simply Farb teaching test prep via the popular online web conferencing tool WebEx. He built no custom software, no new technology. He simply attempted to bring his new teaching approach to students via the Internet. News about a new kind of private tutoring spread quickly, and within a few months Farb was making a decent living teaching online, with monthly revenues of $10,000 to $15,000. But like many entrepreneurs with ambition, Farb didn't build his MVP just to make a living. He had a vision of a more collaborative, more effective kind of teaching for students everywhere. With his initial traction, he was able to raise money from some of the most prestigious investors in Silicon Valley.

When I first met Farb, his company was already on the fast track to success. They had raised venture capital from well-regarded investors, had built an awesome team, and were fresh off an impressive debut at one of Silicon Valley's famous startup competitions.

They were extremely process-oriented and disciplined. Their product development followed a rigorous version of the agile development methodology known as Extreme Programming (described below), thanks to their partnership with a San Francisco–based company called Pivotal Labs. Their early product was hailed by the press as a breakthrough.

There was only one problem: they were not seeing sufficient growth in the use of the product by customers. Grockit is an excellent case study because its problems were not a matter of failure of execution or discipline.

Following standard agile practice, Grockit's work proceeded in a series of *sprints,* or one-month iteration cycles. For each sprint, Farb would prioritize the work to be done that month by writing a series of *user stories,* a technique taken from agile development. Instead of writing a specification for a new feature that described it in technical terms, Farb would write a story that described the feature from the point of view of the customer. That story helped keep the engineers focused on the customer's perspective throughout the development process.

Each feature was expressed in plain language in terms everyone could understand whether they had a technical background or not. Again following standard agile practice, Farb was free to reprioritize these stories at any time. As he learned more about what customers wanted, he could move things around in the *product backlog,* the queue of stories yet to be built. The only limit on this ability to change directions was that he could not interrupt any task that was in progress. Fortunately, the stories were written in such a way that the batch size of work (which I'll discuss in more detail in Chapter 9) was only a day or two.

This system is called agile development for a good reason: teams that employ it are able to change direction quickly, stay light on their feet, and be highly responsive to changes in the business requirements of the product owner (the manager of the process—in this case Farb—who is responsible for prioritizing the stories).

How did the team feel at the end of each sprint? They consistently delivered new product features. They would collect feedback from customers in the form of anecdotes and interviews that indicated that at least some customers liked the new features. There was always a certain amount of data that showed improvement: perhaps the total number of customers was increasing, the total number of questions answered by students was going up, or the number of returning customers was increasing.

However, I sensed that Farb and his team were left with lingering doubts about the company's overall progress. Was the increase in their numbers actually caused by their development efforts? Or could it be due to other factors, such as mentions of Grockit in the press? When I met the team, I asked them this simple question: How do you know that the prioritization decisions that Farb is making actually make sense?

Their answer: "That's not our department. Farb makes the decisions; we execute them."

At that time Grockit was focused on just one customer segment: prospective business school students who were studying for the GMAT. The product allowed students to engage in online study sessions with fellow students who were studying for the same exam. The product was working: the students who completed their studying via Grockit achieved significantly higher scores than they had before. But the Grockit team was struggling with the age-old startup problems: How do we know which features to prioritize? How can we get more customers to sign up and pay? How can we get out the word about our product?

I put this question to Farb: "How confident are you that you are making the right decisions in terms of establishing priorities?" Like most startup founders, he was looking at the available data and making the best educated guesses he could. But this left a lot of room for ambiguity and doubt.

Farb believed in his vision thoroughly and completely, yet he was starting to question whether his company was on pace to realize that vision. The product improved every day, but Farb wanted to make sure those improvements mattered to customers. I believe he deserves a lot of credit for realizing this. Unlike many visionaries, who cling to their original vision no matter what, Farb was willing to put his vision to the test.

Farb worked hard to sustain his team's belief that Grockit was destined for success. He was worried that morale would suffer if anyone thought that the person steering the ship was uncertain about which direction to go. Farb himself wasn't sure if his team would embrace a true learning culture. After all, this was part of the grand bargain of agile development: engineers agree to adapt the product to the business's constantly changing requirements but are not responsible for the quality of those business decisions.

Agile is an efficient system of development from the point of view of the developers. It allows them to stay focused on creating features and technical designs. An attempt to introduce the need to learn into that process could undermine productivity.

(Lean manufacturing faced similar problems when it was introduced in factories. Managers were used to focusing on the utilization rate of each machine. Factories were designed to keep machines running at full capacity as much of the time as possible. Viewed from the perspective of the machine, that is efficient, but from the point of view of the productivity of the entire factory, it is wildly inefficient at times. As they say in systems theory, that which optimizes one part of the system necessarily undermines the system as a whole.)

What Farb and his team didn't realize was that Grockit's progress was being measured by vanity metrics: the total number of customers and the total number of questions answered. That was what was causing his team to spin its wheels; those metrics gave the team the sensation of forward motion even though the company was making little progress. What's interesting is how closely Farb's method followed superficial aspects of the Lean Startup learning milestones: they shipped an early product and established some baseline metrics. They had relatively short iterations, each of which was judged by its ability to improve customer metrics.

However, because Grockit was using the wrong kinds of metrics, the startup was not genuinely improving. Farb was frustrated in his efforts to learn from customer feedback. In every cycle, the type of metrics his team was focused on would change: one month they would look at gross usage numbers, another month registration numbers, and so on. Those metrics would go up and down seemingly on their own. He couldn't draw clear cause-and-effect inferences. Prioritizing work correctly in such an environment is extremely challenging.

Farb could have asked his data analyst to investigate a

particular question. For example, when we shipped feature X, did it affect customer behavior? But that would have required tremendous time and effort. When, exactly, did feature X ship? Which customers were exposed to it? Was anything else launched around that same time? Were there seasonal factors that might be skewing the data? Finding these answers would have required parsing reams and reams of data. The answer often would come weeks after the question had been asked. In the meantime, the team would have moved on to new priorities and new questions that needed urgent attention.

Compared to a lot of startups, the Grockit team had a huge advantage: they were tremendously disciplined. A disciplined team may apply the wrong methodology but can shift gears quickly once it discovers its error. Most important, a disciplined team can experiment with its own working style and draw meaningful conclusions.

## Cohorts and Split-tests

Grockit changed the metrics they used to evaluate success in two ways. Instead of looking at gross metrics, Grockit switched to cohort-based metrics, and instead of looking for cause-and-effect relationships after the fact, Grockit would launch each new feature as a true split-test experiment.

A split-test experiment is one in which different versions of a product are offered to customers at the same time. By observing the changes in behavior between the two groups, one can make inferences about the impact of the different variations. This technique was pioneered by direct mail advertisers. For example, consider a company that sends customers a catalog of products to buy, such as Lands' End or Crate & Barrel. If you wanted to test a catalog design, you could send a new version of it to 50 percent of the customers and send the old standard catalog to the other 50 percent. To assure a scientific result, both catalogs would contain identical products; the only difference would be the changes to the design. To figure out if the new design was effective, all you would have to do was keep track of the sales figures for both groups of customers. (This technique is sometimes called A/B testing after the practice of assigning letter names to each variation.) Although split testing often is thought of as a marketing-specific (or even a direct marketing–specific) practice, Lean Startups incorporate it directly into product development.

These changes led to an immediate change in Farb's understanding of the business. Split testing often uncovers surprising things. For example, many features that make the product better in the eyes of engineers and designers have no impact on customer behavior. This was the case at Grockit, as it has been in every company I have seen adopt this technique. Although working with split tests seems to be more difficult because it requires extra accounting and metrics to keep track of each variation, it almost always saves tremendous amounts of time in the long run by eliminating work that doesn't matter to customers.

Split testing also helps teams refine their understanding of what customers want and don't want. Grockit's team constantly added new ways for their customers to interact with each other in the hope that those social communication tools would increase the product's value. Inherent in those efforts was the belief that customers desired more communication during their studying. When split testing revealed that the extra features did not change customer behavior, it called that belief into question.

The questioning inspired the team to seek a deeper understanding of what customers really wanted. They brainstormed new ideas for product experiments that might have more impact. In fact, many of these ideas were not new. They had simply been overlooked because the company was focused on building social tools. As a result, Grockit tested an intensive solo-studying mode, complete with quests and gamelike levels, so that students could have the choice of studying by themselves or with others. Just as in Farb's original classroom, this proved extremely effective. Without the discipline of split testing, the company might not have had this realization. In fact, over time, through dozens of tests, it became clear that the key to student engagement was to offer them a combination of social and solo features. Students preferred having a choice of how to study.

## Kanban

Following the lean manufacturing principle of *kanban,* or capacity constraint, Grockit changed the product prioritization process. Under the new system, user stories were not considered complete until they led to validated learning. Thus, stories could be cataloged as being in one of four states of development: in the product backlog, actively being built, done (feature complete from a technical point of view), or in the process of being validated. Validated was defined as "knowing whether the story was a good idea to have been done in the first place." This validation usually would come in the form of a split test showing a change in customer behavior but also might include customer interviews or surveys.

The *kanban* rule permitted only so many stories in each of the four states. As stories flow from one state to the other, the buckets fill up. Once a bucket becomes full, it cannot accept more stories. Only when a story has been validated can it be removed from the *kanban* board. If the validation fails and it turns out the story is a bad idea, the relevant feature is removed from the product (see the chart on page 139).

## KANBAN DIAGRAM OF WORK AS IT PROGRESSES FROM STAGE TO STAGE

(No bucket can contain more than three projects at a time.)

| BACKLOG | IN PROGRESS | BUILT | VALIDATED |
|---|---|---|---|
| A | D | F | |
| B | E | | |
| C | | | |

Work on A begins. D and E are in development. F awaits validation.

| BACKLOG | IN PROGRESS | BUILT | VALIDATED |
|---|---|---|---|
| G | | D | F |
| H | B | E | |
| I | C | A | |

F is validated. D and E await validation. G, H, I are new tasks to be undertaken. B and C are being built. A completes development.

| BACKLOG | IN PROGRESS | BUILT | VALIDATED |
|---|---|---|---|
| | G | D | F |
| H → | B → | E | |
| I → | C → | A | |

B and C have been built, but under *kanban,* cannot be moved to the next bucket for validation until A, D, E have been validated. Work cannot begin on H and I until space opens up in the buckets ahead.

I have implemented this system with several teams, and the initial result is always frustrating: each bucket fills up, starting with the "validated" bucket and moving on to the "done" bucket, until it's not possible to start any more work. Teams that are used to measuring their productivity narrowly, by the number of stories they are delivering, feel stuck. The only way to start work on new features is to investigate some of the stories that are done but haven't been validated. That often requires nonengineering efforts: talking to customers, looking at split-test data, and the like.

Pretty soon everyone gets the hang of it. This progress occurs in fits and starts at first. Engineering may finish a big batch of work, followed by extensive testing and validation. As engineers look for ways to increase their productivity, they start to realize that if they include the validation exercise from the beginning, the whole team can be more productive.

For example, why build a new feature that is not part of a split-test experiment? It may save you time in the short run, but it will take more time later to test, during the validation phase. The same logic applies to a story that an engineer doesn't understand. Under the old system, he or she would just build it and find out later what it was for. In the new system, that behavior is clearly counterproductive: without a clear hypothesis, how can a story ever be validated? We saw this behavior at IMVU, too. I once saw a junior engineer face down a senior executive over a relatively minor change. The engineer insisted that the new feature be split-tested, just like any other. His peers backed him up; it was considered absolutely obvious that all features should be routinely tested, no matter who was commissioning them. (Embarrassingly, all too often I was the executive in question.) A solid process lays the foundation for a healthy culture, one where ideas are evaluated by merit and not by job title.

Most important, teams working in this system begin to measure their productivity according to validated learning, not in terms of the production of new features.

## Hypothesis Testing at Grockit

When Grockit made this transition, the results were dramatic. In one case, they decided to test one of their major features, called lazy registration, to see if it was worth the heavy investment they were making in ongoing support. They were confident in this feature because lazy registration is considered one of the design best practices for online services. In this system, customers do not have to register for the service up front. Instead, they immediately begin using the service and are asked to register only after they have had a chance to experience the service's benefit.

For a student, lazy registration works like this: when you come to the Grockit website, you're immediately placed in a study session with other students working on the same test. You don't have to give your name, e-mail address, or credit card number. There is nothing to prevent you from jumping in and getting started immediately. For Grockit, this was essential to testing one of its core assumptions: that customers would be willing to adopt this new way of learning only if they could see proof that it was working early on.

As a result of this hypothesis, Grockit's design required that it manage three classes of users: unregistered guests, registered (trial) guests, and customers who had paid for the premium version of the product. This design required significant extra work to build and maintain: the more classes of users there are, the more work is required to keep track of them, and the more marketing effort is required to create the right incentives to entice customers to upgrade to the next class. Grockit had undertaken this extra effort because lazy registration was considered an industry best practice.

I encouraged the team to try a simple split-test. They took

one cohort of customers and required that they register immediately, based on nothing more than Grockit's marketing materials. To their surprise, this cohort's behavior was exactly the same as that of the lazy registration group: they had the same rate of registration, activation, and subsequent retention. In other words, the extra effort of lazy registration was a complete waste even though it was considered an industry best practice.

Even more important than reducing waste was the insight that this test suggested: customers were basing their decision about Grockit on something other than their use of the product.

Think about this. Think about the cohort of customers who were required to register for the product before entering a study session with other students. They had very little information about the product, nothing more than was presented on Grockit's home page and registration page. By contrast, the lazy registration group had a tremendous amount of information about the product because they had used it. Yet despite this information disparity, customer behavior was exactly the same.

This suggested that improving Grockit's positioning and marketing might have a more significant impact on attracting new customers than would adding new features. This was just the first of many important experiments Grockit was able to run. Since those early days, they have expanded their customer base dramatically: they now offer test prep for numerous standardized tests, including the GMAT, SAT, ACT, and GRE, as well as online math and English courses for students in grades 7 through 12.

Grockit continues to evolve its process, seeking continuous improvement at every turn. With more than twenty employees in its San Francisco office, Grockit continues to operate with the same deliberate, disciplined approach that has been their hallmark all along. They have helped close to a million students and are sure to help millions more.

## THE VALUE OF THE THREE A'S

These examples from Grockit demonstrate each of the three A's of metrics: actionable, accessible, and auditable.

### Actionable

For a report to be considered actionable, it must demonstrate clear cause and effect. Otherwise, it is a vanity metric. The reports that Grockit's team began to use to judge their learning milestones made it extremely clear what actions would be necessary to replicate the results.

By contrast, vanity metrics fail this criterion. Take the number of hits to a company website. Let's say we have 40,000 hits this month—a new record. What do we need to do to get more hits? Well, that depends. Where are the new hits coming from? Is it from 40,000 new customers or from one guy with an extremely active web browser? Are the hits the result of a new marketing campaign or PR push? What is a hit, anyway? Does each page in the browser count as one hit, or do all the embedded images and multimedia content count as well? Those who have sat in a meeting debating the units of measurement in a report will recognize this problem.

Vanity metrics wreak havoc because they prey on a weakness of the human mind. In my experience, when the numbers go up, people think the improvement was caused by their actions, by whatever they were working on at the time. That is why it's so common to have a meeting in which marketing thinks the numbers went up because of a new PR or marketing effort and engineering thinks the better numbers are the result of the new features it added. Finding out what is actually going on is extremely costly, and so most managers simply move on, doing the best they can to form their own judgment on the basis of their experience and the collective intelligence in the room.

Unfortunately, when the numbers go down, it results in a very different reaction: now it's somebody else's fault. Thus, most team members or departments live in a world where their department is constantly making things better, only to have their hard work sabotaged by other departments that just don't get it. Is it any wonder these departments develop their own distinct language, jargon, culture, and defense mechanisms against the bozos working down the hall?

Actionable metrics are the antidote to this problem. When cause and effect is clearly understood, people are better able to learn from their actions. Human beings are innately talented learners when given a clear and objective assessment.

### Accessible

All too many reports are not understood by the employees and managers who are supposed to use them to guide their decision making. Unfortunately, most managers do not respond to this complexity by working hand in hand with the data warehousing team to simplify the reports so that they can understand them better. Departments too often spend their energy learning how to use data to get what they want rather than as genuine feedback to guide their future actions.

There is an antidote to this misuse of data. First, make the reports as simple as possible so that everyone understands them. Remember the saying "Metrics are people, too." The easiest way to make reports comprehensible is to use tangible, concrete units. What is a website hit? Nobody is really sure, but everyone knows what a person visiting the website is: one can practically picture those people sitting at their computers.

This is why cohort-based reports are the gold standard of

learning metrics: they turn complex actions into people-based reports. Each cohort analysis says: among the people who used our product in this period, here's how many of them exhibited each of the behaviors we care about. In the IMVU example, we saw four behaviors: downloading the product, logging into the product from one's computer, engaging in a chat with other customers, and upgrading to the paid version of the product. In other words, the report deals with people and their actions, which are far more useful than piles of data points. For example, think about how hard it would have been to tell if IMVU was being successful if we had reported only on the total number of person-to-person conversations. Let's say we have 10,000 conversations in a period. Is that good? Is that one person being very, very social, or is it 10,000 people each trying the product one time and then giving up? There's no way to know without creating a more detailed report.

As the gross numbers get larger, accessibility becomes more and more important. It is hard to visualize what it means if the number of website hits goes down from 250,000 in one month to 200,000 the next month, but most people understand immediately what it means to lose 50,000 customers. That's practically a whole stadium full of people who are abandoning the product.

Accessibility also refers to widespread access to the reports. Grockit did this especially well. Every day their system automatically generated a document containing the latest data for every single one of their split-test experiments and other leap-of-faith metrics. This document was mailed to every employee of the company: they all always had a fresh copy in their e-mail inboxes. The reports were well laid out and easy to read, with each experiment and its results explained in plain English.

Another way to make reports accessible is to use a technique we developed at IMVU. Instead of housing the analytics or data in a separate system, our reporting data and its infrastructure were considered part of the product itself and were owned by the product development team. The reports were available on our website, accessible to anyone with an employee account.

Each employee could log in to the system at any time, choose from a list of all current and past experiments, and see a simple one-page summary of the results. Over time, those one-page summaries became the de facto standard for settling product arguments throughout the organization. When people needed evidence to support something they had learned, they would bring a printout with them to the relevant meeting, confident that everyone they showed it to would understand its meaning.

## Auditable

When informed that their pet project is a failure, most of us are tempted to blame the messenger, the data, the manager, the gods, or anything else we can think of. That's why the third A of good metrics, "auditable," is so essential. We must ensure that the data is credible to employees.

The employees at IMVU would brandish one-page reports to demonstrate what they had learned to settle arguments, but the process often wasn't so smooth. Most of the time, when a manager, developer, or team was confronted with results that would kill a pet project, the loser of the argument would challenge the veracity of the data.

Such challenges are more common than most managers would admit, and unfortunately, most data reporting systems are not designed to answer them successfully. Sometimes this is the result of a well-intentioned but misplaced desire to protect the privacy of customers. More often, the lack of such supporting documentation is simply a matter of neglect. Most data reporting systems are not built by product development teams, whose job is to prioritize and build product features. They are built by business managers and analysts. Managers who must use these systems can only check to see if the reports are mutually consistent. They all too often lack a way to test if the data is consistent with reality.

The solution? First, remember that "Metrics are people, too." We need to be able to test the data by hand, in the messy real world, by talking to customers. This is the only way to be able to check if the reports contain true facts. Managers need the ability to spot check the data with real customers. It also has a second benefit: systems that provide this level of auditability give managers and entrepreneurs the opportunity to gain insights into why customers are behaving the way the data indicate.

Second, those building reports must make sure the mechanisms that generate the reports are not too complex. Whenever possible, reports should be drawn directly from the master data, rather than from an intermediate system, which reduces opportunities for error. I have noticed that every time a team has one of its judgments or assumptions overturned as a result of a technical problem with the data, its confidence, morale, and discipline are undermined.

○ ○ ○

When we watch entrepreneurs succeed in the mythmaking world of Hollywood, books, and magazines, the story is always structured the same way. First, we see the plucky protagonist having an epiphany, hatching a great new idea. We learn about his or her character and personality, how he or she came to be in the right place at the right time, and how he or she took the dramatic leap to start a business.

Then the photo montage begins. It's usually short, just a few minutes of time-lapse photography or narrative. We see the protagonist building a team, maybe working in a lab, writing on whiteboards, closing sales, pounding on a few keyboards. At the end of the montage, the founders are successful, and the story can move on to more interesting fare: how to split the spoils of their success, who will appear on magazine covers, who sues whom, and implications for the future.

Unfortunately, the real work that determines the success of startups happens during the photo montage. It doesn't make the cut in terms of the big story because it is too boring. Only 5 percent of entrepreneurship is the big idea, the business model, the whiteboard strategizing, and the splitting up of the spoils. The other 95 percent is the gritty work that is measured by innovation accounting: product prioritization decisions, deciding which customers to target or listen to, and having the courage to subject a grand vision to constant testing and feedback.

One decision stands out above all others as the most difficult, the most time-consuming, and the biggest source of waste for most startups. We all must face this fundamental test: deciding when to pivot and when to persevere. To understand what happens during the photo montage, we have to understand how to pivot, and that is the subject of Chapter 8.

# 8

# PIVOT (OR PERSEVERE)

Every entrepreneur eventually faces an overriding challenge in developing a successful product: deciding when to pivot and when to persevere. Everything that has been discussed so far is a prelude to a seemingly simple question: are we making sufficient progress to believe that our original strategic hypothesis is correct, or do we need to make a major change? That change is called a pivot: a structured course correction designed to test a new fundamental hypothesis about the product, strategy, and engine of growth.

Because of the scientific methodology that underlies the Lean Startup, there is often a misconception that it offers a rigid clinical formula for making pivot or persevere decisions. This is not true. There is no way to remove the human element—vision, intuition, judgment—from the practice of entrepreneurship, nor would that be desirable.

My goal in advocating a scientific approach to the creation of startups is to channel human creativity into its most productive form, and there is no bigger destroyer of creative potential than the misguided decision to persevere. Companies that cannot bring themselves to pivot to a new direction on the basis of feedback from the marketplace can get stuck in the land of the living dead, neither growing enough nor dying, consuming resources and commitment from employees and other stakeholders but not moving ahead.

There is good news about our reliance on judgment, though. We are able to learn, we are innately creative, and we have a remarkable ability to see the signal in the noise. In fact, we are so good at this that sometimes we see signals that aren't there. The heart of the scientific method is the realization that although human judgment may be faulty, we can improve our judgment by subjecting our theories to repeated testing.

Startup productivity is not about cranking out more widgets or features. It is about aligning our efforts with a business and product that are working to create value and drive growth. In other words, successful pivots put us on a path toward growing a sustainable business.

## INNOVATION ACCOUNTING LEADS TO FASTER PIVOTS

To see this process in action, meet David Binetti, the CEO of Votizen. David has had a long career helping to bring the American political process into the twenty-first century. In the early 1990s, he helped build USA.gov, the first portal for the federal government. He's also experienced some classic startup failures. When it came time to build Votizen, David was determined to avoid betting the farm on his vision.

David wanted to tackle the problem of civic participation in the political process. His first product concept was a social network of verified voters, a place where people passionate about civic causes could get together, share ideas, and recruit their friends. David built his first minimum viable product for just over $1,200 in about three months and launched it.

David wasn't building something that *nobody* wanted. In fact, from its earliest days, Votizen was able to attract early adopters who loved the core concept. Like all entrepreneurs, David had to refine his product and business model. What made David's challenge especially hard was that he had to make those pivots in the face of moderate success.

David's initial concept involved four big leaps of faith:

1. Customers would be interested enough in the social network to sign up. (Registration)
2. Votizen would be able to verify them as registered voters. (Activation)
3. Customers who were verified voters would engage with the site's activism tools over time. (Retention)
4. Engaged customers would tell their friends about the service and recruit them into civic causes. (Referral)

Three months and $1,200 later, David's first MVP was in customers' hands. In the initial cohorts, 5 percent signed up for the service and 17 percent verified their registered voter status (see the chart below). The numbers were so low that there wasn't enough data to tell what sort of engagement or referral would occur. It was time to start iterating.

| | **INITIAL MVP** |
|---|---|
| Registration | 5% |
| Activation | 17% |
| Retention | Too low |
| Referral | Too low |

David spent the next two months and another $5,000 split testing new product features, messaging, and improving the product's design to make it easier to use. Those tests showed dramatic improvements, going from a 5 percent registration rate to 17 percent and from a 17 percent activation rate to over 90 percent. Such is the power of split testing. This optimization gave David a critical mass of customers with which to measure the next two leaps of faith. However, as shown in the chart below, those numbers proved to be even more discouraging: David achieved a referral rate of only 4 percent and a retention rate of 5 percent.

| | INITIAL MVP | AFTER OPTIMIZATION |
|---|---|---|
| Registration | 5% | 17% |
| Activation | 17% | 90% |
| Retention | Too low | 5% |
| Referral | Too low | 4% |

David knew he had to do more development and testing. For the next three months he continued to optimize, split test, and refine his pitch. He talked to customers, held focus groups, and did countless A/B experiments. As was explained in Chapter 7, in a split test, different versions of a product are offered to different customers at the same time. By observing the changes in behavior between the two groups, one can make inferences about the impact of the different variations. As shown in the chart below, the referral rate nudged up slightly to 6 percent and the retention rate went up to 8 percent. A disappointed David had spent eight months and $20,000 to build a product that wasn't living up to the growth model he'd hoped for.

| | BEFORE OPTIMIZATION | AFTER OPTIMIZATION |
|---|---|---|
| Registration | 17% | 17% |
| Activation | 90% | 90% |
| Retention | 5% | 8% |
| Referral | 4% | 6% |

David faced the difficult challenge of deciding whether to pivot or persevere. This is one of the hardest decisions entrepreneurs face. The goal of creating learning milestones is not to make the decision easy; it is to make sure that there is relevant data in the room when it comes time to decide.

Remember, at this point David has had many customer conversations. He has plenty of learning that he can use to rationalize the failure he has experienced with the current product. That's exactly what many entrepreneurs do. In Silicon Valley, we call this experience getting stuck in the land of the living dead. It happens when a company has achieved a modicum of success—just enough to stay alive—but is not living up to the expectations of its founders and investors. Such companies are a terrible drain of human energy. Out of loyalty, the employees and founders don't want to give in; they feel that success might be just around the corner.

David had two advantages that helped him avoid this fate:

1. Despite being committed to a significant vision, he had done his best to launch early and iterate. Thus, he was facing a pivot or persevere moment just eight months into the life of his company. The more money, time, and creative energy that has been sunk into an idea, the harder it is to pivot. David had done well to avoid that trap.
2. David had identified his leap-of-faith questions explicitly at the outset and, more important, had made quantitative predictions about each of them. It would not have been difficult for him to declare success retroactively from that initial venture. After all, some of his metrics, such as activation, were doing quite well. In terms of gross metrics such as total usage, the company had positive growth. It is only because David focused on actionable metrics for each of his leap-of-faith questions that he was able to

accept that his company was failing. In addition, because David had not wasted energy on premature PR, he was able to make this determination without public embarrassment or distraction.

Failure is a prerequisite to learning. The problem with the notion of shipping a product and then seeing what happens is that you are guaranteed to succeed—at seeing what happens. But then what? As soon as you have a handful of customers, you're likely to have five opinions about what to do next. Which should you listen to?

Votizen's results were okay, but they were not good enough. David felt that although his optimization was improving the metrics, they were not trending toward a model that would sustain the business overall. But like all good entrepreneurs, he did not give up prematurely. David decided to pivot and test a new hypothesis. A pivot requires that we keep one foot rooted in what we've learned so far, while making a fundamental change in strategy in order to seek even greater validated learning. In this case, David's direct contact with customers proved essential.

He had heard three recurring bits of feedback in his testing:

1. "I always wanted to get more involved; this makes it so much easier."
2. "The fact that you prove I'm a voter matters."
3. "There's no one here. What's the point of coming back?"[1]

David decided to undertake what I call a *zoom-in pivot,* refocusing the product on what previously had been considered just one feature of a larger whole. Think of the customer comments above: customers like the concept, they like the voter registration technology, but they aren't getting value out of the social networking part of the product.

David decided to change Votizen into a product called @2gov, a "social lobbying platform." Rather than get customers integrated in a civic social network, @2gov allows them to contact their elected representatives quickly and easily via existing social networks such as Twitter. The customer engages digitally, but @2gov translates that digital contact into paper form. Members of Congress receive old-fashioned printed letters and petitions as a result. In other words, @2gov translates the high-tech world of its customers into the low-tech world of politics.

@2gov had a slightly different set of leap-of-faith questions to answer. It still depended on customers signing up, verifying their voter status, and referring their friends, but the growth model changed. Instead of relying on an engagement-driven business ("sticky" growth), @2gov was more transactional. David's hypothesis was that passionate activists would be willing to pay money to have @2gov facilitate contacts on behalf of voters who cared about their issues.

David's new MVP took four months and another $30,000. He'd now spent a grand total of $50,000 and worked for twelve months. But the results from his next round of testing were dramatic: registration rate 42 percent, activation 83 percent, retention 21 percent, and referral a whopping 54 percent. However, the number of activists willing to pay was less than 1 percent. The value of each transaction was far too low to sustain a profitable business even after David had done his best to optimize it.

Before we get to David's next pivot, notice how convincingly he was able to demonstrate validated learning. He hoped that with this new product, he would be able to improve his leap-of-faith metrics dramatically, and he did (see the chart below).

| | BEFORE PIVOT | AFTER PIVOT |
|---|---|---|
| Engine of growth | Sticky | Paid |
| Registration rate | 17% | 42% |
| Activation | 90% | 83% |
| Retention | 8% | 21% |
| Referral | 6% | 54% |
| Revenue | n/a | 1% |
| Lifetime value (LTV) | n/a | Minimal |

He did this not by working harder but by working smarter, taking his product development resources and applying them to a new and different product. Compared with the previous four months of optimization, the new four months of pivoting had resulted in a dramatically higher return on investment, but David was still stuck in an age-old entrepreneurial trap. His metrics and product were improving, but not fast enough.

David pivoted again. This time, rather than rely on activists to pay money to drive contacts, he went to large organizations, professional fund-raisers, and big companies, which all have a professional or business interest in political campaigning. The companies seemed extremely eager to use and pay for David's service, and David quickly signed letters of intent to build the functionality they needed. In this pivot, David did what I call a *customer segment pivot,* keeping the functionality of the product the same but changing the audience focus. He focused on who pays: from consumers to businesses and nonprofit organizations. In other words, David went from being a business-to-consumer (B2C) company to being a business-to-business (B2B) company. In the process he changed his planned growth model, as well to one where he would be able to fund growth out of the profits generated from each B2B sale.

Three months later, David had built the functionality he had promised, based on those early letters of intent. But when he went back to companies to collect his checks, he discovered more problems. Company after company procrastinated, delayed, and ultimately passed up the opportunity. Although they had been excited enough to sign a letter of intent, closing a real sale was much more difficult. It turned out that those companies were not early adopters.

On the basis of the letters of intent, David had increased his head count, taking on additional sales staff and engineers in anticipation of having to service higher-margin business-to-business accounts. When the sales didn't materialize, the whole team had to work harder to try to find revenue elsewhere. Yet no matter how many sales calls they went on and no matter how much optimization they did to the product, the model wasn't working. Returning to his leap-of-faith questions, David concluded that the results refuted his business-to-business hypothesis, and so he decided to pivot once again.

All this time, David was learning and gaining feedback from his potential customers, but he was in an unsustainable situation. You can't pay staff with what you've learned, and raising money at that juncture would have escalated the problem. Raising money without early traction is not a certain thing. If he had been able to raise money, he could have kept the company going but would have been pouring money into a value-destroying engine of growth. He would be in a high-pressure situation: use investor's cash to make the engine of growth work or risk having to shut down the company (or be replaced).

David decided to reduce staff and pivot again, this time attempting what I call a *platform pivot.* Instead of selling an application to one customer at a time, David envisioned a new growth model inspired by Google's AdWords platform. He built a self-serve sales platform where anyone could become a customer with just a credit card. Thus, no matter what cause you were passionate about, you could go to @2gov's website and @2gov would help you find new people to get involved. As always, the new people were verified registered voters, and so their opinions carried weight with elected officials.

The new product took only one additional month to build and immediately showed results: 51 percent sign-up rate, 92 percent activation rate, 28 percent retention rate, 64 percent referral rate (see the chart below). Most important, 11 percent of these customers were willing to pay 20 cents per message. Most important, this was the beginning of an actual growth model that could work. Receiving 20 cents per message might not sound like much, but the high referral rate meant that @2gov could grow its traffic without spending significant marketing money (this is the viral engine of growth).

| | BEFORE PIVOT | AFTER PIVOT |
|---|---|---|
| Engine of growth | Paid | Viral |
| Registration rate | 42% | 51% |
| Activation | 83% | 92% |
| Retention | 21% | 28% |
| Referral | 54% | 64% |
| Revenue | 1% | 11% |
| Lifetime value (LTV) | Minimal | $0.20 per message |

Votizen's story exhibits some common patterns. One of the most important to note is the acceleration of MVPs. The first MVP took eight months, the next four months, then three, then one. Each time David was able to validate or refute his next hypothesis faster than before.

How can one explain this acceleration? It is tempting to credit it to the product development work that had been going on. Many features had been created, and with them a fair amount of infrastructure. Therefore, each time the company pivoted, it didn't have to start from scratch. But this is not the whole story. For one thing, much of the product had to be discarded between pivots. Worse, the product that remained was classified as a legacy product, one that was no longer suited to the goals of the company. As is usually the case, the effort required to reform a legacy product took extra work. Counteracting these forces were the hard-won lessons David had learned through each milestone. Votizen accelerated its MVP process because it was learning critical things about its customers, market, and strategy.

Today, two years after its inception, Votizen is doing well. They recently raised $1.5 million from Facebook's initial investor Peter Thiel, one of the very few consumer Internet investments he has made in recent years. Votizen's system now can process voter identity in real time for forty-seven states representing 94 percent of the U.S. population and has delivered tens of thousands of messages to Congress. The Startup Visa campaign used Votizen's tools to introduce the Startup Visa Act (S.565), which is the first legislation introduced into the Senate solely as a result of social lobbying. These activities have attracted the attention of established Washington consultants who are seeking to employ Votizen's tools in future political campaigns.

David Binetti sums up his experience building a Lean Startup:

> In 2003 I started a company in roughly the same space as I'm in today. I had roughly the same domain expertise and industry credibility, fresh off the USA.gov success. But back then my company was a total failure (despite

> consuming significantly greater investment), while now I have a business making money and closing deals. Back then I did the traditional linear product development model, releasing an amazing product (it really was) after 12 months of development, only to find that no one would buy it. This time I produced four versions in twelve weeks and generated my first sale relatively soon after that. And it isn't just market timing—two other companies that launched in a similar space in 2003 subsequently sold for tens of millions of dollars, and others in 2010 followed a linear model straight to the dead pool.

## A STARTUP'S RUNWAY IS THE NUMBER OF PIVOTS IT CAN STILL MAKE

Seasoned entrepreneurs often speak of the runway that their startup has left: the amount of time remaining in which a startup must either achieve lift-off or fail. This usually is defined as the remaining cash in the bank divided by the monthly burn rate, or net drain on that account balance. For example, a startup with $1 million in the bank that is spending $100,000 per month has a projected runway of ten months.

When startups start to run low on cash, they can extend the runway two ways: by cutting costs or by raising additional funds. But when entrepreneurs cut costs indiscriminately, they are as liable to cut the costs that are allowing the company to get through its Build-Measure-Learn feedback loop as they are to cut waste. If the cuts result in a slowdown to this feedback loop, all they have accomplished is to help the startup go out of business more slowly.

The true measure of runway is how many pivots a startup has left: the number of opportunities it has to make a fundamental change to its business strategy. Measuring runway through the lens of pivots rather than that of time suggests another way to extend that runway: get to each pivot faster. In other words, the startup has to find ways to achieve the same amount of validated learning at lower cost or in a shorter time. All the techniques in the Lean Startup model that have been discussed so far have this as their overarching goal.

## PIVOTS REQUIRE COURAGE

Ask most entrepreneurs who have decided to pivot and they will tell you that they wish they had made the decision sooner. I believe there are three reasons why this happens.

First, vanity metrics can allow entrepreneurs to form false conclusions and live in their own private reality. This is particularly damaging to the decision to pivot because it robs teams of the belief that it is necessary to change. When people are forced to change against their better judgment, the process is harder, takes longer, and leads to a less decisive outcome.

Second, when an entrepreneur has an unclear hypothesis, it's almost impossible to experience complete failure, and without failure there is usually no impetus to embark on the radical change a pivot requires. As I mentioned earlier, the failure of the "launch it and see what happens" approach should now be evident: you will always succeed—in seeing what happens. Except in rare cases, the early results will be ambiguous, and you won't know whether to pivot or persevere, whether to change direction or stay the course.

Third, many entrepreneurs are afraid. Acknowledging failure can lead to dangerously low morale. Most entrepreneurs' biggest fear is not that their vision will prove to be wrong. More terrifying is the thought that the vision might be deemed wrong without having been given a real chance to prove itself. This fear drives much of the resistance to the minimum viable product, split testing, and other techniques to test hypotheses. Ironically, this fear drives up the risk because testing doesn't occur until the vision is fully represented. However, by that time it is often too late to pivot because funding is running out. To avoid this fate, entrepreneurs need to face their fears and be willing to fail, often in a public way. In fact, entrepreneurs who have a high profile, either because of personal fame or because they are operating as part of a famous brand, face an extreme version of this problem.

A new startup in Silicon Valley called Path was started by experienced entrepreneurs: Dave Morin, who previously had overseen Facebook's platform initiative; Dustin Mierau, product designer and cocreator of Macster; and Shawn Fanning of Napster fame. They decided to release a minimum viable product in 2010. Because of the high-profile nature of its founders, the MVP attracted significant press attention, especially from technology and startup blogs. Unfortunately, their product was not targeted at technology early adopters, and as a result, the early blogger reaction was quite negative. (Many entrepreneurs fail to launch because they are afraid of this kind of reaction, worrying that it will harm the morale of the entire company. The allure of positive press, especially in our "home" industry, is quite strong.)

Luckily, the Path team had the courage to ignore this fear and focus on what their customers said. As a result, they were able to get essential early feedback from actual customers. Path's goal is to create a more personal social network that maintains its quality over time. Many people have had the experience of being overconnected on existing social networks, sharing with past coworkers, high school friends, relatives, and colleagues. Such broad groups make it hard to share intimate moments. Path took an unusual approach. For example, it limited the number of connections to fifty, based on brain research by the anthropologist Robin Dunbar at Oxford. His research suggests that fifty is roughly the number of personal relationships in any person's life at any given time.

For members of the tech press (and many tech early adopters) this "artificial" constraint on the number of connections was anathema. They routinely use new social networking products with thousands of connections. Fifty seemed way too small. As a result, Path endured a lot of public criticism, which was hard to ignore. But customers flocked to the platform, and their feedback was decidedly different from the negativity in the press. Customers liked the intimate moments and consistently wanted features that were not on the original product road map, such as the ability to share how friends' pictures made them feel and the ability to share "video moments."

Dave Morin summed up his experience this way:

> The reality of our team and our backgrounds built up a massive wall of expectations. I don't think it would have mattered what we would have released; we would have been met with expectations that are hard to live up to. But to us it just meant we needed to get our product and our vision out into the market broadly in order to get feedback and to begin iteration. We humbly test our theories and our approach to see what the market thinks. Listen to feedback honestly. And continue to innovate in the directions we think will create meaning in the world.

Path's story is just beginning, but already their courage in facing down critics is paying off. If and when they need to pivot, they won't be hampered by fear. They recently raised $8.5 million in venture capital in a round led by Kleiner Perkins Caufield & Byers. In doing so, Path reportedly turned down an acquisition offer for $100 million from Google.[2]

## THE PIVOT OR PERSEVERE MEETING

The decision to pivot requires a clear-eyed and objective mind-set. We've discussed the telltale signs of the need to pivot: the decreasing effectiveness of product experiments and the general feeling that product development should be more productive. Whenever you see those symptoms, consider a pivot.

The decision to pivot is emotionally charged for any startup and has to be addressed in a structured way. One way to mitigate this challenge is to schedule the meeting in advance. I recommend that every startup have a regular "pivot or persevere" meeting. In my experience, less than a few weeks between meetings is too often and more than a few months is too infrequent. However, each startup needs to find its own pace.

Each pivot or persevere meeting requires the participation of both the product development and business leadership teams. At IMVU, we also added the perspectives of outside advisers who could help us see past our preconceptions and interpret data in new ways. The product development team must bring a complete report of the results of its product optimization efforts over time (not just the past period) as well as a comparison of how those results stack up against expectations (again, over time). The business leadership should bring detailed accounts of their conversations with current and potential customers.

Let's take a look at this process in action in a dramatic pivot done by a company called Wealthfront. That company was founded in 2007 by Dan Carroll and added Andy Rachleff as CEO shortly thereafter. Andy is a well-known figure in Silicon Valley: he is a cofounder and former general partner of the venture capital firm Benchmark Capital and is on the faculty of the Stanford Graduate School of Business, where he teaches a variety of courses on technology entrepreneurship. I first met Andy when he commissioned a case study on IMVU to teach his students about the process we had used to build the company.

Wealthfront's mission is to disrupt the mutual fund industry by bringing greater transparency, access, and value to retail investors. What makes Wealthfront's story unusual, however, is not where it is today but how it began: as an online game.

In Wealthfront's original incarnation it was called kaChing and was conceived as a kind of fantasy league for amateur investors. It allowed anyone to open a virtual trading account and build a portfolio that was based on real market data without having to invest real money. The idea was to identify diamonds in the rough: amateur traders who lacked the resources to become fund managers but who possessed market insight. Wealthfront's founders did not want to be in the online gaming business per se; kaChing was part of a sophisticated strategy in the service of their larger vision. Any student of disruptive innovation would have looked on approvingly: they were following that system perfectly by initially serving customers who were unable to participate in the mainstream market. Over time, they believed, the product would become more and more sophisticated, eventually allowing users to serve (and disrupt) existing professional fund managers.

To identify the best amateur trading savants, Wealthfront built sophisticated technology to rate the skill of each fund manager, using techniques employed by the most sophisticated evaluators of money managers, the premier U.S. university endowments. Those methods allowed them to evaluate not just the returns the managers generated but also the amount of risk they had taken along with how consistent they performed relative to their declared investment strategy. Thus, fund managers who achieved great returns through reckless gambles (i.e., investments outside their area of expertise) would be ranked lower than those who had figured out how to beat the market through skill.

With its kaChing game, Wealthfront hoped to test two leap-of-faith assumptions:

1. A significant percentage of the game players would demonstrate enough talent as virtual fund managers to prove themselves suitable to become managers of real assets (the value hypothesis).
2. The game would grow using the viral engine of growth and generate value using a freemium business model. The game was free to play, but the team hoped that a percentage of the players would realize that they were lousy traders and therefore want to convert to paying customers once Wealthfront started offering real asset management services (the growth hypothesis).

kaChing was a huge early success, attracting more than 450,000 gamers in its initial launch. By now, you should be suspicious of this kind of vanity metric. Many less disciplined companies would have celebrated that success and felt their future was secure, but Wealthfront had identified its assumptions clearly and was able to think more rigorously. By the time Wealthfront was ready to launch its paid financial product, only seven amateur managers had qualified as worthy of managing other people's money, far less than the ideal model had anticipated. After the paid product launched, they were able to measure the conversion rate of gamers into paying customers. Here too the numbers were discouraging: the conversion rate was close to zero. Their model had predicted that hundreds of customers would sign up, but only fourteen did.

The team worked valiantly to find ways to improve the product, but none showed any particular promise. It was time for a pivot or persevere meeting.

If the data we have discussed so far was all that was available at that critical meeting, Wealthfront would have been in trouble. They would have known that their current strategy wasn't working but not what to do to fix it. That is why it was critical that they followed the recommendation earlier in this chapter to investigate alternative possibilities. In this case, Wealthfront had pursued two important lines of inquiry.

The first was a series of conversations with professional money managers, beginning with John Powers, the head of Stanford University's endowment, who reacted surprisingly positively. Wealthfront's strategy was premised on the assumption that professional money managers would be reluctant to join the system because the increased transparency would threaten their sense of authority. Powers had no such concerns. CEO Andy Rachleff then began a series of conversations with other professional investment managers and brought the results back to the company. His insights were as follows:

1. Successful professional money managers felt they had nothing to fear from transparency, since they believed it would validate their skills.
2. Money managers faced significant challenges in managing and scaling their own businesses. They were hampered by the difficulty of servicing their own accounts and therefore had to require high minimum investments as a way to screen new clients.

The second problem was so severe that Wealthfront was fielding cold calls from professional managers asking out of the blue to join the platform. These were classic early adopters who had the vision to see past the current product to something they could use to achieve a competitive advantage.

The second critical qualitative information came out of conversations with consumers. It turned out that they found the blending of virtual and real portfolio management on the ka-Ching website confusing. Far from being a clever way of acquiring customers, the freemium strategy was getting in the way by promoting confusion about the company's positioning.

This data informed the pivot or persevere meeting. With everyone present, the team debated what to do with its future. The current strategy wasn't working, but many employees were nervous about abandoning the online game. After all, it was an important part of what they had signed on to build. They had invested significant time and energy building and supporting those customers. It was painful—as it always is—to realize that that energy had been wasted.

Wealthfront decided it could not persevere as it existed. The company chose instead to celebrate what it had learned. If it had not launched its current product, the team never would have learned what it needed to know to pivot. In fact, the experience taught them something essential about their vision. As Andy says, "What we really wanted to change was not who manages the money but who has access to the best possible talent. We'd originally thought we'd need to build a significant business with amateur managers to get professionals to come on board, but fortunately it turns out that wasn't necessary."

The company pivoted, abandoning the gaming customers altogether and focusing on providing a service that allowed customers to invest with professional managers. On the surface, the pivot seems quite dramatic in that the company changed its positioning, its name, and its partner strategy. It even jettisoned a large proportion of the features it had built. But at its core, a surprising amount stayed the same. The most valuable work the company had done was building technology to evaluate managers' effectiveness, and this became the kernel around which the new business was built. This is also common with pivots; it is not necessary to throw out everything that came before and start over. Instead, it's about repurposing what has been built and what has been learned to find a more positive direction.

Today, Wealthfront is prospering as a result of its pivot, with over $180 million invested on the platform and more than forty professional managers.[3] It recently was named one of *Fast Company*'s ten most innovative companies in finance.[4] The company continues to operate with agility, scaling in line with the growth principles outlined in Chapter 12. Wealthfront is also a leading advocate of the development technique known as continuous deployment, which we'll discuss in Chapter 9.

## FAILURE TO PIVOT

The decision to pivot is so difficult that many companies fail to make it. I wish I could say that every time I was confronted with the need to pivot, I handled it well, but this is far from true. I remember one failure to pivot especially well.

A few years after IMVU's founding, the company was having tremendous success. The business had grown to over $1 million per month in revenue; we had created more than twenty million avatars for our customers. We managed to raise significant new rounds of financing, and like the global economy, we were riding high. But danger lurked around the corner.

Unknowingly, we had fallen into a classic startup trap. We had been so successful with our early efforts that we were ignoring the principles behind them. As a result, we missed the need to pivot even as it stared us in the face.

We had built an organization that excelled at the kinds of

activities described in earlier chapters: creating minimum viable products to test new ideas and running experiments to tune the engine of growth. Before we had begun to enjoy success, many people had advised against our "low-quality" minimum viable product and experimental approach, urging us to slow down. They wanted us to do things right and focus on quality instead of speed. We ignored that advice, mostly because we wanted to claim the advantages of speed. After our approach was vindicated, the advice we received changed. Now most of the advice we heard was that "you can't argue with success," urging us to stay the course. We liked this advice better, but it was equally wrong.

Remember that the rationale for building low-quality MVPs is that developing any features beyond what early adopters require is a form of waste. However, the logic of this takes you only so far. Once you have found success with early adopters, you want to sell to mainstream customers. Mainstream customers have different requirements and are much more demanding.

The kind of pivot we needed is called a customer segment pivot. In this pivot, the company realizes that the product it's building solves a real problem for real customers but that they are not the customers it originally planned to serve. In other words, the product hypothesis is confirmed only partially. (This chapter described such a pivot in the Votizen story, above.)

A customer segment pivot is an especially tricky pivot to execute because, as we learned the hard way at IMVU, the very actions that made us successful with early adopters were diametrically opposed to the actions we'd have to master to be successful with mainstream customers. We lacked a clear understanding of how our engine of growth operated. We had begun to trust our vanity metrics. We had stopped using learning milestones to hold ourselves accountable. Instead, it was much more convenient to focus on the ever-larger gross metrics that were so exciting: breaking new records in signing up paying customers and active users, monitoring our customer retention rate—you name it. Under the surface, it should have been clear that our efforts at tuning the engine were reaching diminishing returns, the classic sign of the need to pivot.

For example, we spent months trying to improve the product's activation rate (the rate at which new customers become active consumers of the product), which remained stubbornly low. We did countless experiments: usability improvements, new persuasion techniques, incentive programs, customer quests, and other game-like features. Individually, many of these new features and new marketing tools were successful. We measured them rigorously, using A/B experimentation. But taken in aggregate, over the course of many months, we were seeing negligible changes in the overall drivers of our engine of growth. Even our activation rate, which had been the center of our focus, edged up only a few percentage points.

We ignored the signs because the company was still growing, delivering month after month of "up and to the right" results. But we were quickly exhausting our early adopter market. It was getting harder and harder to find customers we could acquire at the prices we were accustomed to paying. As we drove our marketing team to find more customers, they were forced to reach out more to mainstream customers, but mainstream customers are less forgiving of an early product. The activation and monetization rates of new customers started to go down, driving up the cost of acquiring new customers. Pretty soon, our growth was flatlining and our engine sputtered and stalled.

It took us far too long to make the changes necessary to fix this situation. As with all pivots, we had to get back to basics and start the innovation accounting cycle over. It felt like the company's second founding. We had gotten really good at optimizing, tuning, and iterating, but in the process we had lost sight of the purpose of those activities: testing a clear hypothesis in the service of the company's vision. Instead, we were chasing growth, revenue, and profits wherever we could find them.

We needed to reacquaint ourselves with our new mainstream customers. Our interaction designers led the way by developing a clear customer archetype that was based on extensive in-person conversations and observation. Next, we needed to invest heavily in a major product overhaul designed to make the product dramatically easier to use. Because of our overfocus on fine-tuning, we had stopped making large investments like these, preferring to invest in lower-risk and lower-yield testing experiments.

However, investing in quality, design, and larger projects did not require that we abandon our experimental roots. On the contrary, once we realized our mistake and executed the pivot, those skills served us well. We created a sandbox for experimentation like the one described in Chapter 12 and had a cross-functional team work exclusively on this major redesign. As they built, they continuously tested their new design head to head against the old one. Initially, the new design performed worse than the old one, as is usually the case. It lacked the features and functionality of the old design and had many new mistakes as well. But the team relentlessly improved the design until, months later, it performed better. This new design laid the foundation for our future growth.

This foundation has paid off handsomely. By 2009, revenue had more than doubled to over $25 million annually. But we might have enjoyed that success earlier if we had pivoted sooner.[5]

## A CATALOG OF PIVOTS

Pivots come in different flavors. The word *pivot* sometimes is used incorrectly as a synonym for *change*. A pivot is a special kind of change designed to test a new fundamental hypothesis about the product, business model, and engine of growth.

### Zoom-in Pivot

In this case, what previously was considered a single feature in a product becomes the whole product. This is the type of pivot Votizen made when it pivoted away from a full social network and toward a simple voter contact product.

### Zoom-out Pivot

In the reverse situation, sometimes a single feature is insufficient to support a whole product. In this type of pivot, what was considered the whole product becomes a single feature of a much larger product.

### Customer Segment Pivot

In this pivot, the company realizes that the product it is building solves a real problem for real customers but that they are not the type of customers it originally planned to serve. In other words, the product hypothesis is partially confirmed, solving the right problem, but for a different customer than originally anticipated.

### Customer Need Pivot

As a result of getting to know customers extremely well, it sometimes becomes clear that the problem we're trying to solve for them is not very important. However, because of this customer intimacy, we often discover other related problems that are important and can be solved by our team. In many cases, these related problems may require little more than repositioning the existing product. In other cases, it may require a completely new product. Again, this a case where the product hypothesis is partially confirmed; the target customer has a problem worth solving, just not the one that was originally anticipated.

A famous example is the chain Potbelly Sandwich Shop, which today has over two hundred stores. It began as an antique store in 1977; the owners started to sell sandwiches as a way to bolster traffic to their stores. Pretty soon they had pivoted their way into an entirely different line of business.

### Platform Pivot

A platform pivot refers to a change from an application to a platform or vice versa. Most commonly, startups that aspire to create a new platform begin life by selling a single application, the so-called killer app, for their platform. Only later does the platform emerge as a vehicle for third parties to leverage as a way to create their own related products. However, this order is not always set in stone, and some companies have to execute this pivot multiple times.

### Business Architecture Pivot

This pivot borrows a concept from Geoffrey Moore, who observed that companies generally follow one of two major business architectures: high margin, low volume (complex systems model) or low margin, high volume (volume operations model).[6] The former commonly is associated with business to business (B2B) or enterprise sales cycles, and the latter with consumer products (there are notable exceptions). In a business architecture pivot, a startup switches architectures. Some companies change from high margin, low volume by going mass market (e.g., Google's search "appliance"); others, originally designed for the mass market, turned out to require long and expensive sales cycles.

### Value Capture Pivot

There are many ways to capture the value a company creates. These methods are referred to commonly as monetization or revenue models. These terms are much too limiting. Implicit in the idea of monetization is that it is a separate "feature" of a product that can be added or removed at will. In reality, capturing value is an intrinsic part of the product hypothesis. Often, changes to the way a company captures value can have far-reaching consequences for the rest of the business, product, and marketing strategies.

### Engine of Growth Pivot

As we'll see in Chapter 10, there are three primary engines of growth that power startups: the viral, sticky, and paid growth models. In this type of pivot, a company changes its growth strategy to seek faster or more profitable growth. Commonly but not always, the engine of growth also requires a change in the way value is captured.

### Channel Pivot

In traditional sales terminology, the mechanism by which a company delivers its product to customers is called the sales channel or distribution channel. For example, consumer packaged goods are sold in a grocery store, cars are sold in dealerships, and much enterprise software is sold (with extensive customization) by consulting and professional services firms. Often, the requirements of the channel determine the price, features, and competitive landscape of a product. A channel pivot is a recognition that the same basic solution could be delivered through a different channel with greater effectiveness. Whenever a company abandons a previously complex sales process to "sell direct" to its end users, a channel pivot is in progress.

It is precisely because of its destructive effect on sales channels that the Internet has had such a disruptive influence in industries that previously required complex sales and distribution channels, such as newspaper, magazine, and book publishing.

### Technology Pivot

Occasionally, a company discovers a way to achieve the same solution by using a completely different technology. Technology pivots are much more common in established businesses. In other words, they are a sustaining innovation, an incremental improvement designed to appeal to and retain an existing customer base. Established companies excel at this kind of pivot because so much is not changing. The customer segment is the same, the customer's problem is the same, the value-capture model is the same, and the channel partners are the same. The only question is whether the new technology can provide superior price and/or performance compared with the existing technology.

## A PIVOT IS A STRATEGIC HYPOTHESIS

Although the pivots identified above will be familiar to students of business strategy, the ability to pivot is no substitute for sound strategic thinking. The problem with providing famous examples of pivots is that most people are familiar only with the successful end strategies of famous companies. Most readers know that Southwest or Walmart is an example of a low-cost disruption in their markets, that Microsoft an example of a platform monopoly, and that Starbucks has leveraged a powerful premium brand. What is generally less well known are the pivots that were required to discover those strategies. Companies have a strong incentive to align their PR stories around the heroic founder and make it seem that their success was the inevitable result of a good idea.

Thus, although startups often pivot into a strategy that seems similar to that of a successful company, it is important not to put too much stock in these analogies. It's extremely difficult to know if the analogy has been drawn properly. Have we copied the essential features or just superficial ones? Will what worked in that industry work in ours? Will what has worked in the past work today? A pivot is better understood as a new strategic hypothesis that will require a new minimum viable product to test.

Pivots are a permanent fact of life for any growing business. Even after a company achieves initial success, it must continue to pivot. Those familiar with the technology life cycle ideas of theorists such as Geoffrey Moore know certain later-stage pivots by the names he has given them: the Chasm, the Tornado, the Bowling Alley. Readers of the disruptive innovation literature spearheaded by Harvard's Clayton Christensen will be familiar with established companies that fail to pivot when they should. The critical skill for managers today is to match those theories to their present situation so that they apply the right advice at the right time.

Modern managers cannot have escaped the deluge of recent books calling on them to adapt, change, reinvent, or upend their existing businesses. Many of the works in this category are long on exhortations and short on specifics.

A pivot is not just an exhortation to change. Remember, it is a special kind of structured change designed to test a new fundamental hypothesis about the product, business model, and engine of growth. It is the heart of the Lean Startup method. It is what makes the companies that follow Lean Startup resilient in the face of mistakes: if we take a wrong turn, we have the tools we need to realize it and the agility to find another path.

○ ○ ○

In Part Two, we have looked at a startup idea from its initial leaps of faith, tested it with a minimum viable product, used innovation accounting and actionable metrics to evaluate the results, and made the decision to pivot or persevere.

I have treated these subjects in great detail to prepare for what comes next. On the page, these processes may seem clinical, slow, and simple. In the real world, something different is needed. We have learned to steer when moving slowly. Now we must learn to race. Laying a solid foundation is only the first step toward our real destination: acceleration.

# Part Three

# ACCELERATE

# Start Your Engines

Most of the decisions startups face are not clear-cut. How often should you release a product? Is there a reason to release weekly rather than daily or quarterly or annually? Product releases incur overhead, and so from an efficiency point of view, releasing often leaves less time to devote to building the product. However, waiting too long to release can lead to the ultimate waste: making something that nobody wants.

How much time and energy should companies invest in infrastructure and planning early on in *anticipation* of success? Spend too much and you waste precious time that could have been spent learning. Spend too little and you may fail to take advantage of early success and cede market leadership to a fast follower.

What should employees spend their days doing? How do we hold people accountable for learning at an organizational level? Traditional departments create incentive structures that keep people focused on excellence in their specialties: marketing, sales, product development. But what if the company's best interests are served by cross-functional collaboration? Startups need organizational structures that combat the extreme uncertainty that is a startup's chief enemy.

The lean manufacturing movement faced similar questions on the factory floor. Their answers are relevant for startups as well, with some modifications.

The critical first question for any lean transformation is: which activities create value and which are a form of waste? Once you understand this distinction, you can begin using lean techniques to drive out waste and increase the efficiency of the value-creating activities. For these techniques to be used in a startup, they must be adapted to the unique circumstances of entrepreneurship. Recall from Chapter 3 that value in a startup is not the creation of stuff, but rather validated learning about how to build a sustainable business. What products do customers really want? How will our business grow? Who is our customer? Which customers should we listen to and which should we ignore? These are the questions that need answering as quickly as possible to maximize a startup's chances of success. That is what creates value for a startup.

In Part Three, we will develop techniques that allow Lean Startups to grow without sacrificing the speed and agility that are the lifeblood of every startup. Contrary to common belief, lethargy and bureaucracy are not the inevitable fate of companies as they achieve maturity. I believe that with the proper foundation, Lean Startups can grow to become lean enterprises that maintain their agility, learning orientation, and culture of innovation even as they scale.

In Chapter 9, we will see how Lean Startups take advantage of the counterintuitive power of small batches. Just as lean manufacturing has pursued a just-in-time approach to building products, reducing the need for in-process inventory, Lean Startups practice *just-in-time scalability,* conducting product experiments without making massive up-front investments in planning and design.

Chapter 10 will explore the metrics startups should use to understand their growth as they add new customers and discover new markets. Sustainable growth follows one of three engines of growth: paid, viral, or sticky. By identifying which engine of growth a startup is using, it can then direct energy where it will be most effective in growing the business. Each engine requires a focus on unique metrics to evaluate the success of new products and prioritize new experiments. When used with the innovation accounting method described in Part Two, these metrics allow startups to figure out when their growth is at risk of running out and pivot accordingly.

Chapter 11 shows how to build an *adaptive organization* by investing in the right amount of process to keep teams nimble as they grow. We will see how techniques from the tool kit of lean manufacturing, such as the Five Whys, help startup teams grow without becoming bureaucratic or dysfunctional. We also will see how lean disciplines set the stage for a startup to transition into an established company driven by operational excellence.

In Chapter 12, we'll come full circle. As startups grow into established companies, they face the same pressures that make it necessary for today's enterprises to find new ways to invest in disruptive innovation. In fact, we'll see that an advantage of a successful startup's rapid growth is that the company can keep its entrepreneurial DNA even as it matures. Today's companies must learn to master a management portfolio of sustainable *and* disruptive innovation. It is an obsolete view that sees startups as going through discrete phases that leave earlier kinds of work—such as innovation—behind. Rather, modern companies must excel at doing multiple kinds of work in parallel. To do so, we'll explore techniques for incubating innovation teams within the context of an established company.

I have included an epilogue called "Waste Not" in which I consider some of the broader implications of the success of the Lean Startup movement, place it in historical context (including cautionary lessons from past movements), and make suggestions for its future direction.

# 9

# BATCH

In the book *Lean Thinking*, James Womack and Daniel Jones recount a story of stuffing newsletters into envelopes with the assistance of one of the author's two young children. Every envelope had to be addressed, stamped, filled with a letter, and sealed. The daughters, age six and nine, knew how they should go about completing the project: "Daddy, first you should fold all of the newsletters. Then you should attach the seal. Then you should put on the stamps." Their father wanted to do it the counterintuitive way: complete each envelope one at a time. They—like most of us—thought that was backward, explaining to him "that wouldn't be efficient!" He and his daughters each took half the envelopes and competed to see who would finish first.

The father won the race, and not just because he is an adult. It happened because the one envelope at a time approach is a faster way of getting the job done even though it seems inefficient. This has been confirmed in many studies, including one that was recorded on video.[1]

The one envelope at a time approach is called "single-piece flow" in lean manufacturing. It works because of the surprising power of small batches. When we do work that proceeds in stages, the "batch size" refers to how much work moves from one stage to the next at a time. For example, if we were stuffing one hundred envelopes, the intuitive way to do it—folding one hundred letters at a time—would have a batch size of one hundred. Single-piece flow is so named because it has a batch size of one.

Why does stuffing one envelope at a time get the job done faster even though it seems like it would be slower? Because our intuition doesn't take into account the extra time required to sort, stack, and move around the large piles of half-complete envelopes when it's done the other way.[2] It seems more efficient to repeat the same task over and over, in part because we expect that we will get better at this simple task the more we do it. Unfortunately, in process-oriented work like this, individual performance is not nearly as important as the overall performance of the system.

Even if the amount of time that each process took was exactly the same, the small batch production approach still would be superior, and for even more counterintuitive reasons. For example, imagine that the letters didn't fit in the envelopes. With the large-batch approach, we wouldn't find that out until nearly the end. With small batches, we'd know almost immediately. What if the envelopes are defective and won't seal? In the large-batch approach, we'd have to unstuff all the envelopes, get new ones, and restuff them. In the small-batch approach, we'd find this out immediately and have no rework required.

All these issues are visible in a process as simple as stuffing envelopes, but they are of real and much greater consequence in the work of every company, large or small. The small-batch approach produces a finished product every few seconds, whereas the large-batch approach must deliver all the products at once, at the end. Imagine what this might look like if the time horizon was hours, days, or weeks. What if it turns out that the customers have decided they don't want the product? Which process would allow a company to find this out sooner?

Lean manufacturers discovered the benefits of small batches decades ago. In the post–World War II economy, Japanese carmakers such as Toyota could not compete with huge American factories that used the latest mass production techniques. Following the intuitively efficient way of building, mass production factories built cars by using ever-larger batch sizes. They would spend huge amounts of money buying machines that could produce car parts by the tens, hundreds, or thousands. By keeping those machines running at peak speed, they could drive down the unit cost of each part and produce cars that were incredibly inexpensive so long as they were completely uniform.

The Japanese car market was far too small for companies such as Toyota to employ those economies of scale; thus, Japanese companies faced intense pressure from mass production. Also, in the war-ravaged Japanese economy, capital was not available for massive investments in large machines.

It was against this backdrop that innovators such as Taiichi Ohno, Shigeo Shingo, and others found a way to succeed by using small batches. Instead of buying large specialized machines that could produce thousands of parts at a time, Toyota used smaller general-purpose machines that could produce a wide variety of parts in small batches. This required figuring out ways to reconfigure each machine rapidly to make the right part at the right time. By focusing on this "changeover time," Toyota was able to produce entire automobiles by using small batches throughout the process.

This rapid changing of machines was no easy feat. As in any lean transformation, existing systems and tools often need to be reinvented to support working in smaller batches. Shigeo Shingo created the concept of SMED (Single-Minute Exchange of Die) in order to enable a smaller batch size of work in early Toyota factories. He was so relentless in rethinking the way machines were operated that he was able to reduce changeover times that previously took hours to less than ten minutes. He did this, not by asking workers to work faster, but by reimagining and restructuring the work that needed to be done. Every investment in better tools and process had a corresponding benefit in terms of shrinking the batch size of work.

Because of its smaller batch size, Toyota was able to produce a much greater diversity of products. It was no longer necessary that each product be exactly the same to gain the economies of scale that powered mass production. Thus, Toyota could serve its smaller, more fragmented markets and still compete with the mass producers. Over time, that capability allowed Toyota to move successfully into larger and larger markets until it became the world's largest automaker in 2008.

The biggest advantage of working in small batches is that quality problems can be identified much sooner. This is the origin of Toyota's famous *andon* cord, which allows any worker to ask for help as soon as they notice any problem, such as a defect in a physical part, stopping the entire production line if it cannot be corrected immediately. This is another very counterintuitive practice. An assembly line works best when it is functioning smoothly, rolling car after car off the end of the line. The *andon* cord can interrupt this careful flow as the line is halted repeatedly. However, the benefits of finding and fixing problems faster outweigh this cost. This process of continuously driving out defects has been a win-win for Toyota and its customers. It is the root cause of Toyota's historic high quality ratings and low costs.

## SMALL BATCHES IN ENTREPRENEURSHIP

When I teach entrepreneurs this method, I often begin with stories about manufacturing. Before long, I can see the questioning looks: what does this have to do with my startup? The theory that is the foundation of Toyota's success can be used to dramatically improve the speed at which startups find validated learning.

Toyota discovered that small batches made their factories more efficient. In contrast, in the Lean Startup the goal is not to produce more stuff efficiently. It is to—as quickly as possible—learn how to build a sustainable business.

Think back to the example of envelope stuffing. What if it turns out that the customer doesn't want the product we're building? Although this is never good news for an entrepreneur, finding out sooner is much better than finding out later. Working in small batches ensures that a startup can minimize the expenditure of time, money, and effort that ultimately turns out to have been wasted.

## Small Batches at IMVU

At IMVU, we applied these lessons from manufacturing to the way we work. Normally, new versions of products like ours are released to customers on a monthly, quarterly, or yearly cycle.

Take a look at your cell phone. Odds are, it is not the very first version of its kind. Even innovative companies such as Apple produce a new version of their flagship phones about once a year. Bundled up in that product release are dozens of new features (at the release of iPhone 4, Apple boasted more than 1,500 changes).

Ironically, many high-tech products are manufactured in advanced facilities that follow the latest in lean thinking, including small batches and single-piece flow. However, the process that is used to design the product is stuck in the era of mass production. Think of all the changes that are made to a product such as the iPhone; all 1,500 of them are released to customers in one giant batch.

Behind the scenes, in the development and design of the product itself, large batches are still the rule. The work that goes into the development of a new product proceeds on a virtual assembly line. Product managers figure out what features are likely to please customers; product designers then figure out how those features should look and feel. These designs are passed to engineering, which builds something new or modifies an existing product and, once this is done, hands it off to somebody responsible for verifying that the new product works the way the product managers and designers intended. For a product such as the iPhone, these internal handoffs may happen on a monthly or quarterly basis.

Think back one more time to the envelope-stuffing exercise. What is the most efficient way to do this work?

At IMVU, we attempted to design, develop, and ship our new features one at a time, taking advantage of the power of small batches. Here's what it looked like.

Instead of working in separate departments, engineers and designers would work together side by side on one feature at a time. Whenever that feature was ready to be tested with customers, they immediately would release a new version of the product, which would go live on our website for a relatively small number of people. The team would be able immediately to assess the impact of their work, evaluate its effect on customers, and decide what to do next. For tiny changes, the whole process might be repeated several times per day. In fact, in the aggregate, IMVU makes about fifty changes to its product (on average) every single day.

Just as with the Toyota Production System, the key to being able to operate this quickly is to check for defects immediately, thus preventing bigger problems later. For example, we had an extensive set of automated tests that assured that after every change our product still worked as designed. Let's say an engineer accidentally removed an important feature, such as the checkout button on one of our e-commerce pages. Without this button, customers no longer could buy anything from IMVU. It's as if our business instantly became a hobby. Analogously to the Toyota *andon* cord, IMVU used an elaborate set of defense mechanisms that prevented engineers from accidentally breaking something important.

We called this our product's immune system because those automatic protections went beyond checking that the product behaved as expected. We also continuously monitored the health of our business itself so that mistakes were found and removed automatically.

Going back to our business-to-hobby example of the missing checkout button, let's make the problem a little more interesting. Imagine that instead of removing the button altogether, an engineer makes a mistake and changes the button's color so that it is now white on a white background. From the point of view of automated functional tests, the button is still there and everything is working normally; from the customer's point of view, the button is gone, and so nobody can buy anything. This class of problems is hard to detect solely with automation but is still catastrophic from a business point of view. At IMVU, our immune system is programmed to detect these business consequences and automatically invoke our equivalent of the *andon* cord.

When our immune system detects a problem, a number of things happen immediately:

1. The defective change is removed immediately and automatically.
2. Everyone on the relevant team is notified of the problem.
3. The team is blocked from introducing any further changes,

preventing the problem from being compounded by future mistakes . . .

4. . . . until the root cause of the problem is found and fixed. (This root cause analysis is discussed in greater detail in Chapter 11.)

At IMVU, we called this *continuous deployment*, and even in the fast-moving world of software development it is still considered controversial.[3] As the Lean Startup movement has gained traction, it has come to be embraced by more and more startups, even those that operate mission-critical applications. Among the most cutting edge examples is Wealthfront, whose pivot was described in Chapter 8. The company practices true continuous deployment—including more than a dozen releases to customers every day—in an SEC-regulated environment.[4]

## Continuous Deployment Beyond Software

When I tell this story to people who work in a slower-moving industry, they think I am describing something futuristic. But increasingly, more and more industries are seeing their design process accelerated by the same underlying forces that make this kind of rapid iteration possible in the software industry. There are three ways in which this is happening:

**1. Hardware becoming software.** Think about what has happened in consumer electronics. The latest phones and tablet computers are little more than a screen connected to the Internet. Almost all of their value is determined by their software. Even old-school products such as automobiles are seeing ever-larger parts of their value being generated by the software they carry inside, which controls everything from the entertainment system to tuning the engine to controlling the brakes. What can be built out of software can be modified much faster than a physical or mechanical device can.

**2. Fast production changes.** Because of the success of the lean manufacturing movement, many assembly lines are set up to allow each new product that comes off the line to be customized completely without sacrificing quality or cost-effectiveness. Historically, this has been used to offer the customer many choices of product, but in the future, this capability will allow the designers of products to get much faster feedback about new versions. When the design changes, there is no excess inventory of the old version to slow things down. Since machines are designed for rapid changeovers, as soon as the new design is ready, new versions can be produced quickly.

**3. 3D printing and rapid prototyping tools.** As just one example, most products and parts that are made out of plastic today are mass produced using a technique called injection molding. This process is extremely expensive and time-consuming to set up, but once it is up and running, it can reproduce hundreds of thousands of identical individual items at an extremely low cost. It is a classic large-batch production process. This has put entrepreneurs who want to develop a new physical product at a disadvantage, since in general only large companies can afford these large production runs for a new product. However, new technologies are allowing entrepreneurs to build small batches of products that are of the same quality as products made with injection molding, but at much lower cost and much, much faster.

The essential lesson is not that everyone should be shipping fifty times per day but that by reducing batch size, we can get through the Build-Measure-Learn feedback loop more quickly than our competitors can. The ability to learn faster from customers is the essential competitive advantage that startups must possess.

## SMALL BATCHES IN ACTION

To see this process in action, let me introduce you to a company in Boise, Idaho, called SGW Designworks. SGW's specialty is rapid production techniques for physical products. Many of its clients are startups.

SGW Designworks was engaged by a client who had been asked by a military customer to build a complex field x-ray system to detect explosives and other destructive devices at border crossings and in war zones.

Conceptually, the system consisted of an advanced head unit that read x-ray film, multiple x-ray film panels, and the framework to hold the panels while the film was being exposed. The client already had the technology for the x-ray panels and the head unit, but to make the product work in rugged military settings, SGW needed to design and deliver the supporting structure that would make the technology usable in the field. The framework had to be stable to ensure a quality x-ray image, durable enough for use in a war zone, easy to deploy with minimal training, and small enough to collapse into a backpack.

This is precisely the kind of product we are accustomed to thinking takes months or years to develop, yet new techniques are shrinking that time line. SGW immediately began to generate the visual prototypes by using 3D computer-aided design (CAD) software. The 3D models served as a rapid communication tool between the client and the SGW team to make early design decisions.

The team and client settled on a design that used an advanced locking hinge to provide the collapsibility required without compromising stability. The design also integrated a suction cup/pump mechanism to allow for fast, repeatable attachment to the x-ray panels. Sounds complicated, right?

*Three days later,* the SGW team delivered the first physical prototypes to the client. The prototypes were machined out of aluminum directly from the 3D model, using a technique called computer numerical control (CNC) and were hand assembled by the SGW team.

The client immediately took the prototypes to its military contact for review. The general concept was accepted with a number of minor design modifications. In the next five days, another full cycle of design iteration, prototyping, and design review was completed by the client and SGW. The first production run of forty completed units was ready for delivery three and a half weeks after the initiation of the development project.

SGW realized that this was a winning model because feedback on design decisions was nearly instantaneous. The team used the same process to design and deliver eight products, serving a wide range of functions, in a twelve-month period. Half of those products are generating revenue today, and the rest are awaiting initial orders, all thanks to the power of working in small batches.

| THE PROJECT TIME LINE | |
|---|---|
| Design and engineering of the initial virtual prototype | 1 day |
| Production and assembly of initial hard prototypes | 3 days |
| Design iteration: two additional cycles | 5 days |
| Initial production run and assembly of initial forty units | 15 days |

## Small Batches in Education

Not every type of product—as it exists today—allows for design change in small batches. But that is no excuse for sticking to outdated methods. A significant amount of work may be needed to enable innovators to experiment in small batches. As was pointed out in Chapter 2, for established companies looking to accelerate their innovation teams, building this platform for experimentation is the responsibility of senior management.

Imagine that you are a schoolteacher in charge of teaching math to middle school students. Although you may teach concepts in small batches, one day at a time, your overall curriculum cannot change very often. Because you must set up the curriculum in advance and teach the same concepts in the same order to every student in the classroom, you can try a new curriculum at most only once a year.

How could a math teacher experiment with small batches? Under the current large-batch system for educating students, it would be quite difficult; our current educational system was designed in the era of mass production and uses large batches extensively.

A new breed of startups is working hard to change all that. In School of One, students have daily "playlists" of their learning tasks that are attuned to each student's learning needs, based on that student's readiness and learning style. For example, Julia is way ahead of grade level in math and learns best in small groups, so her playlist might include three or four videos matched to her aptitude level, a thirty-minute one-on-one tutoring session with her teacher, and a small group activity in which she works on a math puzzle with three peers at similar aptitude levels. There are assessments built into each activity so that data can be fed back to the teacher to choose appropriate tasks for the next playlist.

This data can be aggregated across classes, schools, or even whole districts.

Now imagine trying to experiment with a curriculum by using a tool such as School of One. Each student is working at his or her own pace. Let's say you are a teacher who has a new sequence in mind for how math concepts should be taught. You can see immediately the impact of the change on those of your students who are at that point in the curriculum. If you judge it to be a good change, you could roll it out immediately for every single student; when they get to that part of the curriculum, they will get the new sequence automatically. In other words, tools like School of One enable teachers to work in much smaller batches, to the benefit of their students. (And, as tools reach wide-scale adoption, successful experiments by individual teachers can be rolled out district-, city-, or even nationwide.) This approach is having an impact and earning accolades. *Time* magazine recently included School of One in its "most innovative ideas" list; it was the only educational organization to make the list.[5]

## THE LARGE-BATCH DEATH SPIRAL

Small batches pose a challenge to managers steeped in traditional notions of productivity and progress, because they believe that functional specialization is more efficient for expert workers.

Imagine you're a product designer overseeing a new product and you need to produce thirty individual design drawings. It probably seems that the most efficient way to work is in seclusion, by yourself, producing the designs one by one. Then, when you're done with all of them, you pass the drawings on to the engineering team and let them work. In other words, you work in large batches.

From the point of view of individual efficiency, working in large batches makes sense. It also has other benefits: it promotes skill building, makes it easier to hold individual contributors accountable, and, most important, allows experts to work without interruption. At least that's the theory. Unfortunately, reality seldom works out that way.

Consider our hypothetical example. After passing thirty design drawings to engineering, the designer is free to turn his or her attention to the next project. But remember the problems that came up during the envelope-stuffing exercise. What happens when engineering has questions about how the drawings are supposed to work? What if some of the drawings are unclear? What if something goes wrong when engineering attempts to use the drawings?

These problems inevitably turn into interruptions for the designer, and now those interruptions are interfering with the next large batch the designer is supposed to be working on. If the drawings need to be redone, the engineers may become idle while they wait for the rework to be completed. If the designer is not available, the engineers may have to redo the designs themselves. This is why so few products are actually built the way they are designed.

When I work with product managers and designers in companies that use large batches, I often discover that they have to redo their work five or six times for every release. One product manager I worked with was so inundated with interruptions that he took to coming into the office in the middle of the night so that he could work uninterrupted. When I suggested that he try switching the work process from large-batch to single-piece flow, he refused—because that would be inefficient! So strong is the instinct to work in large batches, that even when a large-batch system is malfunctioning, we have a tendency to blame ourselves.

Large batches tend to grow over time. Because moving the batch forward often results in additional work, rework, delays, and interruptions, everyone has an incentive to do work in ever-larger batches, trying to minimize this overhead. This is called the *large-batch death spiral* because, unlike in manufacturing, there are no physical limits on the maximum size of a batch.[6] It is possible for batch size to keep growing and growing. Eventually, one batch will become the highest-priority project, a "bet the company" new version of the product, because the company has taken such a long time since the last release. But now the managers are incentivized to increase batch size rather than ship the product. In light of how long the product has been in development, why not fix one more bug or add one more feature? Who really wants to be the manager who risked the success of this huge release by failing to address a potentially critical flaw?

I worked at a company that entered this death spiral. We had been working for months on a new version of a really cool product. The original version had been years in the making, and expectations for the next release were incredibly high. But the longer we worked, the more afraid we became of how customers would react when they finally saw the new version. As our plans became more ambitious, so too did the number of bugs, conflicts, and problems we had to deal with. Pretty soon we got into a situation in which we could not ship anything. Our launch date seemed to recede into the distance. The more work we got done, the more work we had to do. The lack of ability to ship eventually precipitated a crisis and a change of management, all because of the trap of large batches.

These misconceptions about batch size are incredibly common. Hospital pharmacies often deliver big batches of medications to patient floors once a day because it's efficient (a single trip, right?). But many of those meds get sent back to the pharmacy when a patient's orders have changed or the patient is moved or discharged, causing the pharmacy staff to do lots of rework and reprocessing (or trashing) of meds. Delivering smaller batches every four hours reduces the total workload for the pharmacy and ensures that the right meds are at the right place when needed.

Hospital lab blood collections often are done in hourly batches; phlebotomists collect blood for an hour from multiple patients and then send or take all the samples to the lab. This adds to turnaround time for test results and can harm test quality. It has become common for hospitals to bring small batches (two patients) or a single-patient flow of specimens to the lab even if they have to hire an extra phlebotomist or two to do so, because the total system cost is lower.[7]

## PULL, DON'T PUSH

Let's say you are out for a drive, pondering the merits of small batches, and find yourself accidentally putting a dent in your new 2011 blue Toyota Camry. You take it into the dealership for repair and wait to hear the bad news. The repair technician tells you that you need to have the bumper replaced. He goes to check their inventory levels and tells you he has a new bumper in stock and they can complete your repair immediately. This is good news for everyone—you because you get your car back sooner and the dealership because they have a happy customer and don't run the risk of your taking the car somewhere else for repair. Also, they don't have to store your car or give you a loaner while they wait for the part to come in.

In traditional mass production, the way to avoid stockouts—not having the product the customer wants—is to keep a large inventory of spares just in case. It may be that the blue 2011

Camry bumper is quite popular, but what about last year's model or the model from five years ago? The more inventory you keep, the greater the likelihood you will have the right product in stock for every customer. But large inventories are expensive because they have to be transported, stored, and tracked. What if the 2011 bumper turns out to have a defect? All the spares in all the warehouses instantly become waste.

Lean production solves the problem of stockouts with a technique called pull. When you bring a car into the dealership for repair, one blue 2011 Camry bumper gets used. This creates a "hole" in the dealer's inventory, which automatically causes a signal to be sent to a local restocking facility called the Toyota Parts Distribution Center (PDC). The PDC sends the dealer a new bumper, which creates another hole in inventory. This sends a similar signal to a regional warehouse called the Toyota Parts Redistribution Center (PRC), where all parts suppliers ship their products. That warehouse signals the factory where the bumpers are made to produce one more bumper, which is manufactured and shipped to the PRC.

The ideal goal is to achieve small batches all the way down to single-piece flow along the entire supply chain. Each step in the line pulls the parts it needs from the previous step. This is the famous Toyota just-in-time production method.[8]

When companies switch to this kind of production, their warehouses immediately shrink, as the amount of just-in-case inventory [called work-in-progress (WIP) inventory] is reduced dramatically. This almost magical shrinkage of WIP is where lean manufacturing gets its name. It's as if the whole supply chain suddenly went on a diet.

Startups struggle to see their work-in-progress inventory. When factories have excess WIP, it literally piles up on the factory floor. Because most startup work is intangible, it's not nearly as visible. For example, all the work that goes into designing the minimum viable product is—until the moment that product is shipped—just WIP inventory. Incomplete designs, not-yet-validated assumptions, and most business plans are WIP. Almost every Lean Startup technique we've discussed so far works its magic in two ways: by converting push methods to pull and reducing batch size. Both have the net effect of reducing WIP.

In manufacturing, pull is used primarily to make sure production processes are tuned to levels of customer demand. Without this, factories can wind up making much more—or much less—of a product than customers really want. However, applying this approach to developing new products is not straightforward. Some people misunderstand the Lean Startup model as simply applying pull to customer wants. This assumes that customers could tell us what products to build and that this would act as the pull signal to product development to make them.[9]

As was mentioned earlier, this is not the way the Lean Startup model works, because customers often don't know what they want. Our goal in building products is to be able to run experiments that will help us learn how to build a sustainable business. Thus, the right way to think about the product development process in a Lean Startup is that it is responding to pull requests in the form of experiments that need to be run.

As soon as we formulate a hypothesis that we want to test, the product development team should be engineered to design and run this experiment as quickly as possible, using the smallest batch size that will get the job done. Remember that although we write the feedback loop as Build-Measure-Learn because the activities happen in that order, our planning really works in the reverse order: we figure out what we need to learn and then work backwards to see what product will work as an experiment to get that learning. Thus, it is not the customer, but rather our *hypothesis about the customer*, that pulls work from product development and other functions. Any other work is waste.

## Hypothesis Pull in Clean Tech

To see this in action, let's take a look at Berkeley-based startup Alphabet Energy. Any machine or process that generates power, whether it is a motor in a factory or a coal-burning power plant, generates heat as a by-product. Alphabet Energy has developed a product that can generate electricity from this waste heat, using a new kind of material called a thermoelectric. Alphabet Energy's thermoelectric material was developed over ten years by scientists at the Lawrence Berkeley National Laboratories.

As with many clean technology products, there are huge challenges in bringing a product like this to market. While working through its leap-of-faith assumptions, Alphabet figured out early that developing a solution for waste thermoelectricity required building a heat exchanger and a generic device to transfer heat from one medium to another as well as doing project-specific engineering. For instance, if Alphabet wanted to build a solution for a utility such as Pacific Gas and Electric, the heat exchanger would have to be configured, shaped, and installed to capture the heat from a power plant's exhaust system.

What makes Alphabet Energy unique is that the company made a savvy decision early on in the research process. Instead of using relatively rare elements as materials, they decided to base their research on silicon wafers, the same physical substance that computer central processing units (CPUs) are made from. As CEO Matthew Scullin explains, "Our thermoelectric is the only one that can use low-cost semiconductor infrastructure for manufacturing." This has enabled Alphabet Energy to design and build its products in small batches.

By contrast, most successful clean technology startups have

had to make substantial early investments. The solar panel provider SunPower had to build in factories to manufacture its panels and partner with installers before becoming fully operational. Similarly, BrightSource raised $291 million to build and operate large-scale solar plants without delivering a watt to a single customer.

Instead of having to invest time and money in expensive fabrication facilities, Alphabet is able to take advantage of the massive existing infrastructure that produces silicon wafers for computer electronics. As a result, Alphabet can go from a product concept to holding a physical version in its hand in just six weeks from end to end. Alphabet's challenge has been to find the combination of performance, price, and physical shape that is a match for early customers. Although its technology has revolutionary potential, early adopters will deploy it only if they can see a clear return on investment.

It might seem that the most obvious market for Alphabet's technology would be power plants, and indeed, that was the team's initial hypothesis. Alphabet hypothesized that simple cycle gas turbines would be an ideal application; these turbines, which are similar to jet engines strapped to the ground, are used by power generators to provide energy for peak demand. Alphabet believed that attaching its semiconductors to those turbines would be simple and cheap.

The company went about testing this hypothesis in small batches by building small-scale solutions for its customers as a way of learning. As with many initial ideas, their hypothesis was disproved quickly. Power companies have a low tolerance for risk, making them unlikely to become early adopters. Because it wasn't weighed down by a large-batch approach, Alphabet was ready to pivot after just three months of investigation.

Alphabet has eliminated many other potential markets as well, leading to a series of customer segment pivots. The company's current efforts are focused on manufacturing firms, which have the ability to experiment with new technologies in separate parts of their factory; this allows early adopters to evaluate the real-world benefits before committing to a larger deployment. These early deployments are putting more of Alphabet's assumptions to the test. Unlike in the computer hardware business, customers are not willing to pay top dollar for maximum performance. This has required significant changes in Alphabet's product, configuring it to achieve the lowest cost per watt possible.

All this experimentation has cost the company a tiny fraction of what other energy startups have consumed. To date, Alphabet has raised approximately $1 million. Only time will tell if they will prevail, but thanks to the power of small batches, they will be able to discover the truth much faster.[10]

○ ○ ○

The Toyota Production System is probably the most advanced system of management in the world, but even more impressive is the fact that Toyota has built the most advanced learning organization in history. It has demonstrated an ability to unleash the creativity of its employees, achieve consistent growth, and produce innovative new products relentlessly over the course of nearly a century.[11]

This is the kind of long-term success to which entrepreneurs should aspire. Although lean production techniques are powerful, they are only a manifestation of a high-functioning organization that is committed to achieving maximum performance by employing the right measures of progress over the long term. Process is only the foundation upon which a great company culture can develop. But without this foundation, efforts to encourage learning, creativity, and innovation will fall flat—as many disillusioned directors of HR can attest.

The Lean Startup works only if we are able to build an organization as adaptable and fast as the challenges it faces. This requires tackling the human challenges inherent in this new way of working; that is the subject of the remainder of Part Three.

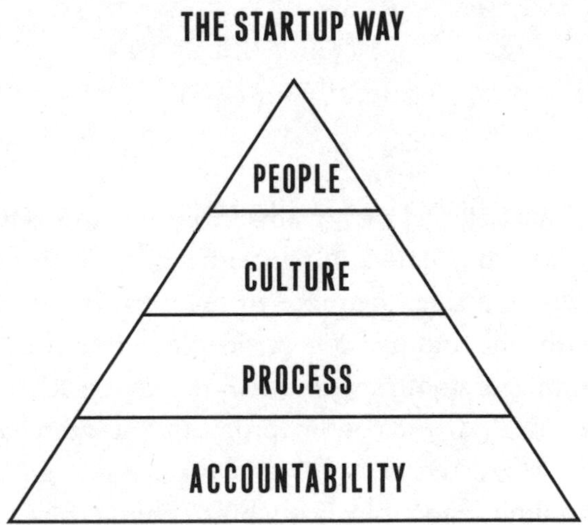

# 10

# GROW

I recently had two startups seek my advice on the same day. As types of businesses, they could not have been more different. The first is developing a marketplace to help traders of collectibles connect with one another. These people are hard-core fans of movies, anime, or comics who strive to put together complete collections of toys and other promotional merchandise related to the characters they love. The startup aspires to compete with online marketplaces such as eBay as well as physical marketplaces attached to conventions and other gatherings of fans.

The second startup sells database software to enterprise customers. They have a next-generation database technology that can supplement or replace offerings from large companies such as Oracle, IBM, and SAP. Their customers are chief information officers (CIOs), IT managers, and engineers in some of the world's largest organizations. These are long-lead-time sales that require salespeople, sales engineering, installation support, and maintenance contracts.

You could be forgiven for thinking these two companies have absolutely nothing in common, yet both came to me with the exact same problem. Each one had early customers and promising early revenue. They had validated and invalidated many hypotheses in their business models and were executing against their product road maps successfully. Their customers had provided a healthy mix of positive feedback and suggestions for improvements. Both companies had used their early success to raise money from outside investors.

The problem was that neither company was growing.

Both CEOs brought me identical-looking graphs showing that their early growth had flatlined. They could not understand why. They were acutely aware of the need to show progress to their employees and investors and came to me because they wanted advice on how to jump-start their growth. Should they invest in more advertising or marketing programs? Should they focus on product quality or new features? Should they try to improve conversion rates or pricing?

As it turns out, both companies share a deep similarity in the way their businesses grow—and therefore a similar confusion about what to do. Both are using the same *engine of growth,* the topic of this chapter.

## WHERE DOES GROWTH COME FROM?

The engine of growth is the mechanism that startups use to achieve sustainable growth. I use the word *sustainable* to exclude all one-time activities that generate a surge of customers but have no long-term impact, such as a single advertisement or a publicity stunt that might be used to jump-start growth but could not sustain that growth for the long term.

Sustainable growth is characterized by one simple rule:

*New customers come from the actions of past customers.*

There are four primary ways past customers drive sustainable growth:

**1. Word of mouth.** Embedded in most products is a natural level of growth that is caused by satisfied customers' enthusiasm for the product. For example, when I bought my first TiVo DVR, I couldn't stop telling my friends and family about it. Pretty soon, my entire family was using one.

**2. As a side effect of product usage.** Fashion or status, such as luxury goods products, drive awareness of themselves whenever they are used. When you see someone dressed in the latest clothes or driving a certain car, you may be influenced to buy that product. This is also true of so-called viral products such as Facebook and PayPal. When a customer sends money to a friend using PayPal, the friend is exposed automatically to the PayPal product.

**3. Through funded advertising.** Most businesses employ advertising to entice new customers to use their products. For this to be a source of sustainable growth, the advertising must be paid for out of revenue, not one-time sources such as investment capital. As long as the cost of acquiring a new customer (the so-called marginal cost) is less than the revenue that customer generates (the marginal revenue), the excess (the marginal profit) can be used to acquire more customers. The more marginal profit, the faster the growth.

**4. Through repeat purchase or use.** Some products are designed to be purchased repeatedly either through a subscription plan (a cable company) or through voluntary repurchases (groceries or lightbulbs). By contrast, many products and services are intentionally designed as one-time events, such as wedding planning.

These sources of sustainable growth power feedback loops that I have termed *engines of growth*. Each is like a combustion engine, turning over and over. The faster the loop turns, the faster the company will grow. Each engine has an intrinsic set of metrics that determine how fast a company can grow when using it.

## THE THREE ENGINES OF GROWTH

We saw in Part Two how important it is for startups to use the right kind of metrics—actionable metrics—to evaluate their progress. However, this leaves a large amount of variety in terms of which numbers one should measure. In fact, one of the most expensive forms of potential waste for a startup is spending time arguing about how to prioritize new development once it has a product on the market. At any time, the company could invest its energy in finding new customers, servicing existing customers better, improving overall quality, or driving down costs. In my experience, the discussions about these kinds of priority decisions can consume a substantial fraction of the company's time.

Engines of growth are designed to give startups a relatively small set of metrics on which to focus their energies. As one of my mentors, the venture capital investor Shawn Carolan, put it, "Startups don't starve; they drown." There are always a zillion new ideas about how to make the product better floating around, but the hard truth is that most of those ideas make a difference only at the margins. They are mere optimizations. Startups have to focus on the big experiments that lead to validated learning. The engines of growth framework helps them stay focused on the metrics that matter.

### The Sticky Engine of Growth

This brings us back to the two startups that kicked off this chapter. Both are using the exact same engine of growth despite being in very different industries. Both products are designed to attract and retain customers for the long term. The underlying mechanism of that retention is different in the two cases. For the collectible company, the idea is to become the number one shopping destination for fanatical collectors. These are people who are constantly hunting for the latest items and the best deals. If the company's product works as designed, collectors who start using it will check constantly and repeatedly to see if new items are for sale as well as listing their own items for sale or trade.

The startup database vendor relies on repeat usage for a very different reason. Database technology is used only as the foundation for a customer's own products, such as a website or a point of sale system. Once you build a product on top of a particular database technology, it is extremely difficult to switch. In the IT industry, such customers are said to be locked in to the vendor they choose. For such a product to grow, it has to offer such a compelling new capability that customers are willing to risk being tied to a proprietary vendor for a potentially long time.

Thus, both businesses rely on having a high customer retention rate. They have an expectation that once you start using their product, you will continue to do so. This is the same dynamic as a mobile telephone service provider: when a customer cancels his or her service, it generally means that he or she is extremely dissatisfied or is switching to a competitor's product. This is in contrast to, say, groceries on a store aisle. In the grocery retail business, customer tastes fluctuate, and if a customer buys a Pepsi this week instead of Coke, it's not necessarily a big deal.

Therefore, companies using the sticky engine of growth track their attrition rate or churn rate very carefully. The churn rate is defined as the fraction of customers in any period who fail to remain engaged with the company's product.

The rules that govern the sticky engine of growth are pretty simple: if the rate of new customer acquisition exceeds the churn rate, the product will grow. The speed of growth is determined by what I call the rate of compounding, which is simply the natural growth rate minus the churn rate. Like a bank account that earns compounding interest, having a high rate of compounding will lead to extremely rapid growth—without advertising, viral growth, or publicity stunts.

Unfortunately, both of these sticky startups were tracking their progress using generic indicators such as the total number of customers. Even the actionable metrics they were using, such as the activation rate and revenue per customer, weren't very helpful because in the sticky engine of growth, these variables have little impact on growth. (In the sticky engine of growth, they are better suited to testing the value hypothesis that was discussed in Chapter 5.)

After our meeting, one of the two startups took me up on my advice to model its customer behavior by using the sticky engine of growth as a template. The results were striking: a 61 percent retention rate and a 39 percent growth rate of new customers. In other words, its churn rate and new customer acquisition balanced each other almost perfectly, leading to a compounding growth rate of just 0.02 percent—almost zero.

This is typical for companies in an engagement business that are struggling to find growth. An insider who worked at the dot-com-era company PointCast once showed me how that company suffered a similar dysfunction. When PointCast was struggling to grow, it was nonetheless incredibly successful in new customer acquisition—just like this sticky startup (39 percent every period). Unfortunately, this growth is being offset by an equivalent amount of churn. Once it is modeled this way, the good news should be apparent: there are plenty of new customers coming in the door. The way to find growth is to focus on existing customers for the product even more engaging to them. For example, the company could focus on getting more and better listings. This would create an incentive for customers to check back often. Alternatively, the company could do something more direct such as messaging them about limited-time sales or special offers. Either way, its focus needs to be on improving customer retention. This goes against the standard intuition in that if a company lacks growth, it should invest more in sales and marketing. This counterintuitive result is hard to infer from standard vanity metrics.

### The Viral Engine of Growth

Online social networks and Tupperware are examples of products for which customers do the lion's share of the marketing. Awareness of the product spreads rapidly from person to person similarly to the way a virus becomes an epidemic. This is distinct from the simple word-of-mouth growth discussed above. Instead, products that exhibit viral growth depend on person-to-person transmission as a necessary consequence of normal product use. Customers are not intentionally acting as evangelists; they are not necessarily trying to spread the word about the product. Growth happens automatically as a side effect of customers using the product. Viruses are not optional.

For example, one of the most famous viral success stories is a company called Hotmail. In 1996, Sabeer Bhatia and Jack Smith launched a new web-based e-mail service that offered customers free accounts. At first, growth was sluggish; with only a small seed investment from the venture capital firm Draper Fisher Jurvetson, the Hotmail team could not afford an extensive marketing campaign. But everything changed when they made one small tweak to the product. They added to the bottom of every single e-mail the message "P.S. Get your free e-mail at Hotmail" along with a clickable link.

Within weeks, that small product change produced massive results. Within six months, Bhatia and Smith had signed up more than 1 million new customers. Five weeks later, they hit the 2 million mark. Eighteen months after launching the service, with 12 million subscribers, they sold the company to Microsoft for $400 million.[1]

The same phenomenon is at work in Tupperware's famous "house parties," in which customers earn commissions by selling the product to their friends and neighbors. Every sales pitch is an opportunity not only to sell Tupperware products but also to persuade other customers to become Tupperware representatives. Tupperware parties are still going strong decades after they started. Many other contemporary companies, such as Pampered Chef (owned by Warren Buffett's Berkshire Hathaway), Southern Living, and Tastefully Simple, have adopted a similar model successfully.

Like the other engines of growth, the viral engine is powered by a feedback loop that can be quantified. It is called the *viral loop,* and its speed is determined by a single mathematical term called the *viral coefficient.* The higher this coefficient is, the faster the product will spread. The viral coefficient measures how many new customers will use a product as a consequence of each new customer who signs up. Put another way, how many friends will each customer bring with him or her? Since each friend is also a new customer, he or she has an opportunity to recruit yet more friends.

For a product with a viral coefficient of 0.1, one in every ten customers will recruit one of his or her friends. This is not a sustainable loop. Imagine that one hundred customers sign up. They will cause ten friends to sign up. Those ten friends will cause one additional person to sign up, but there the loop will fizzle out.

By contrast, a viral loop with a coefficient that is greater than 1.0 will grow exponentially, because each person who signs up will bring, on average, more than one other person with him or her.

To see these effects graphically, take a look at this chart:

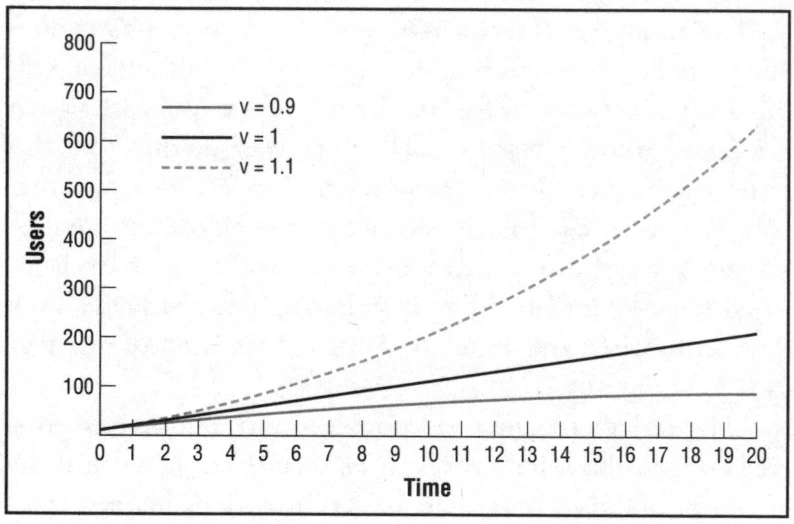


Companies that rely on the viral engine of growth must focus on increasing the viral coefficient more than anything else, because even tiny changes in this number will cause dramatic changes in their future prospects.

A consequence of this is that many viral products do not charge customers directly but rely on indirect sources of revenue such as advertising. This is the case because viral products cannot afford to have any friction impede the process of signing customers up and recruiting their friends. This can make testing the value hypothesis for viral products especially challenging.

The true test of the value hypothesis is always a voluntary

exchange of value between customers and the startup that serves them. A lot of confusion stems from the fact that this exchange can be monetary, as in the case of Tupperware, or nonmonetary, as in the case of Facebook. In the viral engine of growth, monetary exchange does not drive new growth; it is useful only as an indicator that customers value the product enough to pay for it. If Facebook or Hotmail had started charging customers in their early days, it would have been foolish, as it would have impeded their ability to grow. However, it is not true that customers do not give these companies something of value: by investing their time and attention in the product, they make the product valuable to advertisers. Companies that sell advertising actually serve two different groups of customers—consumers and advertisers—and exchange a different currency of value with each.[2]

This is markedly different from companies that actively use money to fuel their expansion, such as a retail chain that can grow as fast as it can fund the opening of new stores at suitable locations. These companies are using a different engine of growth altogether.

### The Paid Engine of Growth

Imagine another pair of businesses. The first makes $1 on each customer it signs up; the second makes $100,000 from each customer it signs up. To predict which company will grow faster, you need to know only one additional thing: how much it costs to sign up a new customer.

Imagine that the first company uses Google AdWords to find new customers online and pays an average of 80 cents each time a new customer joins. The second company sells heavy goods to large companies. Each sale requires a significant time investment from a salesperson and on-site sales engineering to help install the product; these hard costs total up to $80,000 per new customer. Both companies will grow at the exact same rate. Each has the same proportion of revenue (20 percent) available to reinvest in new customer acquisition. If either company wants to increase its rate of growth, it can do so in one of two ways: increase the revenue from each customer or drive down the cost of acquiring a new customer.

That's the paid engine of growth at work.

In relating the IMVU story in Chapter 3, I talked about how we made a major early mistake in setting up the IMVU strategy. We ultimately wound up having to make an engine of growth pivot. We originally thought that our IM add-on strategy would allow the product to grow virally. Unfortunately, customers refused to go along with our brilliant strategy.

Our basic misconception was a belief that customers would be willing to use IMVU as an add-on to existing instant messaging networks. We believed that the product would spread virally through those networks, passed from customer to customer. The problem with that theory is that some kinds of products are not compatible with viral growth.

IMVU's customers didn't want to use the product with their existing friends. They wanted to use it to make new friends. Unfortunately, that meant they did not have a strong incentive to bring new customers to the product; they viewed that as our job. Fortunately, IMVU was able to grow by using paid advertising because our customers were willing to pay more for our product than it cost us to reach them via advertising.

Like the other engines, the paid engine of growth is powered by a feedback loop. Each customer pays a certain amount of money for the product over his or her "lifetime" as a customer. Once variable costs are deducted, this usually is called the customer *lifetime value* (LTV). This revenue can be invested in growth by buying advertising.

Suppose an advertisement costs $100 and causes fifty new customers to sign up for the service. This ad has a *cost per acquisition* (CPA) of $2.00. In this example, if the product has an LTV that is greater than $2, the product will grow. The margin between the LTV and the CPA determines how fast the paid engine of growth will turn (this is called the marginal profit). Conversely, if the CPA remains at $2.00 but the LTV falls below $2.00, the company's growth will slow. It may make up the difference with one-time tactics such as using invested capital or publicity stunts, but those tactics are not sustainable. This was the fate of many failed companies, including notable dot-com flameouts that erroneously believed that they could lose money on each customer but, as the old joke goes, make it up in volume.

Although I have explained the paid engine of growth in terms of advertising, it is far broader than that. Startups that employ an outbound sales force are also using this engine, as are retail companies that rely on foot traffic. All these costs should be factored into the cost per acquisition.

For example, one startup I worked with built collaboration tools for teams and groups. It went through a radical pivot, switching from a tool that was used primarily by hobbyists and small clubs to one that was sold primarily to enterprises, nongovernmental organizations (NGOs), and other extremely large organizations. However, they made that customer segment pivot without changing their engine of growth. Previously, they had done customer acquisition online, using web-based direct marketing techniques. I remember one early situation in which the company fielded a call from a major NGO that wanted to buy its product and roll it out across many divisions. The startup had an "unlimited" pricing plan, its most expensive, that cost only a few hundred dollars per month. The NGO literally could not make the purchase because it had no process in place for buying something so inexpensive. Additionally, the NGO needed substantial help in managing the rollout, educating its staff on the new tool, and tracking the impact of the change; those were all services the company was ill equipped to offer. Changing customer segments required them to switch to hiring a sizable outbound sales staff that spent time attending conferences, educating executives, and authoring white papers. Those much higher costs came with a corresponding reward: the company switched from making only a few dollars per customer to making tens and then hundreds of thousands of dollars per much larger customer. Their new engine of growth led to sustained success.

Most sources of customer acquisition are subject to competition. For example, prime retail storefronts have more foot traffic and are therefore more valuable. Similarly, advertising that is targeted to more affluent customers generally costs more than advertising that reaches the general public. What determines these prices is the average value earned in aggregate by the companies that are in competition for any given customer's attention. Wealthy consumers cost more to reach because they tend to become more profitable customers.

Over time, any source of customer acquisition will tend to have its CPA bid up by this competition. If everyone in an industry makes the same amount of money on each sale, they all will wind up paying most of their marginal profit to the source of acquisition. Thus, the ability to grow in the long term by using the paid engine requires a differentiated ability to monetize a certain set of customers.

IMVU is a case in point. Our customers were not considered very lucrative by other online services: they included a lot of teenagers, low-income adults, and international customers. Other services tended to assume those people would not pay for anything online. At IMVU, we developed techniques for collecting online payments from customers who did not have a credit card, such as allowing them to bill to their mobile phones or send us cash in the mail. Therefore, we could afford to pay more to acquire those customers than our competitors could.

### A Technical Caveat

Technically, more than one engine of growth can operate in a business at a time. For example, there are products that have extremely fast viral growth as well as extremely low customer churn rates. Also, there is no reason why a product cannot have both high margins and high retention. However, in my experience, successful startups usually focus on just one engine of growth, specializing in everything that is required to make it work. Companies that attempt to build a dashboard that includes all three engines tend to cause a lot of confusion because the operations expertise required to model all these effects simultaneously is quite complicated. Therefore, I strongly recommend that startups focus on one engine at a time. Most entrepreneurs already have a strong leap-of-faith hypothesis about which engine is most likely to work. If they do not, time spent out of the building with customers will quickly suggest one that seems profitable. Only after pursuing one engine thoroughly should a startup consider a pivot to one of the others.

## ENGINES OF GROWTH DETERMINE PRODUCT/MARKET FIT

Marc Andreessen, the legendary entrepreneur and investor and one of the fathers of the World Wide Web, coined the term *product/market fit* to describe the moment when a startup finally finds a widespread set of customers that resonate with its product:

> In a great market—a market with lots of real potential customers—the market pulls product out of the startup.

> This is the story of search keyword advertising, Internet auctions, and TCP/IP routers. Conversely, in a terrible market, you can have the best product in the world and an absolutely killer team, and it doesn't matter—you're going to fail.[3]

When you see a startup that has found a fit with a large market, it's exhilarating. It leaves no room for doubt. It is Ford's Model T flying out of the factory as fast as it could be made, Facebook sweeping college campuses practically overnight, or Lotus taking the business world by storm, selling $54 million worth of Lotus 1-2-3 in its first year of operation.

Startups occasionally ask me to help them evaluate whether they have achieved product/market fit. It's easy to answer: if you are asking, you're not there yet. Unfortunately, this doesn't help companies figure out *how* to get closer to product/market fit. How can you tell if you are on the verge of success or hopelessly far away?

Although I don't think Andreessen intended this as part of his definition, to many entrepreneurs it implies that a pivot is a failure event—"our startup has failed to achieve product/market fit." It also implies the inverse—that once our product has achieved product/market fit, we won't have to pivot anymore. Both assumptions are wrong.

I believe the concept of the engine of growth can put the idea of product/market fit on a more rigorous footing. Since each engine of growth can be defined quantitatively, each has a unique set of metrics that can be used to evaluate whether a startup is on the verge of achieving product/market fit. A startup with a viral coefficient of 0.9 or more is on the verge of success. Even better, the metrics for each engine of growth work in tandem with the innovation accounting model discussed in Chapter 7 to give direction to a startup's product development efforts. For example, if a startup is attempting to use the viral engine of growth, it can focus its development efforts on things that might affect customer behavior—on the viral loop—and safely ignore those that do not. Such a startup does not need to specialize in marketing, advertising, or sales functions. Conversely, a company using the paid engine needs to develop those marketing and sales functions urgently.

A startup can evaluate whether it is getting closer to product/market fit as it tunes its engine by evaluating each trip through the Build-Measure-Learn feedback loop using innovation accounting. What really matters is not the raw numbers or vanity metrics but the direction and degree of progress.

For example, imagine two startups that are working diligently to tune the sticky engine of growth. One has a compounding rate of growth of 5 percent, and the other 10 percent. Which company is the better bet? On the surface, it may seem that the larger rate of growth is better, but what if each company's innovation accounting dashboard looks like the following chart?

| COMPOUNDING GROWTH RATE AS OF | COMPANY A | COMPANY B |
|---|---|---|
| Six months ago | 0.1% | 9.8% |
| Five months ago | 0.5% | 9.6% |
| Four months ago | 2.0% | 9.9% |
| Three months ago | 3.2% | 9.8% |
| Two months ago | 4.5% | 9.7% |
| One month ago | 5.0% | 10.0% |

Even with no insight into these two companies' gross numbers, we can tell that company A is making real progress whereas company B is stuck in the mud. This is true even though company B is growing faster than company A right now.

## WHEN ENGINES RUN OUT

Getting a startup's engine of growth up and running is hard enough, but the truth is that every engine of growth eventually runs out of gas. Every engine is tied to a given set of customers and their related habits, preferences, advertising channels, and interconnections. At some point, that set of customers will be exhausted. This may take a long time or a short time, depending on one's industry and timing.

Chapter 6 emphasized the importance of building the minimum viable product in such a way that it contains no additional features beyond what is required by early adopters. Following that strategy successfully will unlock an engine of growth that can reach that target audience. However, making the transition to mainstream customers will require tremendous additional work.[4] Once we have a product that is growing among early adopters, we could in theory stop work in product development entirely. The product would continue to grow until it reached the limits of that early market. Then growth would level off or even stop completely. The challenge comes from the fact that this slowdown might take months or even years to take place. Recall from Chapter 8 that IMVU failed this test—at first—for precisely this reason.

Some unfortunate companies wind up following this strategy inadvertently. Because they are using vanity metrics and traditional accounting, they think they are making progress when they see their numbers growing. They falsely believe they are making their product better when in fact they are having no impact on customer behavior. The growth is all coming from an engine of growth that is working—running efficiently to bring in new customers—not from improvements driven by product development. Thus, when the growth suddenly slows, it provokes a crisis.

This is the same problem that established companies experience. Their past successes were built on a finely tuned engine of growth. If that engine runs its course and growth slows or stops, there can be a crisis if the company does not have new startups incubating within its ranks that can provide new sources of growth.

Companies of any size can suffer from this perpetual affliction. They need to manage a portfolio of activities, simultaneously tuning their engine of growth and developing new sources of growth for when that engine inevitably runs its course. How to do this is the subject of Chapter 12. However, before we can manage that portfolio, we need an organizational structure, culture, and discipline that can handle these rapid and often unexpected changes. I call this an *adaptive organization,* and it is the subject of Chapter 11.

# 11

# ADAPT

When I was the CTO of IMVU, I thought I was doing a good job most of the time. I had built an agile engineering organization, and we were successfully experimenting with the techniques that would come to be known as the Lean Startup. However, on a couple of occasions I suddenly realized that I was failing at my job. For an achievement-oriented person, that is incredibly disarming. Worst of all, you don't get a memo. If you did, it would read something like this:

> Dear Eric,
>
> Congratulations! The job you used to do at this company is no longer available. However, you have been transferred to a new job in the company. Actually, it's not the same company anymore, even though it has the same name and many of the same people. And although the job has the same title, too, and you used to be good at your old job, you're already failing at the new one. This transfer is effective as of six months ago, so this is to alert you that you've already been failing at it for quite some time.
>
> Best of luck!

Every time this happened to me, I struggled to figure out what to do. I knew that as the company grew, we would need additional processes and systems designed to coordinate the company's operations at each larger size. And yet I had also seen many startups become ossified and bureaucratic out of a misplaced desire to become "professional."

Having no system at all was not an option for IMVU and is not an option for you. There are so many ways for a startup to fail. I've lived through the overarchitecture failure, in which attempting to prevent all the various kinds of problems that could occur wound up delaying the company from putting out any product. I've seen companies fail the other way from the so-called Friendster effect, suffering a high-profile technical failure just when customer adoption is going wild. As a department executive, this outcome is worst of all, because the failure is both high-profile and attributable to a single function or department—yours. Not only will the company fail, it will be your fault.

Most of the advice I've heard on this topic has suggested a kind of split-the-difference approach (as in, "engage in a little planning, but not too much"). The problem with this willy-nilly approach is that it's hard to give any rationale for why we should anticipate one particular problem but ignore another. It can feel like the boss is being capricious or arbitrary, and that feeds the common feeling that management's decisions conceal an ulterior motive.

For those being managed this way, their incentives are clear. If the boss tends to split the difference, the best way to influence the boss and get what you want is to take the most extreme position possible. For example, if one group is advocating for an extremely lengthy release cycle, say, an annual new product introduction, you might choose to argue for an equally extremely short release cycle (perhaps weekly or even daily), knowing that the two opinions will be averaged out. Then, when the difference is split, you're likely to get an outcome closer to what you actually wanted in the first place. Unfortunately, this kind of arms race escalates. Rivals in another camp are likely to do the same thing. Over time, everyone will take the most polarized positions possible, which makes splitting the difference ever more difficult and ever less successful. Managers have to take responsibility for knowingly or inadvertently creating such incentives. Although it was not their intention to reward extreme polarization, that's exactly what they are doing. Getting out of this trap requires a significant shift in thinking.

## BUILDING AN ADAPTIVE ORGANIZATION

Should a startup invest in a training program for new employees? If you had asked me a few years ago, I would have laughed and said, "Absolutely not. Training programs are for big companies that can afford them." Yet at IMVU we wound up building a training program that was so good, new hires were productive on their first day of employment. Within just a few weeks, those employees were contributing at a high level. It required a huge effort to standardize our work processes and prepare a curriculum of the concepts that new employees should learn. Every new engineer would be assigned a mentor, who would help the new employee work through a curriculum of systems, concepts, and techniques he or she would need to become productive at IMVU. The performance of the mentor and mentee were linked, so the mentors took this education seriously.

What is interesting, looking back at this example, is that we never stopped work and decided that we needed to build a great training program. Instead, the training program evolved organically out of a methodical approach to evolving our own process. This process of orientation was subject to constant experimentation and revision so that it grew more effective—and less burdensome—over time.

I call this building an *adaptive organization,* one that automatically adjusts its process and performance to current conditions.

## Can You Go Too Fast?

So far this book has emphasized the importance of speed. Startups are in a life-or-death struggle to learn how to build a sustainable business before they run out of resources and die. However, focusing on speed alone would be destructive. To work, startups require built-in speed regulators that help teams find their optimal pace of work.

We saw an example of speed regulation in Chapter 9 with the use of the *andon* cord in systems such as continuous deployment. It is epitomized in the paradoxical Toyota proverb, "Stop production so that production never has to stop." The key to the *andon* cord is that it brings work to a stop as soon as an uncorrectable quality problem surfaces—which forces it to be investigated. This is one of the most important discoveries of the lean manufacturing movement: you cannot trade quality for time. If you are causing (or missing) quality problems now, the resulting defects will slow you down later. Defects cause a lot of rework, low morale, and customer complaints, all of which slow progress and eat away at valuable resources.

So far I have used the language of physical products to describe these problems, but that is simply a matter of convenience. Service businesses have the same challenges. Just ask any manager of a training, staffing, or hospitality firm to show you the playbook that specifies how employees are supposed to deliver the service under various conditions. What might have started out as a simple guide tends to grow inexorably over time.

Pretty soon, orientation is incredibly complex and employees have invested a lot of time and energy in learning the rules. Now consider an entrepreneurial manager in that kind of company trying to experiment with new rules or procedures. The higher-quality the existing playbook is, the easier it will be for it to evolve over time. By contrast, a low-quality playbook will be filled with contradictory or ambiguous rules that cause confusion when anything is changed.

When I teach the Lean Startup approach to entrepreneurs with an engineering background, this is one of the hardest concepts to grasp. On the one hand, the logic of validated learning and the minimum viable product says that we should get a product into customers' hands as soon as possible and that any extra work we do beyond what is required to learn from customers is waste. On the other hand, the Build-Measure-Learn feedback loop is a continuous process. We don't stop after one minimum viable product but use what we have learned to get to work immediately on the next iteration.

Therefore, shortcuts taken in product quality, design, or infrastructure today may wind up slowing a company down tomorrow. You can see this paradox in action at IMVU. Chapter 3 recounted how we wound up shipping a product to customers that was full of bugs, missing features, and bad design. The customers wouldn't even try that product, and so most of that work had to be thrown away. It's a good thing we didn't waste a lot of time fixing those bugs and cleaning up that early version.

However, as our learning allowed us to build products that customers *did* want, we faced slowdowns. Having a low-quality product can inhibit learning when the defects prevent customers from experiencing (and giving feedback on) the product's benefits. In IMVU's case, as we offered the product to more mainstream customers, they were much less forgiving than early adopters had been. Similarly, the more features we added to the product, the harder it became to add even more because of the risk that a new feature would interfere with an existing feature. The same dynamics happen in a service business, since any new rules may conflict with existing rules, and the more rules, the more possibilities for conflict.

IMVU used the techniques of this chapter to achieve scale and quality in a just-in-time fashion.

## THE WISDOM OF THE FIVE WHYS

To accelerate, Lean Startups need a process that provides a natural feedback loop. When you're going too fast, you cause more problems. Adaptive processes force you to slow down and invest in preventing the kinds of problems that are currently wasting time. As those preventive efforts pay off, you naturally speed up again.

Let's return to the question of having a training program for new employees. Without a program, new employees will make mistakes while in their learning curve that will require assistance and intervention from other team members, slowing everyone down. How do you decide if the investment in training is worth the benefit of speed due to reduced interruptions? Figuring this out from a top-down perspective is challenging, because it requires estimating two completely unknown quantities: how much it will cost to build an unknown program against an unknown benefit you might reap. Even worse, the traditional way to make these kinds of decisions is decidedly large-batch thinking. A company either has an elaborate training program or it does not. Until they can justify the return on investment from building a full program, most companies generally do nothing.

The alternative is to use a system called the Five Whys to

make incremental investments and evolve a startup's processes gradually. The core idea of Five Whys is to tie investments directly to the prevention of the most problematic symptoms. The system takes its name from the investigative method of asking the question "Why?" five times to understand what has happened (the root cause). If you've ever had to answer a precocious child who wants to know "Why is the sky blue?" and keeps asking "Why?" after each answer, you're familiar with it. This technique was developed as a systematic problem-solving tool by Taiichi Ohno, the father of the Toyota Production System. I have adapted it for use in the Lean Startup model with a few changes designed specifically for startups.

At the root of every seemingly technical problem is a human problem. Five Whys provides an opportunity to discover what that human problem might be. Taiichi Ohno gives the following example:

> When confronted with a problem, have you ever stopped and asked *why* five times? It is difficult to do even though it sounds easy. For example, suppose a machine stopped functioning:
>
> 1. Why did the machine stop? (There was an overload and the fuse blew.)
> 2. Why was there an overload? (The bearing was not sufficiently lubricated.)
> 3. Why was it not lubricated sufficiently? (The lubrication pump was not pumping sufficiently.)
> 4. Why was it not pumping sufficiently? (The shaft of the pump was worn and rattling.)
> 5. Why was the shaft worn out? (There was no strainer attached and metal scrap got in.)

> Repeating "why" five times, like this, can help uncover the root problem and correct it. If this procedure were not carried through, one might simply replace the fuse or the pump shaft. In that case, the problem would recur within a few months. The Toyota production system has been built on the practice and evolution of this scientific approach. By asking and answering "why" five times, we can get to the real cause of the problem, which is often hidden behind more obvious symptoms.[1]

Note that even in Ohno's relatively simple example the root cause moves away from a technical fault (a blown fuse) and toward a human error (someone forgot to attach a strainer). This is completely typical of most problems that startups face no matter what industry they are in. Going back to our service business example, most problems that at first appear to be individual mistakes can be traced back to problems in training or the original playbook for how the service is to be delivered.

Let me demonstrate how using the Five Whys allowed us to build the employee training system that was mentioned earlier. Imagine that at IMVU we suddenly start receiving complaints from customers about a new version of the product that we have just released.

1. A new release disabled a feature for customers. Why? Because a particular server failed.
2. Why did the server fail? Because an obscure subsystem was used in the wrong way.
3. Why was it used in the wrong way? The engineer who used it didn't know how to use it properly.
4. Why didn't he know? Because he was never trained.
5. Why wasn't he trained? Because his manager doesn't be-

> lieve in training new engineers because he and his team are "too busy."

What began as a purely technical fault is revealed quickly to be a very human managerial issue.

### Make a Proportional Investment

Here's how to use Five Whys analysis to build an adaptive organization: consistently make a proportional investment at each of the five levels of the hierarchy. In other words, the investment should be smaller when the symptom is minor and larger when the symptom is more painful. We don't make large investments in prevention unless we're coping with large problems.

In the example above, the answer is to fix the server, change the subsystem to make it less error-prone, educate the engineer, and, yes, have a conversation with the engineer's manager.

This latter piece, the conversation with the manager, is always hard, especially in a startup. When I was a startup manager, if you told me I needed to invest in training my people, I would have told you it was a waste of time. There were always too many other things to do. I'd probably have said something sarcastic like "Sure, I'd be happy to do that—if you can spare my time for the eight weeks it'll take to set up." That's manager-speak for "No way in hell."

That's why the proportional investment approach is so important. If the outage is a minor glitch, it's essential that we make only a minor investment in fixing it. Let's do the first hour of the eight-week plan. That may not sound like much, but it's a start. If the problem recurs, asking the Five Whys will require that we continue to make progress on it. If the problem does not occur again, an hour isn't a big loss.

I used the example of engineering training because that was

something I was reluctant to invest in at IMVU. At the outset of our venture, I thought we needed to focus all of our energies on building and marketing our product. Yet once we entered a period of rapid hiring, repeated Five Whys sessions revealed that problems caused by lack of training were slowing down product development. At no point did we drop everything to focus solely on training. Instead, we made incremental improvements to the process constantly, each time reaping incremental benefits. Over time, those changes compounded, freeing up time and energy that previously had been lost to firefighting and crisis management.

## Automatic Speed Regulator

The Five Whys approach acts as a natural speed regulator. The more problems you have, the more you invest in solutions to those problems. As the investments in infrastructure or process pay off, the severity and number of crises are reduced and the team speeds up again. With startups in particular, there is a danger that teams will work too fast, trading quality for time in a way that causes sloppy mistakes. Five Whys prevents that, allowing teams to find their optimal pace.

The Five Whys ties the rate of progress to learning, not just execution. Startup teams should go through the Five Whys whenever they encounter any kind of failure, including technical faults, failures to achieve business results, or unexpected changes in customer behavior.

Five Whys is a powerful organizational technique. Some of the engineers I have trained to use it believe that you can derive all the other Lean Startup techniques from the Five Whys. Coupled with working in small batches, it provides the foundation a company needs to respond quickly to problems as they appear, without overinvesting or overengineering.

## THE CURSE OF THE FIVE BLAMES

When teams first adopt Five Whys as a problem-solving tool, they encounter some common pitfalls. We need systems like Five Whys to overcome our psychological limitations because we tend to overreact to what's happening in the moment. We also tend to get frustrated if things happen that we did not anticipate.

When the Five Whys approach goes awry, I call it the Five Blames. Instead of asking why repeatedly in an attempt to understand what went wrong, frustrated teammates start pointing fingers at each other, trying to decide who is at fault. Instead of using the Five Whys to find and fix problems, managers and employees can fall into the trap of using the Five Blames as a means for venting their frustrations and calling out colleagues for systemic failures. Although it's human nature to assume that when we see a mistake, it's due to defects in someone else's department, knowledge, or character, the goal of the Five Whys is to help us see the objective truth that chronic problems are caused by bad process, not bad people, and remedy them accordingly.

I recommend several tactics for escaping the Five Blames. The first is to make sure that everyone affected by the problem is in the room during the analysis of the root cause. The meeting should include anyone who discovered or diagnosed the problem, including customer service representatives who fielded the calls, if possible. It should include anyone who tried to fix the symptom as well as anyone who worked on the subsystems or features involved. If the problem was escalated to senior management, the decision makers who were involved in the escalation should be present as well.

This may make for a crowded room, but it's essential. In my

experience, whoever is left out of the discussion ends up being the target for blame. This is just as damaging whether the scapegoat is a junior employee or the CEO. When it's a junior employee, it's all too easy to believe that that person is replaceable. If the CEO is not present, it's all too easy to assume that his or her behavior is unchangeable. Neither presumption is usually correct.

When blame inevitably arises, the most senior people in the room should repeat this mantra: if a mistake happens, shame on us for making it so easy to make that mistake. In a Five Whys analysis, we want to have a systems-level view as much as possible.

Here's a situation in which this mantra came in handy. Because of the training process we had developed at IMVU through the Five Whys, we routinely asked new engineers to make a change to the production environment on their first day. For engineers trained in traditional development methods, this was often frightening. They would ask, "What will happen to me if I accidentally disrupt or stop the production process?" In their previous jobs, that was a mistake that could get them fired. At IMVU we told new hires, "If our production process is so fragile that you can break it on your very first day of work, shame on us for making it so easy to do so." If they did manage to break it, we immediately would have them lead the effort to fix the problem as well as the effort to prevent the next person from repeating their mistake.

For new hires who came from companies with a very different culture, this was often a stressful initiation, but everyone came through it with a visceral understanding of our values. Bit by bit, system by system, those small investments added up to a robust product development process that allowed all our employees to work more creatively, with greatly reduced fear.

## Getting Started

Here are a few tips on how to get started with the Five Whys that are based on my experience introducing this technique at many other companies.

For the Five Whys to work properly, there are rules that must be followed. For example, the Five Whys requires an environment of mutual trust and empowerment. In situations in which this is lacking, the complexity of Five Whys can be overwhelming. In such situations, I've often used a simplified version that still allows teams to focus on analyzing root causes while developing the muscles they'll need later to tackle the full-blown method.

I ask teams to adopt these simple rules:

1. Be tolerant of all mistakes the first time.
2. Never allow the same mistake to be made twice.

The first rule encourages people to get used to being compassionate about mistakes, especially the mistakes of others. Remember, most mistakes are caused by flawed systems, not bad people. The second rule gets the team started making proportional investments in prevention.

This simplified system works well. In fact, we used it at IMVU in the days before I discovered the Five Whys and the Toyota Production System. However, such a simplified system does not work effectively over the long term, as I found out firsthand. In fact, that was one of the things that drove me to first learn about lean production.

The strength and weakness of the simplified system is that it invites questions such as What counts as the same problem? What kinds of mistakes should we focus on? and Should we fix this individual problem or try to prevent a whole category of related problems? For a team that is just getting started, these questions are thought-provoking and can lay the groundwork for more elaborate methods to come. Ultimately, though, they do need answering. They need a complete adaptive process such as the Five Whys.

### Facing Unpleasant Truths

You will need to be prepared for the fact that Five Whys is going to turn up unpleasant facts about your organization, especially at the beginning. It is going to call for investments in prevention that come at the expense of time and money that could be invested in new products or features. Under pressure, teams may feel that they don't have time to waste on analyzing root causes even though it would give them more time in the long term. The process sometimes will devolve into the Five Blames. At all these junctures, it is essential that someone with sufficient authority be present to insist that the process be followed, that its recommendations be implemented, and to act as a referee if disagreements flare up. Building an adaptive organization, in other words, requires executive leadership to sponsor and support the process.

Often, individual contributors at startups come to my workshops, eager to get started with the Five Whys. I caution against attempting to do that if they do not have the buy-in of the manager or team leader. Proceed cautiously if you find yourself in this situation. It may not be possible to get the entire team together for a true Five Whys inquiry, but you can always follow the simple two-rule version in your own work. Whenever something goes wrong, ask yourself: How could I prevent myself from being in this situation ever again?

## Start Small, Be Specific

Once you are ready to begin, I recommend starting with a narrowly targeted class of symptoms. For example, the first time I used the Five Whys successfully, I used it to diagnose problems with one of our internal testing tools that did not affect customers directly. It may be tempting to start with something large and important because that is where most of the time is being wasted as a result of a flawed process, but it is also where the pressure will be greatest. When the stakes are high, the Five Whys can devolve into the Five Blames quickly. It's better to give the team a chance to learn how to do the process first and then expand into higher-stakes areas later.

The more specific the symptoms are, the easier it will be for everyone to recognize when it's time to schedule a Five Whys meeting. Say you want to use the Five Whys to address billing complaints from customers. In that case, pick a date after which all billing complaints will trigger a Five Whys meeting automatically. Note that this requires that there be a small enough volume of complaints that having this meeting every time one comes in is practical. If there are already too many complaints, pick a subset on which you want to focus. Make sure that the rule that determines which kinds of complaints trigger a Five Whys meeting is simple and ironclad. For example, you might decide that every complaint involving a credit card transaction will be investigated. That's an easy rule to follow. Don't pick a rule that is ambiguous.

At first, the temptation may be to make radical and deep changes to every billing system and process. Don't. Instead, keep the meetings short and pick relatively simple changes at each of the five levels of the inquiry. Over time, as the team gets more comfortable with the process, you can expand it to include more and more types of billing complaints and then to other kinds of problems.

### Appoint a Five Whys Master

To facilitate learning, I have found it helpful to appoint a Five Whys master for each area in which the method is being used. This individual is tasked with being the moderator for each Five Whys meeting, making decisions about which prevention steps to take, and assigning the follow-up work from that meeting. The master must be senior enough to have the authority to ensure that those assignments get done but should not be so senior that he or she will not be able to be present at the meetings because of conflicting responsibilities. The Five Whys master is the point person in terms of accountability; he or she is the primary change agent. People in this position can assess how well the meetings are going and whether the prevention investments that are being made are paying off.

## THE FIVE WHYS IN ACTION

IGN Entertainment, a division of News Corporation, is an online video games media company with the biggest audience of video game players in the world. More than 45 million gamers frequent its portfolio of media properties. IGN was founded in the late 1990s, and News Corporation acquired it in 2005. IGN has grown to employ several hundred people, including almost a hundred engineers.

Recently, I had the opportunity to speak to the product development team at IGN. They had been successful in recent years, but like all the established companies we've seen throughout this book, they were looking to accelerate new product development and find ways to be more innovative. They brought together their engineering, product, and design teams to talk through ways they could apply the Lean Startup model.

This change initiative had the support of IGN's senior management, including the CEO, the head of product development, the vice president of engineering, the publisher, and the head of product. Their previous efforts at Five Whys had not gone smoothly. They had attempted to tackle a laundry list of problem areas nominated by the product team. The issues varied from discrepancies in web analytics to partner data feeds that were not working. Their first Five Whys meeting took an hour, and although they came up with some interesting takeaways, as far as the Five Whys goes, it was a disaster. None of the people who were connected to and knew the most about the issues were at the meeting, and because this was the first time they were doing the Five Whys together, they didn't stick to the format and went off on many tangents. It wasn't a complete waste of time, but it didn't have any of the benefits of the adaptive style of management discussed in this chapter.

## Don't Send Your Baggage through the Five Whys Process

IGN had the experience of trying to solve all of its "baggage" issues that had been causing wasted time for many years. Because this is an overwhelming set of problems, finding fixes quickly proves overwhelming.

In their zeal to get started with the Five Whys, IGN neglected three important things:

1. To introduce Five Whys to an organization, it is necessary to hold Five Whys sessions as new problems come up. Since baggage issues are endemic, they naturally come up as part of the Five Whys analysis and you can take that opportunity to fix them incrementally. If they don't come up organically, maybe they're not as big as they seem.
2. Everyone who is connected to a problem needs to be at the

Five Whys session. Many organizations face the temptation to save time by sparing busy people from the root cause analysis. This is a false economy, as IGN discovered the hard way.

3. At the beginning of each Five Whys session, take a few minutes to explain what the process is for and how it works for the benefit of those who are new to it. If possible, use an example of a successful Five Whys session from the past. If you're brand new, you can use my earlier example about the manager who doesn't believe in training. IGN learned that, whenever possible, it helps to use something that has personal meaning for the team.

After our meeting, the IGN leadership decided to give Five Whys another try. Following the advice laid out in this chapter, they appointed a Five Whys master named Tony Ford, a director of engineering. Tony was an entrepreneur who had come to IGN through an acquisition. He got his start with Internet technology, building websites about video games in the late 1990s. Eventually that led to an opportunity at a startup, TeamXbox, where he served as the lead software developer. TeamXbox was acquired by IGN Entertainment in 2003, and since that time Tony has been a technologist, leader of innovation, and proponent of agile and lean practices there.

Unfortunately, Tony started without picking a narrow problem area on which to focus. This led to early setbacks and frustration. Tony relates, "As the new master I wasn't very good at traversing through the Five Whys effectively, and the problems we were trying to solve were not great candidates in the first place. As you can imagine, these early sessions were awkward and in the end not very useful. I was getting quite discouraged and frustrated." This is a common problem when one tries to tackle too much at once, but it is also a consequence of the fact that these skills take time to master. Luckily, Tony persevered: "Having a Five Whys master is critical in my opinion. Five Whys is easy in theory but difficult in practice, so you need someone who knows it well to shape the sessions for those who don't."

The turnaround came when Tony led a Five Whys session involving a project that had been missing its deadlines. The session was fascinating and insightful and produced meaningful proportional investments. Tony explains: "The success had to do with a more experienced master and more experienced attendees. We all knew what the Five Whys was, and I did a really good job keeping us on track and away from tangents. This was a pivotal moment. Right then I knew the Five Whys was a new tool that was going to have a real impact on our overall success as a team and as a business."

On the surface, Five Whys seems to be about technical problems and preventing mistakes, but as teams drive out these superficial wastes, they develop a new understanding of how to work together. Tony put it this way: "I daresay that I discovered that the Five Whys transcends root cause analysis by revealing information that brings your team closer through a common understanding and perspective. A lot of times a problem can pull people apart; Five Whys does the opposite."

I asked Tony to provide an example of a recent successful Five Whys analysis from IGN. His account of it is listed in the sidebar.

**Why couldn't you add or edit posts on the blogs?**
*Answer:* Any post request (write) to the article content api was returning a 500 error.
*Proportional investment:* Jim—We'll work on the API, but let's make our CMS more forgiving for the user. Allow users to add and edit drafts without errors for a better user experience.

**Why was the content API returning 500 errors?**
*Answer:* The bson_ext gem was incompatible with other gems it depends upon.
*Proportional investment:* King—Remove the gem (already done to resolve the outage).

**Why was the gem incompatible?**
*Answer:* We added a new version of the gem in addition to the existing version and the app started using it unexpectedly.
*Proportional investment:* Bennett—Convert our rails app to use bundler for gem management.

**Why did we add a new version of a gem in production without testing?**
*Answer:* We didn't think we needed a test in these cases.
*Proportional investment:* Bennett and Jim—Write a unit or functional test in the API and CMS that will catch this in the future.

**Why do we add additional gems that we don't intend to use right away?**
*Answer:* In preparation for a code push we wanted to get all new gems ready in the production environment. Even though our code deployments are fully automated, gems are not.
*Proportional investment:* Bennett—Automate gem management and installation into Continuous Integration and Continuous Deployment process.

**Bonus—Why are we doing things in production on Friday nights?**
*Answer:* Because no one says we can't and it was a convenient

time for the developer to prepare for a deployment we'd be doing on Monday.

*Proportional investment:* Tony—Make an announcement to the team. There will be no production changes on Friday, Saturday, or Sunday unless an exception has been made and approved by David (VP Engineering). We will reevaluate this policy when we have a fully automated continuous deployment process in place.

As a result of this Five Whys session and the proportional investments we made, our deployments are easier, quicker, and never again will our process allow a developer to place gems into production systems with unintended consequences. Indeed, we have not had another issue like this. We strengthened our "cluster immune system" as you would say.

Without the Five Whys, we would have never discovered all of the information we did here. My guess is that we would have told that one developer to not do stupid things on Friday nights and moved on. This is what I emphasized earlier, where a good Five Whys session has two outputs, learning and doing. The proportional investments that came out of this session are obviously valuable, but the learnings are much more subtle, but amazing for growing as developers and as a team.

## ADAPTING TO SMALLER BATCHES

Before leaving the topic of building an adaptive organization, I want to introduce one more story. This one concerns a product that you've probably used if you've ever run your own business. It's called QuickBooks, and it is one of Intuit's flagship products.

QuickBooks has been the leading product in its category for many years. As a result, it has a large and dedicated customer base, and Intuit expects it to contribute significantly to its bottom line. Like most personal computer (PC) software of the last two decades, QuickBooks has been launched on an annual cycle, in one giant batch. This was how it worked three years ago, when Greg Wright, the director of product marketing for QuickBooks, joined the team. As you can imagine, there were lots of existing processes in place to ensure a consistent product and an on-time release. The typical release approach was to spend significant up-front time to identify the customers' need:

> Typically the first three to four months of each annual cycle was spent strategizing and planning, without building new features. Once a plan and milestones were established, the team would spend the next six to nine months building. This would culminate in a big launch, and then the team would get its first feedback on whether it had successfully delivered on customers' needs at the end of the process.
>
> So here was the time line: start process in September, first beta release is in June, second beta is in July. The beta is essentially testing to make sure it doesn't crash people's computers or cause them to lose their data—by that time in the process, only major bugs can be fixed. The design of the product itself is locked.

This is the standard "waterfall" development methodology that product development teams have used for years. It is a linear, large-batch system that relies for success on proper forecasting and planning. In other words, it is completely maladapted for today's rapidly changing business environment.

## Year One: Achieving Failure

Greg witnessed this breakdown in 2009, his first year on the QuickBooks team. That year, the company shipped an entirely new system in QuickBooks for online banking, one of its most important features. The team went through rounds of usability testing using mock-ups and nonfunctional prototypes, followed by significant beta testing using sample customer data. At the moment of the launch, everything looked good.

The first beta release was in June, and customer feedback started coming in negative. Although customers were complaining, there wasn't sufficient cause to stop the release because it was technically flawless—it didn't crash computers. At that point, Greg was in a bind. He had no way of knowing how the feedback would translate to real customer behavior in the market. Were these just isolated complaints, or part of a widespread problem? He did know one thing for sure, though: that his team could not afford to miss the deadline.

When the product finally shipped, the results were terrible. It took customers four to five times longer to reconcile their banking transactions than it had with the older version. In the end, Greg's team had failed to deliver on the customer need they were trying to address (despite building the product to specification), and because the next release had to go through the same waterfall process, it took the team nine months to fix. This is a classic case of "achieving failure"—successfully executing a flawed plan.

Intuit uses a tracking survey called the Net Promoter Score[2] to evaluate customer satisfaction with its many products. This is a great source of actionable metrics about what customers really think about a product. In fact, I used it at IMVU, too. One thing that is nice about NPS is that it is very stable over time. Since it is measuring core customer satisfaction, it is not subject to minor fluctuations; it registers only major changes in customer sentiment. That year, the QuickBooks score dropped 20 points, the first time the company had ever moved the needle with the Net Promoter Score. That 20-point drop resulted in significant losses for Intuit and was embarrassing for the company—all because customer feedback came too late in the process, allowing no time to iterate.

Intuit's senior management, including the general manager of the small business division and the head of small business accounting, recognized the need for change. To their credit, they tasked Greg with driving that change. His mission: to achieve startup speed for the development and deployment of QuickBooks.

### Year Two: Muscle Memory

The next chapter of this story illustrates how hard it is to build an adaptive organization. Greg set out to change the QuickBooks development process by using four principles:

1. Smaller teams. Shift from large teams with uniform functional roles to smaller, fully engaged teams whose members take on different roles.
2. Achieve shorter cycle times.
3. Faster customer feedback, testing both whether it crashes customers' computers and the performance of new features/customer experience.
4. Enable and empower teams to make fast and courageous decisions.

On the surface, these goals seem to be aligned with the methods and principles described in previous chapters, but Greg's second year with QuickBooks was not a marked success. For example, he decreed that the team would move to a midyear release milestone, effectively cutting the cycle time and batch size in half. However, this was not successful. Through sheer determination, the team tried valiantly to get an alpha release out in January. However, the problems that afflict large-batch development were still present, and the team struggled to complete the alpha by April. That represented an improvement over the past system because issues could be brought to the surface two months earlier than under the old way, but it did not produce the dramatically better results Greg was looking for.

In fact, over the course of the year, the team's process kept looking more and more like it had in prior years. As Greg put it, "Organizations have muscle memory," and it is hard for people to unlearn old habits. Greg was running up against a system, and making individual changes such as arbitrarily changing the release date were no match for it.

### Year Three: Explosion

Frustrated by the limited progress in the previous year, Greg teamed up with the product development leader Himanshu Baxi. Together they tossed out all the old processes. They made a public declaration that their combined teams would be creating new processes and that they were not going to go back to the old way.

Instead of focusing on new deadlines, Greg and Himanshu invested in process, product, and technology changes that enabled working in smaller batches. Those technical innovations helped them get the desktop product to customers faster for feedback. Instead of building a comprehensive road map at the beginning of the year, Greg kicked off the year with what they called idea/code/solution jams that brought engineers, product managers, and customers together to create a pipeline of ideas. It was scary for Greg as a product manager to start the year without a defined list of what would be in the product release, but he had confidence in his team and the new process.

There were three differences in year three:

- Teams were involved in creating new technologies, processes, and systems.
- Cross-functional teams were formed around new great ideas.
- Customers were involved from the inception of each feature concept.

It's important to understand that the old approach did not lack customer feedback or customer involvement in the planning process. In the true spirit of *genchi gembutsu,* Intuit product managers (PMs) would do "follow-me-homes" with customers to identify problems to solve in the next release. However, the PMs were responsible for all the customer research. They would bring it back to the team and say, "This is the problem we want to solve, and here are ideas for how we could solve it."

Changing to a cross-functional way of working was not smooth sailing. Some team members were skeptical. For example, some product managers felt that it was a waste of time for engineers to spend time in front of customers. The PMs thought that their job was to figure out the customer issue and define what needed to be built. Thus, the reaction of some PMs to the change was: "What's my job? What am I supposed to be doing?" Similarly, some on the engineering side just wanted to be told what to do; they didn't want to talk to customers. As is typically the case in large-batch development, both groups had been willing to sacrifice the team's ability to learn in order to work more "efficiently."

Communication was critical for this change process to succeed. All the team leaders were open about the change they were driving and why they were driving it. Much of the skepticism they faced was based on the fact that they did not have concrete examples of where this had worked in the past; it was an entirely new process for Intuit. They had to explain clearly why the old process didn't work and why the annual release "train" was not setting them up for success. Throughout the change they communicated the process outcomes they were shooting for: earlier customer feedback and a faster development cycle that was decoupled from the annual release time line. They repeatedly emphasized that the new approach was how startup competitors were working and iterating. They had to follow suit or risk becoming irrelevant.

○ ○ ○

Historically, QuickBooks had been built with large teams and long cycle times. For example, in earlier years the ill-fated online banking team had been composed of fifteen engineers, seven quality assurance specialists, a product manager, and at times more than one designer. Now no team is bigger than five people. The focus of each team is iterating with customers as rapidly as possible, running experiments, and then using validated learning to make real-time investment decisions about what to work on. As a result, whereas they used to have five major "branches" of QuickBooks that merged features at the time of the launch, now there are twenty to twenty-five branches. This allows for a much larger set of experiments. Each team works on a new feature for approximately six weeks end to end, testing it with real customers throughout the process.

Although the primary changes that are required in an adaptive organization are in the mind-set of its employees, changing the culture is not sufficient. As we saw in Chapter 9, lean management requires treating work as a system and then dealing with the batch size and cycle time of the whole process. Thus, to achieve lasting change, the QuickBooks team had to invest in tools and platform changes that would enable the new, faster way of working.

For example, one of the major stress points in the attempt to release an early alpha version the previous year was that QuickBooks is a mission-critical product. Many small businesses use it as their primary repository for critical financial data. The team was extremely wary of releasing a minimum viable product that had any risk of corrupting customer data. Therefore, even if they worked in smaller teams with a smaller scope, the burden of all that risk would have made it hard to work in smaller batches.

To get the batch size down, the QuickBooks team had to invest in new technology. They built a virtualization system that allowed them to run multiple versions of QuickBooks on a customer's computer. The second version could access all the customer's data but could not make permanent changes to it. Thus, there was no risk of the new version corrupting the customer's data by accident. This allowed them to isolate new releases to allow selected real customers to test them and provide feedback.

The results in year three were promising. The version of QuickBooks that shipped that year had significantly higher customer satisfaction ratings and sold more units. If you're using QuickBooks right now, odds are you are using a version that was built in small batches. As Greg heads into his fourth year with the QuickBooks team, they are exploring even more ways to drive down batch size and cycle time. As usual, there are possibilities that go beyond technical solutions. For example, the annual sales cycle of boxed desktop software is a significant barrier to truly rapid learning, and so the team has begun experimenting with subscription-based products for the most active customers. With customers downloading updates online, Intuit can release software on a more frequent basis. Soon this program will see the QuickBooks team releasing to customers quarterly.[3]

○ ○ ○

As Lean Startups grow, they can use adaptive techniques to develop more complex processes without giving up their core advantage: speed through the Build-Measure-Learn feedback loop. In fact, one of the primary benefits of using techniques that are derived from lean manufacturing is that Lean Startups, when they grow up, are well positioned to develop operational excellence based on lean principles. They already know how to operate with discipline, develop processes that are tailor-made to their situation, and use lean techniques such as the Five Whys and small batches. As a successful startup makes the transition to an established company, it will be well poised to develop the kind of culture of disciplined execution that characterizes the world's best firms, such as Toyota.

However, successfully growing into an established company is not the end of the story. A startup's work is never done, because as was discussed in Chapter 2, even established companies must struggle to find new sources of growth through disruptive innovation. This imperative is coming earlier in companies' lives. No longer can a successful startup expect to have years after its initial public offering to bask in market-leading success. Today successful companies face immediate pressure from new competitors, fast followers, and scrappy startups. As a result, it no longer makes sense to think of startups as going through discrete phases like the proverbial metamorphosis of a caterpillar to a butterfly. Both successful startups and established companies alike must learn to juggle multiple kinds of work at the same time, pursuing operational excellence *and* disruptive innovation. This requires a new kind of portfolio thinking, which is the subject of Chapter 12.

# 12
# INNOVATE

Conventional wisdom holds that when companies become larger, they inevitably lose the capacity for innovation, creativity, and growth. I believe this is wrong. As startups grow, entrepreneurs can build organizations that learn how to balance the needs of existing customers with the challenges of finding new customers to serve, managing existing lines of business, and exploring new business models—all at the same time. And, if they are willing to change their management philosophy, I believe even large, established companies can make this shift to what I call portfolio thinking.

## HOW TO NURTURE DISRUPTIVE INNOVATION

Successful innovation teams must be structured correctly in order to succeed. Venture-backed and bootstrapped startups naturally have some of these structural attributes as a consequence of being small, independent companies. Internal startup teams require support from senior management to create these structures. Internal or external, in my experience startup teams require three structural attributes: scarce but secure resources, independent authority to develop their business, and a personal stake in the outcome. Each of these requirements is different from those of established company divisions. Keep in mind that structure is merely a prerequisite—it does not guarantee success. But getting the structure wrong can lead to almost certain failure.

## Scarce but Secure Resources

Division leaders in large, established organizations are adept at using politics to enlarge their budgets but know that those budgets are somewhat loose. They often acquire as large a budget as possible and prepare to defend it against incursions from other departments. Politics means that they sometimes win and sometimes lose: if a crisis emerges elsewhere in the organization, their budget might suddenly be reduced by 10 percent. This is not a catastrophe; teams will have to work harder and do more with less. Most likely, the budget has some padding in anticipation of this kind of eventuality.

Startups are different: too much budget is as harmful as too little—as countless dot-com failures can attest—and startups are extremely sensitive to midcourse budgetary changes. It is extremely rare for a stand-alone startup company to lose 10 percent of its cash on hand suddenly. In a large number of cases, this would be a fatal blow, as independent startups are run with little margin for error. Thus, startups are both easier and more demanding to run than traditional divisions: they require much less capital overall, but that capital must be absolutely secure from tampering.

## Independent Development Authority

Startup teams need complete autonomy to develop and market new products within their limited mandate. They have to be able to conceive and execute experiments without having to gain an excessive number of approvals.

I strongly recommend that startup teams be completely cross-functional, that is, have full-time representation from every functional department in the company that will be involved in the creation or launch of their early products. They have to be able to build and ship actual functioning products and services, not just prototypes. Handoffs and approvals slow down the Build-Measure-Learn feedback loop and inhibit both learning and accountability. Startups require that they be kept to an absolute minimum.

Of course, this level of development autonomy is liable to raise fears in a parent organization. Alleviating those fears is a major goal of the method recommended below.

## A Personal Stake in the Outcome

Third, entrepreneurs need a personal stake in the outcome of their creations. In stand-alone new ventures, this usually is achieved through stock options or other forms of equity ownership. Where a bonus system must be used instead, the best incentives are tied to the long-term performance of the new innovation.

However, I do not believe that a personal stake has to be financial. This is especially important in organizations, such as nonprofits and government, in which the innovation is not tied to financial objectives. In these cases, it is still possible for teams to have a personal stake. The parent organization has to make it clear who the innovator is and make sure the innovator receives credit for having brought the new product to life—if it is successful. As one entrepreneur who ran her own division at a major media company told me, "Financial incentives aside, I always felt that because my name was on the door, I had more to lose and more to prove than someone else. That sense of ownership is not insignificant."

This formula is effective in for-profit companies as well. At

Toyota, the manager in charge of developing a new vehicle from start to finish is called the *shusa,* or chief engineer:

> *Shusa* are often called heavy-weight project managers in the U.S. literature, but this name understates their real roles as design leaders. Toyota employees translate the term as chief engineer, and they refer to the vehicle under development as the *shusa*'s car. They assured us that the *shusa* has final, absolute authority over every aspect of vehicle development.[1]

On the flip side, I know an extremely high-profile technology company that has a reputation for having an innovative culture, yet its track record of producing new products is disappointing. The company boasts an internal reward system that is based on large financial and status awards to teams that do something extraordinary, but those awards are handed out by senior management on the basis of—no one knows what. There are no objective criteria by which a team can gauge whether it will win this coveted lottery. Teams have little confidence that they will receive any long-term ownership of their innovations. Thus, teams rarely are motivated to take real risks, instead focusing their energies on projects that are expected to win the approval of senior management.

## CREATING A PLATFORM FOR EXPERIMENTATION

Next, it is important to focus on establishing the ground rules under which autonomous startup teams operate: how to protect the parent organization, how to hold entrepreneurial managers accountable, and how to reintegrate an innovation back into the parent organization if it is successful. Recall the "island of freedom" that enabled the SnapTax team—in Chapter 2—to successfully create a startup within Intuit. That's what a platform for experimentation can do.

## Protecting the Parent Organization

Conventionally, advice about internal innovators focuses on protecting the startup from the parent organization. I believe it is necessary to turn this model on its head.

Let me begin by describing a fairly typical meeting from one of my consulting clients, a large company. Senior management had gathered to make decisions about what to include in the next version of its product. As part of the company's commitment to being data-driven, it had tried to conduct an experiment on pricing. The first part of the meeting was taken up with interpreting the data from the experiment.

One problem was that nobody could agree on what the data meant. Many custom reports had been created for the meeting; the data warehouse team was at the meeting too. The more they were asked to explain the details of each row on the spreadsheet, the more evident it became that nobody understood how those numbers had been derived. What we were left looking at was the number of gross sales of the product at a variety of different price points, broken down by quarter and by customer segment. It was a lot of data to try to comprehend.

Worse, nobody was sure which customers had been exposed to the experiment. Different teams had been responsible for implementing it, and so different parts of the product had been updated at different times. The whole process had taken many months, and by this point, the people who had conceived the experiment had been moved to a division separate from that of the people who had executed it.

You should be able to spot the many problems with this

situation: the use of vanity metrics instead of actionable metrics, an overly long cycle time, the use of large batch sizes, an unclear growth hypothesis, a weak experimental design, a lack of team ownership, and therefore very little learning.

Listening in, I assumed this would be the end of the meeting. With no agreed-on facts to help make the decision, I thought nobody would have any basis for making the case for a particular action. I was wrong. Each department simply took whatever interpretation of the data supported its position best and started advocating on its own behalf. Other departments would chime in with alternative interpretations that supported their positions, and so on. In the end, decisions were not made based on data. Instead, the executive running the meeting was forced to base decisions on the most plausible-sounding arguments.

It seemed wasteful to me how much of the meeting had been spent debating the data because, in the end, the arguments that carried the day could have been made right at the start. It was as if each advocate sensed that he or she was about to be ambushed; if another team managed to bring clarity to the situation, it might undermine that person, and so the rational response was to obfuscate as much as possible. What a waste.

Ironically, meetings like this had given data-driven decision making and experimentation a bad name inside the company, and for good reason. The data warehousing team was producing reports that nobody read or understood. The project teams felt the experiments were a waste of time, since they involved building features halfway, which meant they were never any good. "Running an experiment" seemed to them to be code for postponing a hard decision. Worst of all, the executive team experienced the meetings as chronic headaches. Their old product prioritization meetings might have been little more than a battle of opinions, but at least the executives understood what was going on. Now they had to go through a ritual that involved complex math and reached no definite outcome, and then they ended up having a battle of opinions anyway.

## Rational Fears

However, at the heart of this departmental feud was a very rational fear. This company served two customer segments: a business-to-business enterprise segment and a consumer segment. In the B2B segment, the company employed sales staff to sell large volumes of the product to other companies, whereas the consumer segment was driven mostly by one-off purchases made by individuals. The bulk of the company's current revenue came from B2B sales, but growth in that segment had been slowing. Everyone agreed there was tremendous potential for growth in the consumer segment, but so far little had materialized.

Part of the cause of this lack of growth was the current pricing structure. Like many companies that sell to large enterprises, this one published a high list price and then provided heavy discounts to "favored" corporate clients who bought in bulk. Naturally, every salesperson was encouraged to make all of his or her clients feel favored. Unfortunately, the published list price was much too high for the consumer segment.

The team in charge of growing the consumer segment wanted to run experiments with a lower price structure. The team in charge of the enterprise segment was nervous that this would cannibalize or otherwise diminish its existing relationships with its customers. What if those customers discovered that individuals were getting a lower price than they were?

Anyone who has been in a multisegment business will recognize that there are many possible solutions to this problem, such as creating tiered feature sets so that different customers are able to purchase different "levels" of the product (as in airline seating) or even supporting different products under separate brand names. Yet the company was struggling to implement any of those solutions. Why? Out of fear of endangering the current business, each proposed experiment would be delayed, sabotaged, and obfuscated.

It's important to emphasize that this fear is well founded. Sabotage is a rational response from managers whose territory is threatened. This company is not a random, tiny startup with nothing to lose. An established company has a lot to lose. If the revenue from the core business goes down, heads will roll. This is not something to be taken lightly.

## The Dangers of Hiding Innovation inside the Black Box

The imperative to innovate is unrelenting. Without the ability to experiment in a more agile manner, this company eventually would suffer the fate described in *The Innovator's Dilemma*: ever-higher profits and margins year after year until the business suddenly collapsed.

We often frame internal innovation challenges by asking, How can we protect the internal startup from the parent organization? I would like to reframe and reverse the question: How can we protect the parent organization from the startup? In my experience, people defend themselves when they feel threatened, and no innovation can flourish if defensiveness is given free rein. In fact, this is why the common suggestion to hide the innovation team is misguided. There are examples of one-time successes using a secret skunkworks or off-site innovation team, such as the building of the original IBM PC in Boca Raton, Florida, completely separate from mainline IBM. But these examples should serve mostly as cautionary tales, because they have rarely led to sustainable innovation.[2] Hiding from the parent organization can have long-term negative consequences.

Consider it from the point of view of the managers who have the innovation sprung on them. They are likely to feel betrayed and more than a little paranoid. After all, if something of this magnitude could be hidden, what else is waiting in the shadows? Over time, this leads to more politics as managers are incentivized to ferret out threats to their power, influence, and careers. The fact that the innovation was a success is no justification for this dishonest behavior. From the point of view of established managers, the message is clear: if you are not on the inside, you are liable to be blindsided by this type of secret.

It is unfair to criticize these managers for their response; the criticism should be aimed at senior executives who failed to design a supportive system in which to operate and innovate. I believe this is one reason why companies such as IBM lost their leadership position in the new markets that they developed using a black box such as the PC business; they are unable to re-create and sustain the culture that led to the innovation in the first place.

## Creating an Innovation Sandbox

The challenge here is to create a mechanism for empowering innovation teams out in the open. This is the path toward a sustainable culture of innovation over time as companies face repeated existential threats. My suggested solution is to create a sandbox for innovation that will contain the impact of the new innovation but not constrain the methods of the startup team. It works as follows:

1. Any team can create a true split-test experiment that affects only the sandboxed parts of the product or service (for a multipart product) or only certain customer segments or territories (for a new product). However:

2. One team must see the whole experiment through from end to end.
3. No experiment can run longer than a specified amount of time (usually a few weeks for simple feature experiments, longer for more disruptive innovations).
4. No experiment can affect more than a specified number of customers (usually expressed as a percentage of the company's total mainstream customer base).
5. Every experiment has to be evaluated on the basis of a single standard report of five to ten (no more) actionable metrics.
6. Every team that works inside the sandbox and every product that is built must use the same metrics to evaluate success.
7. Any team that creates an experiment must monitor the metrics and customer reactions (support calls, social media reaction, forum threads, etc.) while the experiment is in progress and abort it if something catastrophic happens.

At the beginning, the sandbox has to be quite small. In the company above, the sandbox initially contained only the pricing page. Depending on the types of products the company makes, the size of the sandbox can be defined in different ways. For example, an online service might restrict it to certain pages or user flows. A retail operation might restrict it to certain stores or geographic areas. Companies trying to bring an entirely new product to market might build the restriction around customers in certain segments.

Unlike in a concept test or market test, customers in the sandbox are considered real and the innovation team is allowed to attempt to establish a long-term relationship with them. After all, they may be experimenting with those early adopters for a long time before their learning milestones are accomplished.

Whenever possible, the innovation team should be cross-functional and have a clear team leader, like the Toyota *shusa.* It should be empowered to build, market, and deploy products or features in the sandbox without prior approval. It should be required to report on the success or failure of those efforts by using standard actionable metrics and innovation accounting.

This approach can work even for teams that have never before worked cross-functionally. The first few changes, such as a price change, may not require great engineering effort, but they require coordination across departments: engineering, marketing, customer service. Teams that work this way are more productive as long as productivity is measured by their ability to create customer value and not just stay busy.

True experiments are easy to classify as successes or failures because top-level metrics either move or they don't. Either way, the team learns immediately whether its assumptions about how customers will behave are correct. By using the same metrics each time, the team builds literacy about those metrics across the company. Because the innovation team is reporting on its progress by using the system of innovation accounting described in Part Two, anyone who reads those reports is getting an implicit lesson in the power of actionable metrics. This effect is extremely powerful. Even if someone wants to sabotage the innovation team, he or she will have to learn all about actionable metrics and learning milestones to do it.

The sandbox also promotes rapid iteration. When people have a chance to see a project through from end to end and the work is done in small batches and delivers a clear verdict quickly, they benefit from the power of feedback. Each time they fail to move the numbers, they have a real opportunity to act on their findings immediately. Thus, these teams tend to converge on optimal solutions rapidly even if they start out with really bad ideas.

As we saw earlier, this is a manifestation of the principle of small batches. Functional specialists, especially those steeped in waterfall or stage-gate development, have been trained to work in extremely large batches. This causes even good ideas to get bogged down by waste. By making the batch size small, the sandbox method allows teams to make cheap mistakes quickly and start learning. As we'll see below, these small initial experiments can demonstrate that a team has a viable new business that can be integrated back into the parent company.

### Holding Internal Teams Accountable

We already discussed learning milestones in detail in Chapter 7. With an internal startup team, the sequence of accountability is the same: build an ideal model of the desired disruption that is based on customer archetypes, launch a minimum viable product to establish a baseline, and then attempt to tune the engine to get it closer to the ideal.

Operating in this framework, internal teams essentially act as startups. As they demonstrate success, they need to become integrated into the company's overall portfolio of products and services.

## CULTIVATING THE MANAGEMENT PORTFOLIO

There are four major kinds of work that companies must manage.[3] As an internal startup grows, the entrepreneurs who created the original concept must tackle the challenge of scale. As new mainstream customers are acquired and new markets are conquered, the product becomes part of the public face of the company, with important implications for PR, marketing, sales, and business development. In most cases, the product will attract competitors: copycats, fast followers, and imitators of all stripes.

Once the market for the new product is well established, procedures become more routine. To combat the inevitable commoditization of the product in its market, line extensions, incremental upgrades, and new forms of marketing are essential. In this phase, operational excellence takes on a greater role, as an important way to increase margins is to lower costs. This may require a different type of manager: one who excels in optimization, delegation, control, and execution. Company stock prices depend on this kind of predictable growth.

There is a fourth phase as well, one dominated by operating costs and legacy products. This is the domain of outsourcing, automation, and cost reduction. Nonetheless, infrastructure is still mission-critical. Failure of facilities or important infrastructure or the abandonment of loyal customers could derail the whole company. However, unlike the growth and optimization phase, investments in this area will not help the company achieve top-line growth. Managers of this kind of organization suffer the fate of baseball umpires: criticized when something goes wrong, unappreciated when things are going well.

We tend to speak of these four phases of businesses from the perspective of large companies, in which they may represent entire divisions and hundreds or even thousands of people. That's logical, as the evolution of the business in these kinds of extreme cases is the easiest to observe. However, all companies engage in all four phases of work all the time. As soon as a product hits the marketplace, teams of people work hard to advance it to the next phase. Every successful product or feature began life in research and development (R&D), eventually became a part of the company's strategy, was subject to optimization, and in time became old news.

The problem for startups and large companies alike is that employees often follow the products they develop as they move from phase to phase. A common practice is for the inventor of a new product or feature to manage the subsequent resources, team, or division that ultimately commercializes it. As a result, strong creative managers wind up getting stuck working on the growth and optimization of products rather than creating new ones.

This tendency is one of the reasons established companies struggle to find creative managers to foster innovation in the first place. Every new innovation competes for resources with established projects, and one of the scarcest resources is talent.

## Entrepreneur Is a Job Title

The way out of this dilemma is to manage the four kinds of work differently, allowing strong cross-functional teams to develop around each area. When products move from phase to phase, they are handed off between teams. Employees can choose to move with the product as part of the handoff or stay behind and begin work on something new. Neither choice is necessarily right or wrong; it depends on the temperament and skills of the person in question.

Some people are natural inventors who prefer to work without the pressure and expectations of the later business phases. Others are ambitious and see innovation as a path toward senior management. Still others are particularly skilled at the management of running an established business, outsourcing, and bolstering efficiencies and wringing out cost reductions. People should be allowed to find the kinds of jobs that suit them best.

In fact, entrepreneurship should be considered a viable career path for innovators inside large organizations. Managers who can lead teams by using the Lean Startup methodology should not have to leave the company to reap the rewards of their skills or have to pretend to fit into the rigid hierarchies of established functional departments. Instead, they should have a business card that says simply "Entrepreneur" under the name. They should be held accountable via the system of innovation accounting and promoted and rewarded accordingly.

After an entrepreneur has incubated a product in the innovation sandbox, it has to be reintegrated into the parent organization. A larger team eventually will be needed to grow it, commercialize it, and scale it. At first, this team will require the continued leadership of the innovators who worked in the sandbox. In fact, this is a positive part of the process in that it gives the innovators a chance to train new team members in the new style of working that they mastered in the original sandbox.

Ideally, the sandbox will grow over time; that is, rather than move the team out of the sandbox and into the company's standard routines, there may be opportunities to enlarge the scope of the sandbox. For example, if only certain aspects of the product were subject to experimentation in the sandbox, new features can be added. In the online service described earlier, this could be accomplished by starting with a sandbox that encompassed the product pricing page. When those experiments succeeded, the company could add the website's home page to the sandbox. It subsequently might add the search functionality or the overall web design. If only certain customers or certain numbers of customers were targeted initially, the product's reach could be increased. When such changes are contemplated, it's important that senior management consider whether the teams working in the sandbox can fend for themselves politically in the parent organization. The sandbox was designed to protect them and the parent organization, and any expansion needs to take this into account.

Working in the innovation sandbox is like developing startup muscles. At first, the team will be able to take on only modest experiments. The earliest experiments may fail to produce much learning and may not lead to scalable success. Over time, those teams are almost guaranteed to improve as long as they get the constant feedback of small-batch development and actionable metrics and are held accountable to learning milestones.

Of course, any innovation system eventually will become the victim of its own success. As the sandbox expands and the company's revenue grows as a result of the sandbox's innovations, the cycle will have to begin again. The former innovators will become guardians of the status quo. When the product makes up the whole sandbox, it inevitably will become encumbered with the additional rules and controls needed for mission-critical operation. New innovation teams will need a new sandbox within which to play.

## Becoming the Status Quo

This last transition is especially hard for innovators to accept: their transformation from radical outsiders to the embodiment of the status quo. I have found it disturbing in my career. As you can guess from the techniques I advocate as part of the Lean Startup, I have always been a bit of a troublemaker at the companies at which I have worked, pushing for rapid iteration, data-driven decision making, and early customer involvement. When these ideas were not part of the dominant culture, it was simple (if frustrating) to be an advocate. All I had to do was push as hard as humanly possible for my ideas. Since the dominant culture found them heretical, they would compromise with me a "reasonable" amount. Thanks to the psychological phenomenon of anchoring, this led to a perverse incentive: the more radical my suggestion was, the more likely it was that the reasonable compromise would be closer to my true goal.

Fast-forward several years to when I was running product development. When we'd hire new people, they had to be indoctrinated into the Lean Startup culture. Split testing, continuous deployment, and customer testing were all standard practice. I needed to continue to be a strong advocate for my ideas, making sure each new employee was ready to give them a try. But for the people who had been working there awhile, those ideas had become part of the status quo.

Like many entrepreneurs, I was caught between constant evangelizing for my ideas and constantly entertaining suggestions for ways they could be improved. My employees faced the same incentive I had exploited years before: the more radical the suggestion is, the more likely it is that the compromise will move in the direction they desire. I heard it all: suggestions that we go back to waterfall development, use more quality assurance (QA), use less QA, have more or less customer involvement, use more vision and less data, or interpret data in a more statistically rigorous way.

It took a constant effort to consider these suggestions seriously. However, responding dogmatically is unhelpful. Compromising by automatically splitting the difference doesn't work either.

I've found that every suggestion should be subjected to the same rigorous scientific inquiry that led to the creation of the Lean Startup in the first place. Can we use the theory to predict the results of the proposed change? Can we incubate the change in a small team and see what happens? Can we measure its impact? Whenever they could be implemented, these approaches have allowed me to increase my own learning and, more important, the productivity of the companies I have worked with. Many of the Lean Startup techniques that we pioneered at IMVU are not my original contributions. Rather, they were conceived, incubated, and executed by employees who brought their own creativity and talent to the task.

Above all, I faced this common question: How do we know that "your way" of building a company will work? What other companies are using it? Who has become rich and famous as a result? These questions are sensible. The titans of our industry are all working in a slower, more linear way. Why are we doing something different?

It is these questions that require the use of theory to answer. Those who look to adopt the Lean Startup as a defined set of steps or tactics will not succeed. I had to learn this the hard way. In a startup situation, things constantly go wrong. When that happens, we face the age-old dilemma summarized by Deming: How do we know that the problem is due to a special cause versus a systemic cause? If we're in the middle of adopting a new way of working, the temptation will always be to blame the new system for the problems that arise. Sometimes that tendency is correct, sometimes not. Learning to tell the difference requires theory. You have to be able to predict the outcome of the changes you make to tell if the problems that result are really problems.

For example, changing the definition of productivity for a team from functional excellence—excellence in marketing, sales, or product development—to validated learning will cause problems. As was indicated earlier, functional specialists are accustomed to measuring their efficiency by looking at the proportion of time they are busy doing their work. A programmer expects to be coding all day long, for example. That is why many traditional work environments frustrate these experts: the constant interruption of meetings, cross-functional handoffs, and explanations for endless numbers of bosses all act as a drag on efficiency. However, the individual efficiency of these specialists is not the goal in a Lean Startup. Instead, we want to force teams to work cross-functionally to achieve validated learning. Many of the techniques for doing this—actionable metrics, continuous deployment, and the overall Build-Measure-Learn feedback loop—necessarily cause teams to suboptimize for their individual functions. It does not matter how fast we can build. It does not matter how fast we can measure. What matters is how fast we can get through the entire loop.

In my years teaching this system, I have noticed this pattern every time: switching to validated learning feels worse before it feels better. That's the case because the problems caused by the old system tend to be intangible, whereas the problems of the new system are all too tangible. Having the benefit of theory is the antidote to these challenges. If it is known that this loss of productivity is an inevitable part of the transition, it can be managed actively. Expectations can be set up front. In my consulting practice, for example, I have learned to raise these issues from day one; otherwise, they are liable to derail the whole effort once it is under way. As the change progresses, we can use the root cause analysis and fast response techniques to figure out which problems need prevention. Ultimately, the Lean Startup is a framework, not a blueprint of steps to follow. It is designed to be adapted to the conditions of each specific company. Rather than copy what others have done, techniques such as the Five Whys allow you to build something that is perfectly suited to your company.

The best way to achieve mastery of and explore these ideas is to embed oneself in a community of practice. There is a thriving community of Lean Startup meetups around the world as well as online, and suggestions for how you can take advantage of these resources listed in the last chapter of this book, "Join the Movement."

13

# EPILOGUE: WASTE NOT

This year marks the one hundredth anniversary of Frederick Winslow Taylor's *The Principles of Scientific Management*, first published in 1911. The movement for scientific management changed the course of the twentieth century by making possible the tremendous prosperity that we take for granted today. Taylor effectively invented what we now consider simply management: improving the efficiency of individual workers, management by exception (focusing only on unexpectedly good or bad results), standardizing work into tasks, the task-plus-bonus system of compensation, and—above all—the idea that work can be studied and improved through conscious effort. Taylor invented modern white-collar work that sees companies as systems that must be managed at more than the level of the individual. There is a reason all past management revolutions have been led by engineers: management is human systems engineering.

In 1911 Taylor wrote: "In the past, the man has been first; in the future, the system must be first." Taylor's prediction has come to pass. We are living in the world he imagined. And yet, the revolution that he unleashed has been—in many ways—too successful. Whereas Taylor preached science as a way of thinking, many people confused his message with the rigid techniques he advocated: time and motion studies, the differential piece-rate system, and—most galling of all—the idea that workers should be treated as little more than automatons. Many of these ideas proved extremely harmful and required the efforts of later theorists and managers to undo. Critically, lean manufacturing rediscovered the wisdom and initiative hidden in every factory worker and redirected Taylor's notion of efficiency away from the individual task and toward the corporate organism as a whole. But each of these subsequent revolutions has embraced Taylor's core idea that work can be studied scientifically and can be improved through a rigorous experimental approach.

In the twenty-first century, we face a new set of problems that Taylor could not have imagined. Our productive capacity greatly exceeds our ability to know what to build. Although there was a tremendous amount of invention and innovation in the early twentieth century, most of it was devoted to increasing the productivity of workers and machines in order to feed, clothe, and house the world's population. Although that project is still incomplete, as the millions who live in poverty can attest, the solution to that problem is now strictly a political one. We have the capacity to build almost anything we can imagine. The big question of our time is not Can it be built? but Should it be built? This places us in an unusual historical moment: our future prosperity depends on the quality of our collective imaginations.

In 1911, Taylor wrote:

> We can see our forests vanishing, our water-powers going to waste, our soil being carried by floods into the sea; and the end of our coal and our iron is in sight. But our larger wastes of human effort, which go on every day through such of our acts as are blundering, ill-directed, or inefficient . . . are less visible, less tangible, and are but vaguely appreciated.
>
> We can see and feel the waste of material things. Awkward, inefficient, or ill-directed movements of men,

> however, leave nothing visible or tangible behind them. Their appreciation calls for an act of memory, an effort of the imagination. And for this reason, even though our daily loss from this source is greater than from our waste of material things, the one has stirred us deeply, while the other has moved us but little.[1]

A century on, what can we say about those words? On the one hand, they feel archaic. We of the twenty-first century are hyperaware of the importance of efficiency and the economic value of productivity gains. Our workplaces are—at least when it comes to the building of material objects—incredibly well organized compared with those of Taylor's day.

On the other hand, Taylor's words strike me as completely contemporary. For all of our vaunted efficiency in the making of things, our economy is still incredibly wasteful. This waste comes not from the inefficient organization of work but rather from working on the wrong things—and on an industrial scale. As Peter Drucker said, "There is surely nothing quite so useless as doing with great efficiency what should not be done at all."[2]

And yet we are doing the wrong things efficiently all the time. It is hard to come by a solid estimate of just how wasteful modern work is, but there is no shortage of anecdotes. In my consulting and travels talking about the Lean Startup, I hear the same message consistently from employees of companies big and small. In every industry we see endless stories of failed launches, ill-conceived projects, and large-batch death spirals. I consider this misuse of people's time a criminally negligent waste of human creativity and potential.

What percentage of all this waste is preventable? I think a much larger proportion than we currently realize. Most people I meet believe that in their industry at least, projects fail for good reasons: projects are inherently risky, market conditions are unpredictable, "big company people" are intrinsically uncreative. Some believe that if we just slowed everything down and used a more careful process, we could reduce the failure rate by doing fewer projects of higher quality. Others believe that certain people have an innate gift of knowing the right thing to build. If we can find enough of these visionaries and virtuosos, our problems will be solved. These "solutions" were once considered state of the art in the nineteenth century, too, before people knew about modern management.

The requirements of an ever-faster world make these antique approaches unworkable, and so the blame for failed projects and businesses often is heaped on senior management, which is asked to do the impossible. Alternatively, the finger of blame is pointed at financial investors or the public markets for overemphasizing quick fixes and short-term results. We have plenty of blame to go around, but far too little theory to guide the actions of leaders and investors alike.

The Lean Startup movement stands in contrast to this hand-wringing. We believe that most forms of waste in innovation are preventable once their causes are understood. All that is required is that we change our collective mind-set concerning how this work is to be done.

It is insufficient to exhort workers to try harder. Our current problems are caused by trying too hard—at the wrong things. By focusing on functional efficiency, we lose sight of the real goal of innovation: to learn that which is currently unknown. As Deming taught, what matters is not setting quantitative goals but fixing the method by which those goals are attained. The Lean Startup movement stands for the principle that the scientific method can be brought to bear to answer the most pressing innovation question: How can we build a sustainable organization around a new set of products or services?

## ORGANIZATIONAL SUPERPOWERS

A participant at one of my workshops came up to me a few months afterward to relate the following story, which I am paraphrasing: "Knowing Lean Startup principles makes me feel like I have superpowers. Even though I'm just a junior employee, when I meet with corporate VPs and GMs in my large company, I ask them simple questions and very quickly help them see how their projects are based on fundamental hypotheses that are testable. In minutes, I can lay out a plan they could follow to scientifically validate their plans before it's too late. They consistently respond with 'Wow, you are brilliant. We've never thought to apply that level of rigor to our thinking about new products before.'"

As a result of these interactions, he has developed a reputation within his large company as a brilliant employee. This has been good for his career but very frustrating for him personally. Why? Because although he *is* quite brilliant, his insights into flawed product plans are due not to his special intelligence but to having a theory that allows him to predict what will happen and propose alternatives. He is frustrated because the managers he is pitching his ideas to do not see the system. They wrongly conclude that the key to success is finding brilliant people like him to put on their teams. They are failing to see the opportunity he is really presenting them: to achieve better results systematically by changing their beliefs about how innovation happens.

### Putting the System First: Some Dangers

Like Taylor before us, our challenge is to persuade the managers of modern corporations to put the system first. However, Taylorism should act as a cautionary tale, and it is important to learn the lessons of history as we bring these new ideas to a more mainstream audience.

Taylor is remembered for his focus on systematic practice rather than individual brilliance. Here is the full quote from *The Principles of Scientific Management* that includes the famous line about putting the system first:

> In the future it will be appreciated that our leaders must be trained right as well as born right, and that no great man can (with the old system of personal management) hope to compete with a number of ordinary men who have been properly organized so as efficiently to cooperate.
>
> In the past the man has been first; in the future the system must be first. This in no sense, however, implies that great men are not needed. On the contrary, the first object of any good system must be that of developing first-class men; and under systematic management the best man rises to the top more certainly and more rapidly than ever before.[3]

Unfortunately, Taylor's insistence that scientific management does not stand in opposition to finding and promoting the best individuals was quickly forgotten. In fact, the productivity gains to be had through the early scientific management tactics, such as time and motion study, task-plus-bonus, and especially functional foremanship (the forerunner of today's functional departments), were so significant that subsequent generations of managers lost sight of the importance of the people who were implementing them.

This has led to two problems: (1) business systems became overly rigid and thereby failed to take advantage of the adaptability, creativity, and wisdom of individual workers, and (2) there has been an overemphasis on planning, prevention, and procedure, which enable organizations to achieve consistent results in a mostly static world. On the factory floor, these problems have been tackled head on by the lean manufacturing movement, and those lessons have spread throughout many modern corporations. And yet in new product development, entrepreneurship, and innovation work in general we are still using an outdated framework.

My hope is that the Lean Startup movement will not fall into the same reductionist trap. We are just beginning to uncover the rules that govern entrepreneurship, a method that can improve the odds of startup success, and a systematic approach to building new and innovative products. This in no way diminishes the traditional entrepreneurial virtues: the primacy of vision, the willingness to take bold risks, and the courage required in the face of overwhelming odds. Our society needs the creativity and vision of entrepreneurs more than ever. In fact, it is precisely because these are such precious resources that we cannot afford to waste them.

## Product Development Pseudoscience

I believe that if Taylor were alive today, he would chuckle at what constitutes the management of entrepreneurs and innovators. Although we harness the labor of scientists and engineers who would have dazzled any early-twentieth-century person with their feats of technical wizardry, the management practices we use to organize them are generally devoid of scientific rigor. In fact, I would go so far as to call them pseudoscience.

We routinely green-light new projects more on the basis of intuition than facts. As we've seen throughout this book, that is not the root cause of the problem. All innovation begins with vision. It's what happens next that is critical. As we've seen, too many innovation teams engage in success theater, selectively finding data that support their vision rather than exposing the elements of the vision to true experiments, or, even worse, staying in stealth mode to create a data-free zone for unlimited "experimentation" that is devoid of customer feedback or external accountability of any kind. Anytime a team attempts to demonstrate cause and effect by placing highlights on a graph of gross metrics, it is engaging in pseudoscience. How do we know that the proposed cause and effect is true? Anytime a team attempts to justify its failures by resorting to learning as an excuse, it is engaged in pseudoscience as well.

If learning has taken place in one iteration cycle, let us demonstrate it by turning it into validated learning in the next cycle. Only by building a model of customer behavior and then showing our ability to use our product or service to change it over time can we establish real facts about the validity of our vision.

Throughout our celebration of the success of the Lean Startup movement, a note of caution is essential. We cannot afford to have our success breed a new pseudoscience around pivots, MVPs, and the like. This was the fate of scientific management, and in the end, I believe, that set back its cause by decades. Science came to stand for the victory of routine work over creative work, mechanization over humanity, and plans over agility. Later movements had to be spawned to correct those deficiencies.

Taylor believed in many things that he dubbed scientific but that our modern eyes perceive as mere prejudice. He believed in the inherent superiority in both intelligence and character of aristocratic men over the working classes and the superiority of men over women; he also thought that lower-status people should be supervised strictly by their betters. These beliefs are part and parcel of Taylor's time, and it is tempting to forgive him for having been blind to them.

Yet when our time is viewed through the lens of future practice, what prejudices will be revealed? In what forces do we place undue faith? What might we risk losing sight of with this initial success of our movement?

It is with these questions that I wish to close. As gratifying as it is for me to see the Lean Startup movement gain fame and recognition, it is far more important that we be right in our prescriptions. What is known so far is just the tip of the iceberg. What is needed is a massive project to discover how to unlock the vast stores of potential that are hidden in plain sight in our modern workforce. If we stopped wasting people's time, what would they do with it? We have no real concept of what is possible.

Starting in the late 1880s, Taylor began a program of experimentation to discover the optimal way to cut steel. In the course of that research, which lasted more than twenty-five years, he and his colleagues performed more than twenty thousand individual experiments. What is remarkable about this project is that it had no academic backing, no government R&D budget. Its entire cost was paid by industry out of the immediate profits generated from the higher productivity the experiments enabled. This was only one experimental program to uncover the hidden productivity in just one kind of work. Other scientific management disciples spent years investigating bricklaying, farming, and even shoveling. They were obsessed with learning the truth and were not satisfied with the folk wisdom of craftspersons or the parables of experts.

Can any of us imagine a modern knowledge-work manager with the same level of interest in the methods his or her employees use? How much of our current innovation work is guided by catchphrases that lack a scientific foundation?

## A New Research Program

What comparable research programs could we be engaged in to discover how to work more effectively?

For one thing, we have very little understanding of what stimulates productivity under conditions of extreme uncertainty. Luckily, with cycle times falling everywhere, we have many opportunities to test new approaches. Thus, I propose that we create startup testing labs that could put all manner of product development methodologies to the test.

How might those tests be conducted? We could bring in small cross-functional teams, perhaps beginning with product and engineering, and have them work to solve problems by using different development methodologies. We could begin with problems with clear right answers, perhaps drawn from the many international programming competitions that have developed databases of well-defined problems with clear solutions. These competitions also provide a clear baseline of how long it should take for various problems to be solved so that we could establish clearly the individual problem-solving prowess of the experimental subjects.

Using this kind of setup for calibration, we could begin to vary the conditions of the experiments. The challenge will be to increase the level of uncertainty about what the right answer is while still being able to measure the quality of the outcome objectively. Perhaps we could use real-world customer problems and then have real consumers test the output of the teams' work. Or perhaps we could go so far as to build minimum viable products for solving the same set of problems over and over again to quantify which produces the best customer conversion rates.

We also could vary the all-important cycle time by choosing more or less complex development platforms and distribution channels to test the impact of those factors on the true productivity of the teams.

Most of all, we need to develop clear methods for holding teams accountable for validated learning. I have proposed one method in this book: innovation accounting using a well-defined financial model and engine of growth. However, it is naive to assume that this is the best possible method. As it is adopted in more and more companies, undoubtedly new techniques will be suggested, and we need to be able to evaluate the new ideas as rigorously as possible.

All these questions raise the possibilities of public-private partnerships between research universities and the entrepreneurial communities they seek to foster. It also suggests that universities may be able to add value in more ways than by being simply financial investors or creators of startup incubators, as is the current trend. My prediction is that wherever this research is conducted will become an epicenter of new entrepreneurial practice, and universities conducting this research therefore may be able to achieve a much higher level of commercialization of their basic research activities.[4]

## THE LONG-TERM STOCK EXCHANGE

Beyond simple research, I believe our goal should be to change the entire ecosystem of entrepreneurship. Too much of our startup industry has devolved into a feeder system for giant media companies and investment banks. Part of the reason established companies struggle to invest consistently in innovation is intense pressure from public markets to hit short-term profitability and growth targets. Mostly, this is a consequence of the accounting methods we have developed for evaluating managers, which focus on the kinds of gross "vanity" metrics discussed in Chapter 7. What is needed is a new kind of stock exchange, designed to trade in the stocks of companies that are organized to sustain long-term thinking. I propose that we create a Long-Term Stock Exchange (LTSE).

In addition to quarterly reports on profits and margins,

companies on the LTSE would report using innovation accounting on their internal entrepreneurship efforts. Like Intuit, they would report on the revenue they were generating from products that did not exist a few years earlier. Executive compensation in LTSE companies would be tied to the company's long-term performance. Trading on the LTSE would have much higher transaction costs and fees to minimize day trading and massive price swings. In exchange, LTSE companies would be allowed to structure their corporate governance to facilitate greater freedom for management to pursue long-term investments. In addition to support for long-term thinking, the transparency of the LTSE will provide valuable data about how to nurture innovation in the real world. Something like the LTSE would accelerate the creation of the next generation of great companies, built from the ground up for continuous innovation.

## IN CONCLUSION

As a movement, the Lean Startup must avoid doctrines and rigid ideology. We must avoid the caricature that science means formula or a lack of humanity in work. In fact, science is one of humanity's most creative pursuits. I believe that applying it to entrepreneurship will unlock a vast storehouse of human potential.

What would an organization look like if all of its employees were armed with Lean Startup organizational superpowers?

For one thing, everyone would insist that assumptions be stated explicitly and tested rigorously not as a stalling tactic or a form of make-work but out of a genuine desire to discover the truth that underlies every project's vision.

We would not waste time on endless arguments between the defenders of quality and the cowboys of reckless advance;

instead, we would recognize that speed and quality are allies in the pursuit of the customer's long-term benefit. We would race to test our vision but not to abandon it. We would look to eliminate waste not to build quality castles in the sky but in the service of agility and breakthrough business results.

We would respond to failures and setbacks with honesty and learning, not with recriminations and blame. More than that, we would shun the impulse to slow down, increase batch size, and indulge in the curse of prevention. Instead, we would achieve speed by bypassing the excess work that does not lead to learning. We would dedicate ourselves to the creation of new institutions with a long-term mission to build sustainable value and change the world for the better.

Most of all, we would stop wasting people's time.

# 14

# JOIN THE MOVEMENT

In the past few years, the Lean Startup movement has gone global. The number of resources available for aspiring entrepreneurs is incredible. Here, I'll do my best to list just a few of the best events, books, and blogs for further reading and further practice. The rest is up to you. Reading is good, action is better.

The most important resources are local. Gone are the days where you had to be in Silicon Valley to find other entrepreneurs to share ideas and struggles with. However, being embedded in a startup ecosystem is still an important part of entrepreneurship. What's changed is that these ecosystems are springing up in more and more startup hubs around the world.

I maintain an official website for *The Lean Startup* at http://theleanstartup.com, where you can find additional resources, including case studies and links to further reading. You will also find links there to my blog, *Startup Lessons Learned,* as well as videos, slides, and audio from my past presentations.

## Lean Startup Meetups

Chances are there is a Lean Startup meetup group near you. As of this writing, there are over a hundred, with the largest in

San Francisco, Boston, New York, Chicago, and Los Angeles. You can find a real-time map of groups here: http://lean-startup.meetup.com/. You can also find a list of cities where people are interested in starting a new group, and tools to set one up yourself.

### The Lean Startup Wiki

Not every Lean Startup group uses Meetup.com to organize, and a comprehensive list of events and other resources is maintained by volunteers on the Lean Startup Wiki: http://leanstartup.pbworks.com/

### The Lean Startup Circle

The largest community of practice around the Lean Startup is happening online, right now, on the Lean Startup Circle mailing list. Founded by Rich Collins, the list has thousands of entrepreneurs sharing tips, resources, and stories every day. If you have a question about how Lean Startup might apply to your business or industry, it's a great place to start: http://leanstartupcircle.com/

### The Startup Lessons Learned Conference

For the past two years, I have run a conference called Startup Lessons Learned. More details are available here: http://sllconf.com

## REQUIRED READING

Steve Blank's book *The Four Steps to the Epiphany* is the original book about customer development. When I was building

IMVU, a dog-eared copy of this book followed me everywhere. It is an indispensable guide. You can get a copy here: http://ericri.es/FourSteps or read my review of it here: http://www.startuplessonslearned.com/2008/11/what-is-customer-development.html. Steve also maintains an active and excellent blog at http://steveblank.com/

Brant Cooper and Patrick Vlaskovits have created a short but excellent book called *The Entrepreneur's Guide to Customer Development,* which provides a gentle introduction to the topic. You can buy it here: http://custdev.com or read my review here: http://www.startuplessonslearned.com/2010/07/entrepreneurs-guide-to-customer.html

When I first began blogging about entrepreneurship, it was not nearly as common an occupation as it is now. Very few bloggers were actively working on new ideas about entrepreneurship, and together we debated and refined these ideas online.

Dave McClure, founder of the venture firm 500 Startups, writes a blog at http://500hats.typepad.com/. 500 Startups has an excellent blog as well: http://blog.500startups.com/. Dave's "Startup Metrics for Pirates" presentation laid out a framework for thinking about and measuring online services that greatly influenced the concept of "engines of growth." You can see the original presentation here: http://500hats.typepad.com/500blogs/2008/09/startup-metri-2.html as well as my original reaction here: http://www.startuplessonslearned.com/2008/09/three-drivers-of-growth-for-your.html

Sean Ellis writes the *Startup Marketing Blog,* which has been influential in my thinking about how to integrate marketing into startups: http://startup-marketing.com/

Andrew Chen's blog *Futuristic Play* is one of the best sources for thoughts on viral marketing, startup metrics, and design: http://andrewchenblog.com/

Babak Nivi writes the excellent blog *Venture Hacks* and was an early Lean Startup evangelist: http://venturehacks.com/. He's since gone on to create Angel List, which matches startups and investors around the world: http://angel.co/

Other fantastic Lean Startup blogs include:

- Ash Maurya has emerged as a leader in helping bootstrapped online businesses apply Lean Startup ideas. His blog is called *Running Lean,* and he also has released an eBook of the same name. Both can be found here: http://www.runningleanhq.com/
- Sean Murphy on early-stage software startups: http://www.skmurphy.com/blog/
- Brant Cooper's *Market by Numbers:* http://market-by-numbers.com/
- Patrick Vlaskovits on technology, customer development, and pricing: http://vlaskovits.com/
- The KISSmetrics Marketing Blog: http://blog.kissmetrics.com/ and Hiten Shah's http://hitenism.com

## FURTHER READING

Clayton M. Christensen's *The Innovator's Dilemma* and *The Innovator's Solution* are classics. In addition, Christensen's more recent work is also extremely helpful for seeing the theory of disruptive innovation in practice, including *The Innovator's Prescription* (about disrupting health care) and *Disrupting Class* (about education).
http://ericri.es/ClaytonChristensen

Geoffrey A. Moore's early work is famous among all entrepreneurs, especially *Crossing the Chasm* and *Inside the Tornado.* But

he has continued to refine his thinking, and I have found his latest work, *Dealing with Darwin: How Great Companies Innovate at Every Phase of Their Evolution,* especially useful.
http://ericri.es/DealingWithDarwin

*The Principles of Product Development Flow: Second Generation Lean Product Development* by Donald G. Reinertsen.
http://ericri.es/pdflow

*The Toyota Way* by Jeffrey Liker.
http://ericri.es/thetoyotaway

*Lean Thinking: Banish Waste and Create Wealth in Your Corporation, Revised and Updated* by James P. Womack and Daniel T. Jones.
http://ericri.es/LeanThinking

*The People's Tycoon: Henry Ford and the American Century* by Steven Watts.
http://ericri.es/ThePeoplesTycoon

*The One Best Way: Frederick Winslow Taylor and the Enigma of Efficiency* by Robert Kanigel.
http://ericri.es/OneBestWay

*The Principles of Scientific Management* by Frederick Winslow Taylor.
http://ericri.es/ScientificManagement

*Extreme Programming Explained: Embrace Change* by Kent Beck and Cynthia Andres.
http://ericri.es/EmbraceChange

*Toyota Production System: Beyond Large-Scale Production* by Taiichi Ohno.
http://ericri.es/TaiichiOhno

The idea of the Build-Measure-Learn feedback loop owes a lot to ideas from maneuver warfare, especially John Boyd's OODA (Observe-Orient-Decide-Act) Loop. The most accessible introduction to Boyd's ideas is *Certain to Win: The Strategy of John Boyd, Applied to Business* by Chet Richards.
http://ericri.es/CertainToWin

*Out of the Crisis* by W. Edwards Deming.
http://ericri.es/OutOfTheCrisis

*My Years with General Motors* by Alfred Sloan.
http://ericri.es/MyYears

*Billy, Alfred, and General Motors: The Story of Two Unique Men, a Legendary Company, and a Remarkable Time in American History* by William Pelfrey.
http://ericri.es/BillyAlfred

*The Practice of Management* by Peter F. Drucker.
http://ericri.es/PracticeOfManagement

*Getting to Plan B: Breaking Through to a Better Business Model* by John Mullins and Randy Komisar.
http://ericri.es/GettingToPlanB

# Endnotes

## Introduction

1. For an up-to-date listing of Lean Startup meetups or to find one near you, see http://lean-startup.meetup.com or the Lean Startup Wiki: http://leanstartup.pbworks.com/Meetups. See also Chapter 14, "Join the Movement."

## Chapter 1. Start

1. Manufacturing statistics and analysis are drawn from the blog *Five Thirty Eight*: http://www.fivethirtyeight.com/2010/02/us-manufacturing-is-not-dead.html

## Chapter 2. Define

1. *The Innovator's Dilemma* is a classic text by Clayton Christensen about the difficulty established companies have with disruptive innovation. Along with its sequel, *The Innovator's Solution,* it lays out specific suggestions for how established companies can create autonomous divisions to pursue startup-like innovation. These specific structural prerequisites are discussed in detail in Chapter 12.
2. For more about SnapTax, see http://blog.turbotax.intuit.com/turbotax-press-releases/taxes-on-your-mobile-phone-it%E2%80%99s-a-snap/01142011–4865 and http://mobilized.allthingsd.com/20110204/exclusive-intuit-sees-more-than-350000-downloads-for-snaptax-its-smartphone-tax-filing-app/
3. Most information relating to Intuit and SnapTax comes from

private interviews with Intuit management and employees. Information about Intuit's founding comes from Suzanne Taylor and Kathy Schroeder's *Inside Intuit: How the Makers of Quicken Beat Microsoft and Revolutionized an Entire Industry* (Cambridge, Mass.: Harvard Business Press, 2003).

## Chapter 3. Learn

1. The original five founders of IMVU were Will Harvey, Marcus Gosling, Matt Danzig, Mel Guymon, and myself.
2. Usage in the United States was even more concentrated; see http://www.businessweek.com/technology/tech_stats/im050307.htm
3. To hear more about IMVU's early conversations with customers that led to our pivot away from the add-on strategy, see: http://mixergy.com/ries-lean/
4. A word of caution: demonstrating validated learning requires the right kind of metrics, called *actionable metrics,* which are discussed in Chapter 7.
5. This case was written by Bethany Coates under the direction of Professor Andy Rachleff. You can get a copy here: http://hbr.org/product/imvu/an/E254-PDF-ENG

## Chapter 4. Experiment

1. Some entrepreneurs have adopted this slogan as their startup philosophy, using the acronym JFDI. A recent example can be seen at http://www.cloudave.com/1171/what-makes-an-entrepreneur-four-letters-jfdi/
2. http://techcrunch.com/2009/11/02/amazon-closes-zappos-deal-ends-up-paying-1–2-billion/
3. I want to thank Caroline Barlerin and HP for allowing me to include my experimental analysis of this new project.
4. Information about Kodak Gallery comes from interviews conducted by Sara Leslie.
5. The VLS story was recounted by Elnor Rozenrot, formerly of Innosight Ventures. Additional detail was provided by Akshay Mehra. For more on the VLS, see the article in *Harvard Business Review*: http://hbr.org/2011/01/new-business-models-in-emerging

-markets/ar/1 or press coverage at http://economictimes.indiatimes.com/news/news-by-company/corporate-trends/village-laundry-services-takes-on-the-dhobi/articleshow/5325032.cms

6. For more on the early efforts of the CFPB, see the *Wall Street Journal*'s April 13, 2011, article "For Complaints, Don't Call Consumer Bureau Yet"; http://online.wsj.com/article/SB10001424052748703551304576260772357440148.html. Many dedicated public servants are currently working hard to incorporate this experimental approach in the public sector under the leadership of President Obama. I would like to thank Aneesh Chopra, Chris Vein, Todd Park, and David Forrest for introducing me to these groundbreaking efforts.

### Chapter 5. Leap

1. For example, CU Community, which began at Columbia University, had an early head start. See http://www.slate.com/id/2269131/. This account of Facebook's founding is drawn from David Kirkpatrick's *The Facebook Effect* (New York: Simon & Schuster, 2011).
2. Actual engagement numbers from 2004 are hard to find, but this pattern has been consistent throughout Facebook's public statements. For example, Chris Hughes reported in 2005 that "60% log in daily. About 85% log in at least once a week, and 93% log in at least once a month." http://techcrunch.com/2005/09/07/85-of-college-students-use-facebook/
3. I first heard the term *leap of faith* applied to startup assumptions by Randy Komisar, a former colleague and current partner at the venture firm Kleiner Perkins Caufield & Byers. He expands on the concept in his book *Getting to Plan B,* coauthored with John Mullins.
4. http://www.forbes.com/2009/09/17/venture-capital-ipod-intelligent-technology-komisar.html
5. "A carefully researched table compiled for *Motor* magazine by Charles E. Duryea, himself a pioneer carmaker, revealed that from 1900 to 1908, 501 companies were formed in the United States for the purpose of manufacturing automobiles. Sixty percent of them folded outright within a couple of years; another

6 percent moved into other areas of production." This quote is from the Ford biography *The People's Tycoon: Henry Ford and the American Century* by Steven Watts (New York: Vintage, 2006).

6. Jeffrey K. Liker, *The Toyota Way*. New York: McGraw-Hill, 2003, p. 223.
7. http://www.autofieldguide.com/articles/030302.html
8. In the customer development model, this is called *customer discovery*.
9. For more on the founding of Intuit, see Suzanne Taylor and Kathy Schroeder, *Inside Intuit*.
10. For more on the Lean UX movement, see http://www.cooper.com/journal/2011/02/lean_ux_product_stewardship_an.html and http://www.slideshare.net/jgothelflean-ux-getting-out-of-the-deliverables-business

## Chapter 6. Test

1. http://www.pluggd.in/groupon-story-297/
2. "Groupon's $6 Billion Gambler," *Wall Street Journal;* http://online.wsj.com/article_email/SB10001424052748704828104576021481410635432-lMyQjAxMTAwMDEwODExNDgyWj.html
3. The term *minimum viable product* has been in use since at least 2000 as part of various approaches to product development. For an academic example, see http://www2.cs.uidaho.edu/~billjunk/Publications/DynamicBalance.pdf

   See also Frank Robinson of PMDI, who refers to a version of the product that is the smallest needed to sell to potential customers (http://productdevelopment.com/howitworks/mvp.html). This is similar to Steve Blank's concept of the "minimum feature set" in customer development (http://steveblank.com/2010/03/04/perfection-by-subtraction-the-minimum-feature-set/). My use of the term here has been generalized to any version of a product that can begin the process of learning, using the Build-Measure-Learn feedback loop. For more, see http://www.startuplessonslearned.com/2009/08/minimum-viable-product-guide.html
4. Many people have written about this phenomenon, using varying terminology. Probably the most widely read is Geoffrey Moore's *Crossing the Chasm*. For more, see Eric Von Hippel's research into

what he termed "lead users"; his book *The Sources of Innovation* is a great place to start. Steve Blank uses the term *earlyvangelist* to emphasize the evangelical powers of these early customers.

5. "To the casual observer, the Dropbox demo video looked like a normal product demonstration," Drew says, "but we put in about a dozen Easter eggs that were tailored for the Digg audience. References to Tay Zonday and 'Chocolate Rain' and allusions to *Office Space* and XKCD. It was a tongue-in-cheek nod to that crowd, and it kicked off a chain reaction. Within 24 hours, the video had more than 10,000 Diggs." http://answers.oreilly.com/topic/1372-marketing-lessons-from-dropbox-a-qa-with-ceo-drew-houston/. You can see the original video as well as the reaction from the Digg community at http://digg.com/software/Google_Drive_killer_coming_from_MIT_Startup. For more on Dropbox's success, see "Dropbox: The Hottest Startup You've Never Heard Of" at http://tech.fortune.cnn.com/2011/03/16/cloud-computing-for-the-rest-of-us/
6. This description courtesy of Lifehacker: http://lifehacker.com/5586203/food-on-the-table-builds-menus-and-grocery-lists-based-on-your-familys-preferences
7. This list was compiled by my colleague, Professor Tom Eisenmann at Harvard Business School, Launching Technology Ventures for a case that he authored on Aardvark for his new class. For more, see http://platformsandnetworks.blogspot.com/2011/01/launching-tech-ventures-part-i-course.html
8. http://www.robgo.org/post/568227990/product-leadership-series-user-driven-design-at
9. http://venturebeat.com/2010/02/11/confirmed-google-buys-social-search-engine-aardvark-for-50-million/
10. This is the heart of the *Innovator's Dilemma* by Clayton Christensen.
11. For more, see http://bit.ly/DontLaunch

## Chapter 7. Measure

1. By contrast, Google's main competitor Overture (eventually bought by Yahoo) had a minimum account size of $50, which deterred us from signing up, as it was too expensive.
2. For more details about Farb's entrepreneurial journey, see

this Mixergy interview: http://mixergy.com/farbood-nivi-grockit-interview/

## Chapter 8. Pivot (or Persevere)

1. http://www.slideshare.net/dbinetti/lean-startup-at-sxsw-votizen-pivot-case-study
2. For more on Path, see http://techcrunch.com/2011/02/02/google-tried-to-buy-path-for-100-million-path-said-no/ and http://techcrunch.com/2011/02/01kleiner-perkins-leads-8–5-million-round-for-path/
3. Includes approximately $30 million of assets under management and approximately $150 million of assets under administration, as of April 1, 2011.
4. For more on Wealthfront, see the case study written by Sarah Milstein at http://www.startuplessonslearned.com/2010/07/case-study-kaching-anatomy-of-pivot.html. For more on Wealthfront's recent success, see http://bits.blogs.ntimes.com/2010/10/19/wealthfront-loses-the-sound-effects/
5. IMVU's results have been shared publicly on a few occasions. For 2008, see http://www.worldsinmotion.biz/2008/06/imvu_reaches_20_million_regist.php; for 2009 see http://www.imvu.com/about/press_releases/press_release_20091005_1.php, and for 2010 see http://techcrunch.com/2010/04/24/imvu-revenue/
6. Business architecture is a concept explored in detail in Moore's *Dealing with Darwin.* "Organizational structure based on prioritizing one of two business models (Complex systems model and Volume operations model). Innovation types are understood and executed in completely different ways depending on which model an enterprise adopts." For more, see http://www.dealingwithdarwin.com/theBook/darwinDictionary.php

## Chapter 9. Batch

1. http://lssacademy.com/2008/03/24/a-response-to-the-video-skeptics/

2. If you're having trouble accepting this fact, it really is helpful to watch it on video. One extremely detail-oriented blogger took one video and broke it down, second-by-second, to see where the time went: "You lose between 2 and 5 seconds every time you move the pile around between steps. Also, you have to manage the pile several times during a task, something you don't have to do nearly as much with [single-piece flow]. This also has a factory corollary: storing, moving, retrieving, and looking for work in progress inventory." See the rest of the commentary here: http://lssacademy.com/2008/03/24/a-response-to-the-video-skeptics/
3. Timothy Fitz, an early IMVU engineer, deserves credit for having coined the term *continuous deployment* in a blog post: http://timothyfitz.wordpress.com/2009/02/10/continuous-deployment-at-imvu-doing-the-impossible-fifty-times-a-day/. The actual development of the continuous deployment system is the work of too many different engineers at IMVU for me to give adequate credit here. For details on how to get started with continuous deployment, see http://radar.oreilly.com/2009/03/continuous-deployment-5-eas.html
4. For technical details of Wealthfront's continuous deployment setup, see http://eng.wealthfront.com/2010/05/deployment-infrastructure-for.html and http://eng.wealthfront.com/2011/03/lean-startup-stage-at-sxsw.html
5. This description of School of One was provided by Jennifer Carolan of NewSchools Venture Fund.
6. For more on the large-batch death spiral, see *The Principles of Product Development Flow: Second Generation Lean Product Development* by Donald G. Reinertsen: http://bit.ly/pdflow
7. These lean health care examples are courtesy of Mark Graban, author of *Lean Hospitals* (New York: Productivity Press, 2008).
8. This illustrative story about pull is drawn from *Lean Production Simplified* by Pascal Dennis (New York: Productivity Press, 2007).
9. For an example of this misunderstanding at work, see http://www.oreillygmt.eu/interview/fatboy-in-a-lean-world/
10. Information about Alphabet Energy comes from interviews conducted by Sara Leslie.

11. For more on Toyota's learning organization, see *The Toyota Way* by Jeffrey Liker.

## Chapter 10. Grow

1. The Hotmail story, along with many other examples, is recounted in Adam L. Penenberg's *Viral Loop*. For more on Hotmail, also see http://www.fastcompany.com/magazine/27/neteffects.html
2. For more on the four customer currencies of time, money, skill, and passion, see http://www.startuplessonslearned.com/2009/12/business-ecology-and-four-customer.html
3. http://pmarca-archive.posterous.com/the-pmarca-guide-to-startups-part-4-the-only
4. This is the lesson of Geoffrey Moore's bestselling book *Crossing the Chasm* (New York: Harper Paperbacks, 2002).

## Chapter 11. Adapt

1. *Toyota Production System: Beyond Large-Scale Production* by Taiichi Ohno (New York: Productivity Press, 1988).
2. For more on Net Promoter Score, see http://www.startuplessonslearned.com/2008/11/net-promoter-score-operational-tool-to.html and *The Ultimate Question* by Fred Reichheld (Cambridge, Mass.: Harvard Business Press, 2006).
3. Information about QuickBooks comes from interviews conducted by Marisa Porzig.

## Chapter 12. Innovate

1. Jeffrey Liker, John E. Ettlie, and John Creighton Campbell, *Engineered in Japan: Japanese Technology-Management Practices* (New York: Oxford University Press, 1995), p. 196.
2. For one account, see *PC Magazine*'s "Looking Back: 15 Years of PC Magazine" by Michael Miller, http://www.pcmag.com/article2/0,2817,35549,00.asp
3. The following discussion owes a great deal to Geoffrey Moore's *Dealing with Darwin* (New York: Portfolio Trade, 2008). I have had success implementing this framework in companies of many different sizes.

**Chapter 13. Epilogue: Waste Not**

1. http://www.ibiblio.org/eldritch/fwt/ti.html
2. http://www.goodreads.com/author/quotes/66490.Peter_Drucker
3. http://www.ibiblio.org/eldritch/fwt/ti.html
4. In fact, some such research has already begun. For more on Lean Startup research programs, see Nathan Furr's Lean Startup Research Project at BYU, http://nathanfurr.com/2010/09/15/the-lean-startup-research-project/, and Tom Eisenmann of Harvard Business School's Launching Technology Ventures project, http://platformsandnetworks.blogspot.om/2011/01/launching-tech-ventures-part-iv.html

# Disclosures

I have worked with the following companies named in this book either as a consultant, adviser, or investor. I have a relationship or equity interest in each of them.

Aardvark
Dropbox
Food on the Table
Grockit
IMVU
Intuit
Votizen
Wealthfront

I have additional interests in companies through my affiliations with venture capital firms. I have invested in or worked with the following firms as either a consultant or as a limited partner. Through these firms, I have equity and relationship interests in many more companies beyond those listed above.

500 Startups
Floodgate
Greylock Partners
Kleiner Perkins Caufield & Byers
Seraph Group

# Acknowledgments

I owe a tremendous debt of gratitude to the many people who have helped make *The Lean Startup* a reality. First and foremost are the thousands of entrepreneurs around the world who have tested these ideas, challenged them, refined them, and improved them. Without their relentless—and mostly unheralded—work every day, none of this would be possible. Thank you.

Real startups involve failure, embarrassing mistakes, and constant chaos. In my research for this book, I discovered that most entrepreneurs and managers would prefer not to have the real story of their daily work told in public. Therefore, I am indebted to the courageous entrepreneurs who consented to have their stories told, many of whom spent hours in tedious interviews and fact-checking conversations. Thank you.

I have been grateful throughout my career to have mentors and collaborators who have pushed me to accomplish more than I could have on my own. Will Harvey is responsible for both recruiting me to Silicon Valley in the first place and for trusting me with the opportunity to try out many of these ideas for the first time at IMVU. I am grateful to my other IMVU cofounders Marcus Gosling, Matt Danzig, and Mel Guymon as well as the many IMVU employees who did so much of the work I discussed. Of course, none of that would have been possible without the support of millions of IMVU customers over the years.

I'd also like to thank David Millstone, Ken Duda, Fernando Paiz, Steve Weinstein, Owen Mahoney, Ray Ocampo, and Jason Altieri for their help along the way.

We all owe Steve Blank a debt for the work he did developing the theory of customer development at a time when it was considered heretical in startup and VC circles. As I mentioned in the Introduction, Steve was an early investor in and adviser to IMVU. For the past seven years, he has been an adviser, mentor, and collaborator to me personally. I want to thank him for his encouragement, support, and friendship.

The Lean Startup movement is made up of many more thinkers, practitioners, and writers than just me. I want to thank Dave McClure, Ash Maurya, Brant Cooper, Patrick Vlaskovits, Sean Ellis, Andrew Chen, Sean Murphy, Trevor Owens, Hiten Shah, and Kent Beck for their ideas, support, and evangelism. Several investors and venture capitalists were early supporters and adopters. I would like to thank Mike Maples and Ann Miura-Ko (Floodgate), Steve Anderson (Baseline), Josh Kopelman (First Round Capital), Ron Conway (SV Angel), and Jeff Clavier (SoftTech VC).

As you can imagine, this book involved a tremendous amount of feedback, iteration, and testing. I received invaluable, in-depth early feedback from Laura Crescimano, Lee Hoffman, Professor Tom Eisenmann, and Sacha Judd. Thanks also to Mitch Kapor, Scott Cook, Shawn Fanning, Mark Graban, Jennifer Carolan, Manuel Rosso, Tim O'Reilly, and Reid Hoffman for their suggestions, feedback, and support. I owe a special note of thanks to Ruth Kaplan and Ira Fay for their wisdom and friendship.

Throughout the process of writing the book, I had the benefit of a custom-built testing platform to run split-test experiments on everything from cover design to subtitles to actual bits of the book (you can see the results of these experiments at http://lean

.st). Pivotal Labs built this software for me; they are the premier practitioners of agile development. Special thanks to Rob Mee, Ian McFarland, and—most important—Parker Thompson, who worked tirelessly to build, experiment, and learn with me.

Thanks also to IMVU cofounder Marcus Gosling, one of the most talented designers I know, who designed this book's cover, after countless iterations.

One of the premier web and user experience design firms, Digital Telepathy, designed and built the website for http://theleanstartup.com, using their unique Iterative Performance Design process. It's awesome. Learn more at http://www.dtelepathy.com/

I was extremely fortunate to have the support of three legendary institutions at various points in my journey. Much of the research that went into this book was generously underwritten by the Kauffman Foundation. At Kauffman, I want to especially thank Bo Fishback and Nick Seguin for their support. I spent the past year as an entrepreneur-in-residence at Harvard Business School, where I enjoyed the opportunity to test my ideas against some of the brightest minds in business. I am especially grateful to Professors Tom Eisenmann and Mike Roberts for their sponsorship and support, as well as to the students of the HBS Startup Tribe. I also had the opportunity to spend a brief time with an office at the premier venture capital firm in Silicon Valley, Kleiner Perkins Caufield & Byers, where I received an in-depth education into how entrepreneurship is nurtured at the highest levels. Thanks to Chi-Hua Chien, Randy Komisar, Matt Murphy, Bing Gordon, Aileen Lee, and Ellen Pao, and to my officemate and EIR, Cyriac Roeding.

My research team helped me document case studies, interview hundreds of startups, and filter thousands of stories. I want to thank Marisa Porzig, who logged countless hours documenting, cross-referencing, and investigating. Additional case studies were developed by Sara Gaviser Leslie and Sarah Milstein.

Traditional publishing is a complicated and insular business. I benefited from advice and connections from many people. Tim Ferriss and Ramit Sethi set me straight early on. I am also grateful to Peter Sims, Paul Michelman, Mary Treseler, Joshua-Michéle Ross, Clara Shih, Sarah Milstein, Adam Penenberg, Gretchen Rubin, Kate Lee, Hollis Heimbouch, Bob Sutton, Frankie Jones, Randy Komisar, and Jeff Rosenthal.

At Crown, the herculean task of turning this idea into the book you are reading fell to a huge team of people. My editor, Roger Scholl, saw the vision of this book from the very beginning and shepherded it through the entire process. I want to also thank Tina Constable, Tara Gilbride, and Meredith McGinnis and everyone else who worked on making this book a reality.

Those who had the misfortune of reading an early draft know just how much gratitude I owe to Laureen Rowland, who provided essential editorial help on an unbelievably tight schedule. If you enjoyed any part of this book, she deserves your thanks.

My adviser, partner, and *consigliere* throughout the publishing process has been my phenomenal agent, Christy Fletcher. She has the uncanny ability to predict the future, make things happen, and keep every stakeholder happy—all at the same time. She truly understands the modern media landscape and has helped me navigate its crazy waters at every turn. At Fletcher and Company, I also want to thank Alyssa Wolff, who has been a tireless advocate and gatekeeper, and Melissa Chinchillo, who is working to bring this book to new regions and languages.

I know it is a cliché to say, "None of this would have been possible without the constant support of my loving family." But in this case, it is simply the truth. My parents, Vivian Reznik and Andrew Ries, have always supported my love of technology while still insisting on the importance of a liberal arts education. Without their constant love and support, I would never have had the courage to step into the void of entrepreneurship or have found my own voice as a writer. I know my grandparents have been with me every step of this journey—they believed deeply in the power of writing and took supreme joy in my sisters' and my every accomplishment. To my sisters Nicole and Amanda and my brother-in-law Dov, I can only say: thank you for supporting me all these years.

My wife, Tara Sophia Mohr, has been a constant source of joy and comfort every step of the way. She has experienced every stress, every high, and every low through this very lengthy process. Tara, you are an incredibly brilliant, strong, and compassionate woman. Words cannot express how much I appreciate your steadfast support, your overwhelming love, and the daily adventure that is our life together. Thank you.

# Index

## About the Author

ERIC RIES is an entrepreneur and author of the popular blog *Startup Lessons Learned.* He cofounded and served as CTO of IMVU, his third startup. He is a frequent speaker at business events, has advised a number of startups, large companies, and venture capital firms on business and product strategy, and is an entrepreneur-in-residence at Harvard Business School. His Lean Startup methodology has been written about in the *New York Times,* the *Wall Street Journal,* the *Harvard Business Review,* the *Huffington Post,* and many blogs. He lives in San Francisco.